Business Impacts of Web Accessibility

Electronic Business

Herausgegeben von Christine Strauss

Band 3

PETER LANG
Frankfurt am Main · Berlin · Bern · Bruxelles · New York · Oxford · Wien

Marie-Luise Leitner

Business Impacts of Web Accessibility

A Holistic Approach

PETER LANG
Internationaler Verlag der Wissenschaften

Bibliographic Information published by the Deutsche Nationalbibliothek
The Deutsche Nationalbibliothek lists this publication in the Deutsche Nationalbibliografie; detailed bibliographic data is available in the internet at http://dnb.d-nb.de.

Cover design:
Olaf Glöckler, Atelier Platen, Friedberg

ISSN 1868-646X
ISBN 978-3-631-59526-8
© Peter Lang GmbH
Internationaler Verlag der Wissenschaften
Frankfurt am Main 2010
All rights reserved.

All parts of this publication are protected by copyright. Any utilisation outside the strict limits of the copyright law, without the permission of the publisher, is forbidden and liable to prosecution. This applies in particular to reproductions, translations, microfilming, and storage and processing in electronic retrieval systems.

www.peterlang.de

Acknowledgements

This work would not have been possible without the help of many people. First of all, I would like to thank my supervisor and mentor, Ao. Univ.-Prof. Dr. Christine Strauss for her professional and personal support over the last couple of years. The critical discussions with her always opened up new doors for me, the motivation she provided me with and the freedom I had in executing my work were crucial for the finalization of this work.

I also would like to thank my second reviewer, Ao. Univ.-Prof. Dr. Christian Stummer for his valuable comments about my work. Moreover, I owe thanks to Ao. Univ.-Prof. Dr. Klaus Miesenberger who offered me the possibility to work in a European web accessibility project.

Special thanks go to my colleagues, Lea and Marita, for their detailed and valuable comments on this work, Christoph, for all the fruitful comments and challenging discussions especially about methodological aspects, Kornelia, my second coder, for her perfect support, Maria, for her valuable help in the tourism sector, Manuela, for proof reading the manuscript, Christine, for sharing her experiences, Rudi, for his precious inputs from the computer science perspective, and Michaela and Petra, for all the motivation and understanding they provided me with over the last years.

Finally, I would like to thank my family for all their love, support, and education.

This work is part of the „Web Accessibility Quality Management" Project (Project Nr. 12461) funded by the Austrian National Bank.

Table of Contents

1 Introduction 11
   1.1 Objectives and research contribution 11
   1.2 Research design 16
   1.3 Research approach 18
      1.3.1 Organization 19
      1.3.2 Authority 19

2 Current state of web accessibility 23
   2.1 Background 23
   2.2 Users and support 25
      2.2.1 User groups 25
      2.2.2 Assistive devices 26
   2.3 Technical specifications 28
      2.3.1 Web Content Accessibility Guidelines 1.0 28
      2.3.2 Web Content Accessibility Guidelines 2.0 29
      2.3.3 Search engine ranking 30
   2.4 Legal regulations 31
      2.4.1 European Union 31
      2.4.2 United States 33
      2.4.3 Austria 33
   2.5 Business relevance 33
      2.5.1 Web 2.0 impact 34
      2.5.2 Business aspects 36

3 Case study research methodology 41
   3.1 Research questions 43
   3.2 Case selection 44
   3.3 Research instruments 47
      3.3.1 Evaluation of web presences 49
      3.3.2 Semi-structured interviews 50
   3.4 Field research 52
   3.5 Data analysis 52
      3.5.1 Within-case analysis 53
      3.5.2 Cross-case analysis 55
   3.6 Enfolding literature 55

4 Within case analyses: Empirical evidence and results 57
   4.1 Case 1: Tourism 57
      4.1.1 Sector overview 57
      4.1.2 Web site evaluation 59
      4.1.3 Qualitative analysis 62
      4.1.4 Summary and interpretation 70

- 4.2 Case 2: Financial services ... 72
  - 4.2.1 Sector overview ... 72
  - 4.2.2 Web site evaluation ... 75
  - 4.2.3 Qualitative analysis ... 75
  - 4.2.4 Summary and interpretation ... 95
- 4.3 Case 3: Information ... 96
  - 4.3.1 Sector overview ... 96
  - 4.3.2 Web site evaluation ... 99
  - 4.3.3 Qualitative analysis ... 100
  - 4.3.4 Summary and interpretation ... 109

5 Cross-case analysis ... 111
- 5.1 Purpose ... 111
- 5.2 Reasons for accessibility implementation ... 113
  - 5.2.1 Economic motivations ... 113
  - 5.2.2 Social motivations ... 114
  - 5.2.3 Technical motivations ... 117
- 5.3 Changes after accessibility implementation ... 119
  - 5.3.1 Economic changes ... 119
  - 5.3.2 Social changes ... 120
  - 5.3.3 Technical changes ... 121
- 5.4 Reasons for failure of implementation ... 124
  - 5.4.1 Design and layout ... 124
  - 5.4.2 Argumentation ... 125
- 5.5 Incentives for accessibility implementation ... 126
  - 5.5.1 External incentives ... 126
  - 5.5.2 Internal incentives ... 126
- 5.6 The web accessibility implementation process model ... 127
  - 5.6.1 Initiation ... 128
  - 5.6.2 Implementation ... 133
  - 5.6.3 Application ... 135
- 5.7 Web site evaluation ... 139
- 5.8 Discussion ... 143

6 Business model for a web accessibility quality mark ... 147
- 6.1 Conformity assessment in Europe ... 148
  - 6.1.1 Terminology ... 148
  - 6.1.2 Historical background ... 150
  - 6.1.3 Outcomes ... 152
- 6.2 Course of action ... 154

6.3 Business model for web site certification 156
  6.3.1 Business models – literature overview 156
  6.3.2 Analysis of existing quality marks 158
  6.3.3 Structure, roles, and relationships 163
  6.3.4 Implementation scenarios 169
  6.3.5 Scenario analysis 172
  6.3.6 Business model and implementation plan 173
  6.3.7 Person certification 176
 6.4 Summary and interpretation 178
7 Conclusion 181
 7.1 Key findings 182
 7.2 Limitations 185
 7.3 Future Work 186
8 References 189
9 List of Tables 205
10 List of Figures 207
11 Appendix 209

1 Introduction

*"The power of the web is in its universality.
Access by everyone regardless of disability is an essential aspect."*

Tim Berners-Lee, Founder of the WWW, Director of the W3C

Information technology captures a vital part in the life of many people as an increasing number of people are joining the digital highway. Moreover, information and communication technologies (ICT) may improve personal autonomy and quality of life (e.g., Council of the European Union 2008). Worldwide, almost every 5th person has Internet access. In the European Union, the Internet penetration rate was even 48.1% in 2008 (World Internet Usage Statistics 2008).

Although the World Wide Web has become an indispensable source of information and services, the universal accessibility of the Internet, that Tim Berners-Lee originally envisioned, has not been realized yet. People with motor, cognitive, visual, or auditory impairments cannot use the Internet without the help of assistive devices, such as screen readers or Braille displays, that require accessible web sites (Sierkowski 2002). The Internet – originally based on the idea of offering equal opportunities to each and everybody – has emerged as a medium for the creation of digital divide as it excludes certain groups of people by not providing adequate accessibility.

1.1 Objectives and research contribution

In the area of computer science, web accessibility has become an established research field. Recent technical studies on web accessibility evaluation (e.g., Williams and Rattray 2003; Loiacono and McCoy 2004; Hackett and Parmanto 2005; Snaprud and Sawicka 2007), the development of evaluation tools and methods (e.g., O'Grady and Harrison 2003; Kelly et al. 2005; Brajnik 2006; Krüger 2008), and human computer interaction (HCI) and usability (e.g., Petrie et al. 2006) account for the importance of web accessibility in the area of computer science. Moreover, in recent years, research on accessible tourism (e.g., Pühretmair 2004) and accessible mobile use (e.g., Vigo et al. 2008) has been conducted.

Apart from the area of computer science, web accessibility plays a role in various scientific disciplines (cf. Figure 1). Legal regulations on European (cf. i2010 Initiative, Mandate 376) and national level (e.g., Austrian e-Government Act) have considered accessible design of web sites. In the field of education and pedagogy, there are attempts to develop curricula for web accessibility in higher education (e.g., Ortner and Miesenberger 2005; Matausch et al. 2006) as well as to create accessible learning environments for students (e.g., Johnson and Ruppert 2002).

Sociological research covers browsing behavior of people with impairments and the development of easy-to-read texts (e.g., Petz and Tronbacke 2008). Web accessibility plays a role in engineering when it comes to construction and design of assistive devices and smart environments. Finally, in the area of ethics, web accessibility takes over a major part, dealing with social responsibility, e-inclusion and human rights issues (Europe's Information Society 2008).

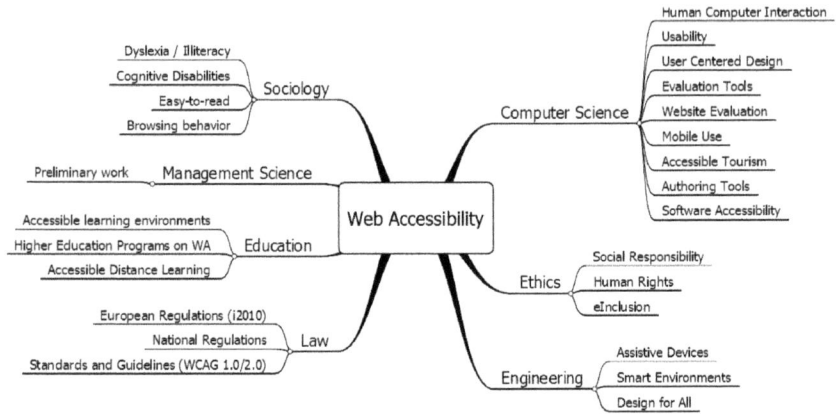

Figure 1: Web accessibility - the big picture

By contrast, the issue of web accessibility has gained little attention in the area of economics, business or management science so far, even though its implementation especially in organizations of the private sector justifies also business and management research to be considered. Previous research about web accessibility in management science focused on theoretical models for benefit analysis (Puhl 2008) and cost-benefit scenarios (Heerdt and Strauss 2004). These synthetic approaches included cost-benefit estimations but were not based on empirical data. Furthermore, the experiences of organizations with web accessibility implementation have not been examined so far. This contribution draws on a holistic approach to fill this research gap and analyzes the impact of web accessibility implementation by means of exploratory case study research and therefore constitutes a first holistic management science approach on web accessibility. This work considers an interdisciplinary set of literature derived from management, marketing, information science, organizational theory, and psychology that explains the emerging phenomena in the course of web accessibility implementation in an organization in the private sector. The diversity in theories enables a ubiquitous understanding of the enduring effects of web accessibility implementation.

Legal obligations and the implications of social responsibility may intensify the pressure on organizations to make their web sites accessible. Nevertheless, managers will still require facts and figures about web accessibility costs, benefits, savings or expenditures, as well as amortization and financial plans, for their decision making process. Social pressure on its own is unlikely to suffice in convincing organizations of the benefits of implementing web accessibility. Decisions on new information and communication technologies are usually taken by the Chief Information Officer (CIO) of an organization. However, the support of the Chief Executive Officer (CEO) is crucial and requires efficiency considerations or benchmarks. In case of web accessibility implementation, these measures have not been developed so far which is the reason why they are tackled in this contribution' approach.

The first part of this contribution introduces a web accessibility implementation process (WAIP) model and identifies business impacts of web accessibility implementation by means of exploratory case study research in three major industry sectors. This part constitutes a first managerial approach to identify the experiences of organizations with web accessibility and generates a sound basis for management decision recommendations.

Due to the fact that the accessibility of web presences is not visible by a layperson, its business impacts can only be fully exploited when appropriate measures for quality assurance are given. A quality mark for accessible web presences constitutes a means to foster visibility and awareness to the general public and may therefore be the only impartial possibility for organizations to communicate their accessibility efforts. This communication represents the basis for further exploitation of business benefits.

A recent study on the availability of barrier-free media content in Austria resulted in 23 out of 50 organizations stating that their web site was accessible (Karmasin.Motivforschung 2006). This rather positive self assessment must be called into question, as no recognized certificate or quality mark currently exists for accessible web sites in Austria; the absence of such a certification implies that an impartial assessment is not possible for the time being. Moreover, research on the use of accessibility logos in e-business and financial web sites has shown that web sites make exaggerated claims of their level of accessibility (Petrie 2005).

In recent years, web accessibility quality marks have been developed and implemented on a national basis in several European countries. Despite the fact that these quality marks are all based on the Web Content Accessibility Guidelines 1.0 (W3C 1999) published by the World Wide Web Consortium, different evaluation procedures, implementations and levels of conformity have led to considerable heterogeneity within the European context. The European Commission has attempted to create a unified web accessibility quality mark in order to avoid further fragmentation. However, the development of a distinct European framework for a web accessibility quality mark has been hampered by the diverging interests of the various stakeholders and by the extensive harmonization process involving the existing quality marks.

The second part of this contribution explores viable alternatives for implementing the European web accessibility quality mark in Austria. This contribution applies a look-ahead approach that assumes the release of a normative document and an evaluation methodology in the near future. A scenario analysis includes the development of four alternatives and their evaluation in terms of six criteria. Moreover, a business model for the development and implementation of an Austrian web accessibility quality mark is introduced.

Having specified the main objectives of the two studies presented in this contribution, two central research questions (RQ) can be derived:

RQ 1) What business impact can be obtained from an implementation of accessible web presences in private sector organizations?

RQ 2) How does a business model for an Austrian web accessibility quality mark have to be configured in order to be applied in a European context?

The two research questions relate to the two research gaps that are covered in this work. Table 1 depicts the research gaps and the corresponding research contributions and indicates the section in which these contributions can be found.

Research gap	Contribution	Section

1. Lack of examination of business perspective of web accessibility implementation	1a. Identification of business experiences of profit-oriented organizations with web accessibility implementation in the financial services, information, and tourism sector. Four main aspects have been identified:
	   i. reasons for implementation
	   ii. changes after implementation
	   iii. incentives for implementation
	   iv. reasons for failure of implementation
		4

	1b. Identification of similarities and differences across sectors.	5
	1c. Development of a web accessibility implementation process (WAIP) model for organizations based on case study research data.	5
2. Lack of business model for an Austrian web accessibility quality mark	2a. Development and evaluation of four implementation alternatives for a web accessibility quality mark by means of scenario analysis.	6
	2b. Development of a business model for an Austrian web accessibility quality mark that complies with European structures.	6

Table 1: Research gaps and corresponding research contributions

Due to the fact that this work looks at the issue of web accessibility from two different perspectives, it can be referred to as a **holistic business analysis of web accessibility**. This holistic approach includes two independent studies that have a strong relationship between each other.

1. Determination of business impacts of web accessibility implementation for organizations:
   An exploratory case study analysis in three business sectors identifies the business impacts of web accessibility implementation for private organizations and develops a web accessibility implementation process model.

2. Development of a business model for an Austrian web accessibility quality mark:
   Viable implementation alternatives for a web accessibility quality mark are analyzed by means of scenario technique. Business model specifications for a quality mark that fits into a European framework are developed.

These two perspectives are closely interrelated. In the course of this research, the connection of both perspectives has become increasingly obvious. Organizations need a quality mark in order to communicate and promote their accessibility efforts to the public. Moreover, the quality assurance dimension and credibility is fostered by a quality mark. On the other hand, the success of a web accessibility quality mark is reliant on organizations willing to consider accessibility for their web presences. Thus, a dependency between these two studies has been identified that justifies the holistic approach in this work.

1.2 Research design

Figure 2 depicts the possible perspectives that can be considered when analyzing web accessibility from a business angle. As already stated before, two perspectives are covered in this work: (i) organization and (ii) authority. The customer perspective represents a third possibility that is added for reasons of completeness but is out of scope of this contribution.

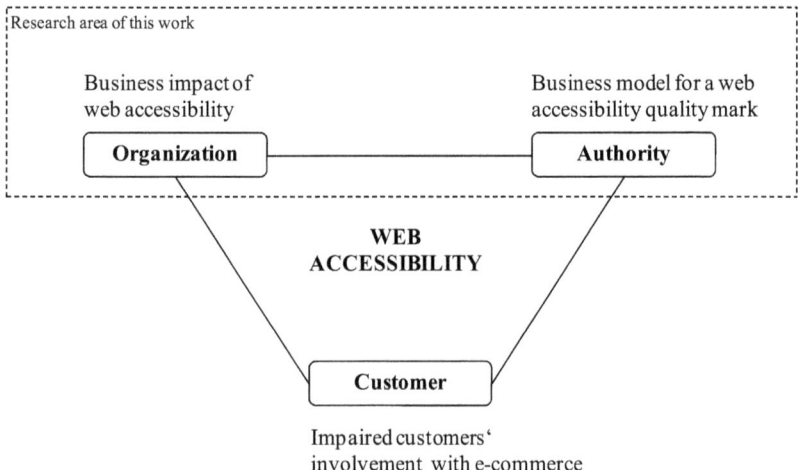

Figure 2: Research design

These three perspectives represent elements that are assembled to a new holistic web accessibility business approach.

From an organizational perspective, the business and economic impacts of web accessibility implementation take over a central criterion in the decision making process. Therefore, this section covers the determination and realization of case studies on the business and economic impacts of web accessibility implementation into an organization. These case studies are intended to show if web accessibility implementation entails business opportunities and benefits for organizations in the b2c sector. Moreover, the experiences and problems organizations face with web accessibility implementation are analyzed. The findings represent a knowledge database and constitute an important support for organizations intending to consider web accessibility for themselves.

Authorities (e.g., the government, European standardization bodies) have established regulations and guidelines concerning accessible web sites. For reasons of verifiability and controllability of conformance with these regulations, a quality mark is needed that, on the one hand, contributes to an increase in awareness, visibility, and positive image claimed by organizations and customers, and, on the other hand, controls the conformance with guidelines set by authorities. Several European member states have already established web accessibility quality marks. Due to a lack of such a quality mark in Austria, this section covers the development of a flexible business model for an Austrian web accessibility quality mark that fits into a possible European framework and at the same time facilitates and accelerates a national implementation.

The consumer behavior in e-commerce, especially the constructs of customer satisfaction and loyalty have been analyzed in numerous studies (e.g., Hallowell 1996; Srinivasan et al. 2002; Anderson and Srinivasan 2003; Sarv et al. 2003). Moreover, some studies, like the work of Baker et al. (2002) and Baker et al. (2007) deal with disabled shoppers in physical shopping environment but not in e-commerce. For these reasons, ongoing research considers the online shopping behavior of visually impaired customers within a small explorative case study which gives insight in the current e-shopping situation of these customers and reflects their needs in terms of online shopping. However, this case study is mentioned only for the sake of completeness and not within the scope of this contribution.

The three players described, organization, authority, and customer, are closely related to one another.

Authority – Organization: The demonstration of business impacts of web accessibility may encourage organizations to implement accessible web sites themselves. The external visibility of this effort is required if organizations want to profit from image enhancements due to the new accessible web site. Visibility can in turn only be reached with an objective quality mark that certifies the compliance with certain accessibility criteria. On the other hand, it is in the authority's interest to have as many organizations implementing web accessibility as possible in order to promote the quality mark. Moreover, authorities may want to have a maximum compliance with European and national standards and regulations which can in turn be fulfilled by encouraging organizations of web accessibility implementation.

Organization – Customer: People with disabilities, the elderly generation and people using browsers on mobile devices profit from accessible web sites as they facilitate and sometimes even enable Internet usage for them. This customer group is dependent on organizations with accessible web sites. In turn, organizations attract these customers who represent a new market potential and high purchasing power.

Customer – Authority: This relationship is strongly influenced by social and ethical issues. Authorities, such as the government, take over social responsibility for people with impairments by passing laws about equal treatment. In turn, customers with disabilities may embrace awareness raising issues of web accessibility, one of which is the establishment of a quality mark.

1.3 Research approach

The research approach for the study on organization and the study on authority conducted in this contribution and their dependencies are depicted in Figure 3. Moreover, the elements where empiric inquiry has been conducted are separated from subsequent interpretation and provision of solutions.

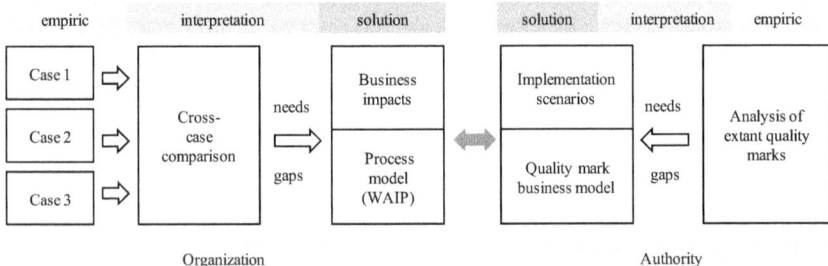

Figure 3: Research approach

Both the organizational and the authority study include an empiric part. After independent analysis of three cases in the organizational study, a cross-case comparison identifies business needs and gaps of organizations in terms of web accessibility implementation which are subsequently taken as a basis for business impact and process model development. The authority study empirically analyzes extant quality marks. This analysis in connection with extensive literature research leads to an identification of needs and gaps of authorities on which the formulation of implementation scenarios and the quality mark business model is based. Both studies have strong interrelations. A quality mark constitutes the only possibility for organizations to fully exploit business benefits from web accessibility implementation as it represents a means for both quality assurance and external communication. The research approach for each study is further explained in sections 1.3.1 and 1.3.2.

1.3.1 Organization

An extensive literature research in the field of web accessibility revealed various technical studies about web site accessibility evaluation (e.g., Loiacono and McCoy 2004; Hackett and Parmanto 2005; Petrie 2005) but very few studies on business and managerial benefits of web accessibility (Heerdt and Strauss 2004; Puhl 2008). Yin's case study research was chosen as an exploratory methodology for addressing this research gap (Yin 2003).

The case study research model comprises the analysis of private organizations in the b2c segment of three industry sectors with high relevance in electronic business (European Commission 2007): (i) tourism, (ii) financial services, and (iii) information. In each of the three sectors, the impact of web accessibility is analyzed focusing on two extreme situations (Eisenhardt 1989), namely organizations which have successfully implemented web accessibility and organizations which have failed in web accessibility implementation. For reasons of internal validity, comparability, repeatability, and profound data analysis, the data collection methods used for this case study research (semi-structured interviews, questionnaires, observations, archives, etc.) have to follow a well-structured conceptual framework (Miles and Huberman 2005). Furthermore, a consistent application of the same variables and issues in each case is required in order to ensure comparability. In each of the three industry sectors, semi-structured interviews have been conducted following the conceptual framework. Each interview has been audio-taped and transcribed. Every organization analyzed had distinct experiences with web accessibility implementation which resulted in a library of show cases that may assist other organizations considering web accessibility implementation in their decision making process. The coding and analysis of the interviews and the subsequent cross-case comparisons resulted in the development of business indicators for web accessibility implementation and a web accessibility implementation process (WAIP) model.

1.3.2 Authority

Literature research has revealed that various web accessibility quality marks partially based on different evaluation criteria have been established by some European Union member states (e.g., France, Spain, and the Netherlands). In a first step, these quality marks were analyzed in terms of their processes, actors, roles, evaluation criteria and issuing details. Moreover, a detailed analysis of laws and regulations of web accessibility in the EU member states as well as the various issuing, certification and accreditation processes has been conducted. This way, a quality mark framework for a potential Austrian web accessibility quality mark could be established.

With the help of scenario analysis techniques, different implementation scenarios were compared in terms of six evaluation criteria. Based on these results, a suggestion for an e-business model for an Austrian web accessibility quality mark could be made. Additionally, considerations for a possible implementation of this quality mark have been taken in order to facilitate and accelerate the realization of such approaches at the national level and to encourage other European countries to adopt selected elements for their own initiation.

Having explained the relationships between the two studies and the research approach used, the following paragraphs will give a roadmap for this work; the sections' main content is briefly illustrated and their dependencies are defined. Moreover, the target audience which may benefit from reading the respective sections is identified. Figure 4 displays the roadmap for this book.

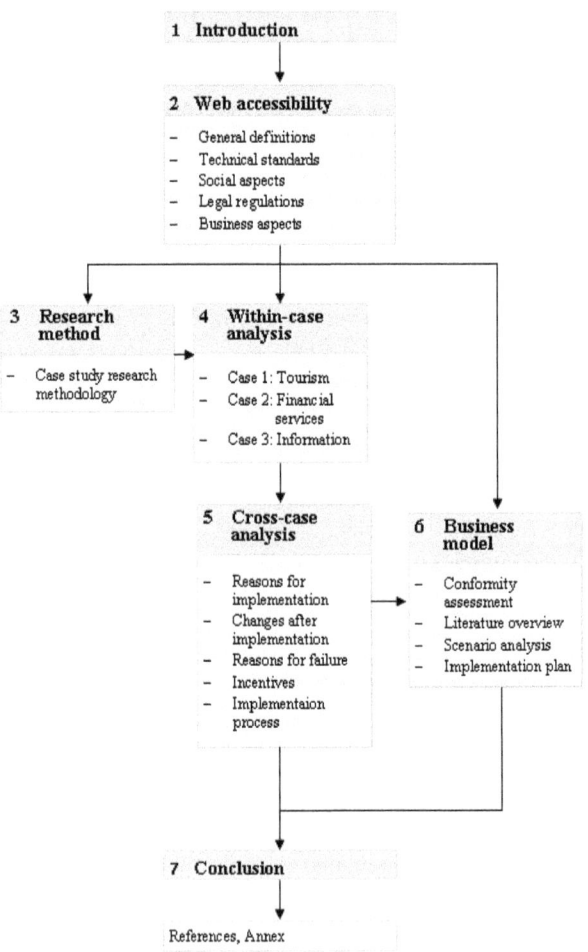

Figure 4: Roadmap

This contribution starts by giving an overview of the web accessibility concept in section 2. Beginning with an explanation of how people with disabilities use the web and which assistive devices they are dependent on, section 2 particularly covers a literature overview of the technical guidelines, the legal regulations, and the social and business aspects of web accessibility. Hence, this section gives a consolidated overview of the main aspects of the web accessibility concept and therefore provides a sound basis for understanding the subsequent sections. Section 2 may also be considered by readers solely interested in web accessibility and its spheres of influence as the whole web accessibility concept is depicted in an aggregate way. Moreover, practitioners intending to update their knowledge about web accessibility belong to the reader target group of this section.

Section 3, 4, 5, and 6 comprise the main focus of this book. The case study conceptualization and theory is presented in section 3. Section 4 analyzes each of the three cases and represents the basis for the cross-case analysis given in section 5. The reader may therefore consider each of the three sections separately, depending on the extent of his interest. Examples of possible target groups for this contribution are specified in the following paragraphs.

Practitioners, for instance CEOs or heads of department of organizations in the financial services, information, and tourism sector who intend to implement web accessibility may consider the respective case analysis in section 4 in order to learn about experiences of other organizations in their sector. For the same group of persons of organizations in other sectors than the analyzed ones, cross-case analysis in section 5 may be of interest as common patterns across all sectors are identified.

Moreover, researchers from various disciplines, e.g., management science, business informatics, psychology, and pedagogy may be interested in section 3 to 5. Researchers interested in the application on case study methodology, or the business investigation of the web accessibility phenomenon may consider these sections. In addition, researchers in innovation and marketing who intend to do further research on interdisciplinary patterns may take sections 4 and 5 into consideration. Lecturers teaching case study research or web accessibility issues will find valuable inputs for their classes in this work.

Public authorities and governmental bodies will rather consider section 6. For reasons of understanding of the holistic business analysis, the consideration of every study is essential.

In the concluding management summary, the most important findings are summed up and interpreted. Moreover, limitations of the study and directions for possible future research are discussed.

2 Current state of web accessibility

> *"For people without disabilities, technology makes things convenient, for people with disabilities, it makes things possible."*
>
> Judith E. Heumann, Secretary of State, US Department of Education

Section 2 gives a consolidated overview of the web accessibility concept and briefly covers the variety of disciplines this concept has influence in. After a confine of the notions usability and accessibility, it is explained how people with disabilities use the web and which assistive devices they are dependent on. This is followed by a brief overview of the current state of web accessibility in terms of technical, social and legal aspects. Finally, web 2.0 and business aspects of web accessibility are addressed.

2.1 Background

Design for All is an attempt to describe products, systems and services that can be used by everyone in each and every circumstance. In the last years, many synonyms for the term *Design for All* have emerged in different countries (e.g., *Universal Design* in the USA, *Inclusive Design* in Britain and Ireland and *Barrier-free Design* in Germany) (Darzentas and Miesenberger 2005). Ronald Mace, founder of the Center for Universal Design at the North Carolina State University defines *Universal Design* as the "design of products and environment to be usable by all people, to the greatest extent possible, without the need for adaptation or specialized design"[1]. In this concept, both the notions "accessibility" and "usability" are hidden which necessitates a detailed definition of both terms and their confine from each other.

One aspect of the *Design for All* concept is the design of services that can be used by everyone – in other words, the *accessibility* of IT services, one of which is the Internet. Web sites are accessible when individuals with disabilities can access and use them as effectively as people without disabilities (Section508 1998). The notion of web accessibility has existed for over a decade and generally means "that people with disabilities can perceive, understand, navigate, and interact with the Web, and that they can contribute to the Web" (W3C 2005b, p. 1).

Usability is defined as "the extent to which a product can be used by specified users to achieve specified goals with effectiveness, efficiency, and satisfaction in a specified context of use" (International Standards Organization 1994).

---

1 Available at http://www.design.ncsu.edu/cud/about_ud/about_ud.htm (last access 23/10/09).

The confine of the term web accessibility from usability is not always obvious. Both concepts are used in relation to web sites. Thatcher et al. (2003) define accessibility as a subset of usability and, as a consequence, state that accessibility problems represent special types of usability problems. Shneiderman (2003) points out that accessibility is a first but not sufficient step to ensure usability.

Petrie and Kheir (2007) further analyze the relationship between accessibility and usability and come up with four different sets of possibilities that are summarized in Table 2.

Relationship Accessibility - Usability	Definition	Literature
Two distinct, non intersecting sets	Accessibility affects disabled users; usability affects non-disabled users.	Petrie and Kheir (2007)
Accessibility as subset of usability	All accessibility problems also affect non-disabled users.	Thatcher et al (2003)
Usability as subset of accessibility	All usability problems also affect disabled users.	Shneiderman (2003)
Two overlapping sets	Pure accessibility problems, pure usability problems, universal usability problems;	Petrie and Kheir (2007)

Table 2: Relationship between accessibility and usability (after Petrie and Kheir 2007)

Firstly, accessibility and usability may be considered as two "distinct, non-intersecting sets" (Petrie and Kheir 2007, p. 398). In this case, accessibility only affects people with disabilities and usability only affects people without disabilities – a scenario that is often applied in web development practice. However, a correct application of headings and structural elements is an accessibility feature from which non-disabled users may also benefit. Secondly, they refer to Thatcher et al. (2003) who define accessibility as a subset of usability, which means that all accessibility problems will also affect non-disabled users. However, to give an example, poor color contrast may pose problems for people with color deficiencies but may not be problematic for non-disabled people. This implies that accessibility cannot be considered as a subset of usability. Thirdly, Petrie and Kheir (2007) refer to Shneiderman's (2003) concept of universal usability, who defines usability as a subset of accessibility. This means that the problems of people with disabilities are the same as the problems of people without disabilities. Finally, Petrie and Kheir (2007) suggest the consideration of accessibility and usability as two overlapping sets with three categories: pure accessibility problems, pure usability problems and universal usability problems. Pure accessibility problems only affect people with disabilities (e.g., alternative texts for graphics), pure usability problems are only encountered by users without disabilities and universal usability problems affect disabled and non-disabled users. In this book, Petrie and Kheir's (2007) definition of the relationship between accessibility and usability as two overlapping sets is taken over as it encompasses the full range of possible accessibility and usability problems.

The conceptualization above leads to the conclusion that usability does not necessarily lead to web accessibility and vice versa[2]. Still, Sullivan and Matson (2000) who have tested 50 web pages for usability and accessibility have found a relationship between the two states[3]. Petrie and Kheir (2007) detected about 14% overlap in usability and accessibility problems of visually impaired users and non-disabled sighted users.

For effective and efficient web site usage, people with disabilities are dependent on the use of assistive technologies (e.g., refreshable Braille display, screen reader, head mouse, eye gaze system) that help to compensate their particular kind of disability (cf. Section 2.2.2). Elderly people may also have similar problems (e.g., diminishing eye sight, arthritis) that require the use of assistive devices (e.g., screen magnifier). These assistive devices can in turn only be used efficiently in combination with accessible web sites.

The World Wide Web Consortium (W3C) has developed a first set of guidelines to ensure accessible web sites in 1999 (W3C 1999). In spite of this, most of the current web sites do not comply with these guidelines and can therefore not be used efficiently by people with disabilities.

2.2 Users and support

2.2.1 User groups

The W3C uses a broad definition on disability, including the following groups (W3C 2005a): (i) visual disabilities (blindness, low vision, color blindness); (ii) hearing impairments (including deafness); (iii) physical and motor disabilities; (iv) speech disabilities; (v) cognitive and neurological disabilities (dyslexia and dyscalculia, attention deficit disorder, intellectual disabilities, memory impairments, mental health disabilities, seizure disorders), and (vi) multiple disabilities.

It can be estimated that in the EU at least 50 million people, which is about 10% of the population, have some type of disability (Burnett and Baker 2001; European Disability Forum 2001). People with impairments may be more dependent on using the Internet as the main source of information, since other sources, like

---

2 On the one hand, drop-down menus with JavaScript lead to a higher usability of web pages but do not lead to more accessible websites. On the other hand, accessibility features (e.g., styleswitcher, zoom) may hamper the usability of websites.
3 The value obtained was on the borderline of significance which implies that there is only a weak possibility that a relationship between accessibility and usability exists.

printed information or personal advice, may be difficult or even impossible to access. It is difficult to assess the ratio of people with disabilities surfing the Internet (ENAT 2007).

People with temporary handicaps (e.g., broken arms or legs) should also be counted to the target group of web accessibility as they have the same problems as people with disabilities.

Accessible web is also of high value for elderly people, a user group that is becoming increasingly important from an economic point of view. The world population, particularly in developed countries, is aging rapidly; the EU estimates that by 2030 24.7% of the EU population will be older than 65 years (VID 2006). Many age-related conditions, such as vision impairments, hearing loss, motor skill diminishment, memory and processing problems are similar to those experienced by the disabled. Moreover, elderly people tend to have a combination of multiple sensory losses and functional impairments. They often have cognitive problems, are overwhelmed with the information flow and have trouble comprehending the user interface (Arch 2008). Currently, only 10% of people older than 65 years use the Internet (Europe's Information Society 2008). In the near future, this number will increase dramatically, due to two developments: (i) an increase in the Internet penetration in this age group, and (ii) a more Internet-accustomed elderly generation in the years to come.

Another user group that benefits significantly from web accessibility is the group of the mobile device users. In the age of smart phones and PDAs, these users are facing similar barriers as people with disabilities (e.g., they rarely use the mouse, they often do not or cannot load images) (W3C 2008b). All the same, mobile internet use is becoming increasingly popular but still suffers from accessibility and usability problems (W3C 2009b).

People with economic or social constraints may also profit from accessible web sites. They often have out-dated modems or poor Internet connections that cannot load large web sites easily.
Predominantly, accessible web sites are constructed for people with disabilities, but – referring to the concept of *Design for All* (cf. section 2.1) – they also offer facilitations for the average, non-disabled Internet user.

2.2.2 Assistive devices

For people with disabilities, the web offers various opportunities for participating in societal life. Online shopping, daily information retrieval, e-government services, and communication possibilities are among the main advantages of the web. Inaccessible web sites are not compatible with assistive technologies and therefore hamper web access for people with disabilities. This chapter will give a short overview of the assistive technologies most commonly used and the problems the users are confronted with when accessing web sites.

Visually impaired people use screen reader software that presents the content displayed on the screen to the user in text. This text can be made available to the user on a "refreshable Braille display" (a tactile hardware device) or through "speech output". For text-input, visually impaired people use the keyboard; for "reading" of text elements they prefer speech output and for navigation and control of spelling they tend to use Braille display. One of the biggest problems for visually impaired users is non-textual content on web sites that does not have a text alternative (alt attribute), e.g., pictures or graphics without appropriate values of the alt-attribute. Moreover, blind users are dependent on a clear web page structure with headings and list attributes as this facilitates web site orientation and navigation. Dependent on the kind and degree of disability, people with low vision may use screen magnifiers that zoom parts of the screen in different sizes. Common problems that people with low vision have to cope with when using a web site are, for example, low color contrast, text that cannot be magnified, and unstructured sites that make navigation difficult.

A lot of motor impaired people cannot use the mouse and/or a standard keyboard. They may use alternative input devices instead, e.g. different sensing devices, head mouse, mouth stick, track ball, or accessible keyboard. Device independent implementation represents a prerequisite for the utilization of these tools. Deaf and hard-of-hearing people face two main problems. The language used on web sites often cannot be understood in enough detail. A solution for this problem could be the usage of "easy to read" texts or the use of sign language videos. In addition, audio files would need a textual alternative. Cognitive impaired people and people with learning difficulties are often confronted with too complex texts and a navigation structure that is not consistent. "Easy to read" texts and a well structured navigation are the most important requirements for this target group.

Some assistive devices, originally developed to provide assistance for people with disabilities, have become common goods over the years, as their utility for the average user has been detected. The first typewriter was developed by Pelegrino Turri in 1808 in order to enable his blind girlfriend to write love letters legibly. Alexander Graham Bell (also known as "father of the deaf") invented the telephone for his wife who suffered from hearing loss (Chamber of Commerce for Individuals with Disabilities 2008). Remote controls for TV sets or speech output of any type (e.g., navigation systems) have also originally been constructed in order to assist people with impairments. In the best possible case, accessible web sites may undergo a similar development.

2.3 Technical specifications

The World Wide Web Consortium (W3C) has developed a holistic set of guidelines and techniques for web accessibility which encompasses (i) web content (WCAG 1.0, WCAG 2.0), (ii) user agents (UAAG), (iii) authoring tools (ATAG), (iv) web applications (WAI-ARIA), and (v) the evaluation of test results (EARL). As the focus of this work lies on the accessibility of web content, the Web Content Accessibility Guidelines 1.0 and 2.0 (WCAG 1.0 and 2.0) are analyzed in further detail. In sections 2.3.1 and 2.3.2, the main content of both guidelines is briefly explained.

2.3.1 Web Content Accessibility Guidelines 1.0

The WCAG 1.0 have been created in 1999 and, by now, represent a de facto standard in Europe (W3C 1999). The WCAG 1.0 are guidelines for accessible web content (text, images, forms, sounds) and mainly refer to HTML and CSS techniques that were common techniques at the time of WCAG 1.0 publication. The WCAG 1.0 summarize 14 guidelines that represent general principles of accessible web design (W3C 1999). Each guideline has one or more checkpoints which explain its application in a specific area. Table 3 summarizes the core techniques of WCAG 1.0.

Area	Technique
Images & animations	Use the alt attribute to describe the function of each visual.
Image maps	Use the client-side map and text for hotspots.
Multimedia	Provide captioning and transcripts of audio and descriptions of video.
Hypertext links	Use text that makes sense when read out of context.
Page organization	Use headings, lists, and consistent structure. Use **CSS** for layout and style where possible.
Graphs & charts	Summarize or use the "longdesc" attribute.
Scripts, applets, plug-ins	Provide alternative content in case active features are inaccessible or unsupported.
Frames	Use the "noframes" element and meaningful titles.
Tables	Make line-by-line reading sensible. Summarize.
Check your work	Validate. Use tools, checklist, and guidelines at http://www.w3.org/TR/WCAG

Table 3 : Core Techniques of WCAG 1.0 (W3C 1999)

Based on their relevance for accessible web design, the checkpoints are divided into three priority groups:

(i) Priority 1 "must criteria" (have to be satisfied to ensure basic access),
(ii) Priority 2 "should criteria" (should be satisfied in order to remove significant barriers), and

(iii) Priority 3 "may criteria" (may be met to further improve access to web sites).

Analogously, three levels of conformance are defined by the WCAG 1.0 guidelines (W3C 1999):

(i) Conformance level A: Satisfaction of all priority 1 criteria
(ii) Conformance level AA: Satisfaction of all priority 2 criteria
(iii) Conformance level AAA: Satisfaction of all priority 3 criteria

Due to the fast development of new technologies and techniques in the information society (e.g., Web 2.0), the WCAG 1.0 needed to be updated and expanded (cf. section 2.3.2) which led to the introduction of the Web Content Accessibility Guidelines 2.0 (WCAG 2.0).

2.3.2 Web Content Accessibility Guidelines 2.0

In December 2008, the W3C published the WCAG 2.0, an expansion and amelioration of WCAG 1.0 (W3C 2008c) which responds to many changes and developments of both web technologies and assistive technologies that have taken place since the publication of version 1.0. WCAG 2.0 contains success criteria that are intended to be testable and not technology specific.
There are four core principles of WCAG 2.0 which are divided into guidelines (W3C 2008c):
(i) Perceivability: information must be presentable to users in ways they can perceive
  Guideline 1.1: Text Alternatives
  Guideline 1.2: Time-based Media
  Guideline 1.3: Adaptable Content
  Guideline 1.4: Distinguishable Content
(ii) Operability: user interface components and navigation must be operable
  Guideline 2.1: Keyboard Accessibility
  Guideline 2.2: Adjustable Timing
  Guideline 2.3: Avoid Seizures
  Guideline 2.4: Navigability
(iii) Understandability: information and the operation of user interface must be understandable
  Guideline 3.1: Readability
  Guideline 3.2: Predictability
  Guideline 3.3: Input Assistance
(iv) Robustness: content must be robust enough that it can be interpreted reliably by a wide variety of user agents, including assistive technologies
  Guideline 4.1: Compatibility

The release of a draft version of WCAG 2.0 almost 10 years after the publication of WCAG 1.0 has been accompanied by some criticism. Clark (2006) criticized the size of the documentation and its comprehensibility. W3C responded to this criticism in an updated version of WCAG 2.0 (Kelly et al. 2008).

Following these guidelines shall ensure an accessible web page, even if such a page can hardly ever be simultaneously barrier-free for all groups of the disabled as some accessibility issues are very difficult to realize (e.g., sign-language translation for every text element of a web site). The inexperienced user only notices that a web page is not accessible when being faced with a barrier, otherwise, at first sight, the accessibility is not detectable. Therefore, it is particularly difficult to raise awareness of the issue. At the moment there is no widespread quality benchmark (e.g. accessibility certification) that allows a web site owner to promote accessibility. The WCAG 1.0 logo of W3C is based on self assessment and thus may lead to misuse.

2.3.3 Search engine ranking

A technical effect of following the guidelines described in sections 2.3.1 and 2.3.2 can be observed in connection with search engines. If a web site is verified accessible, people with disabilities, such as visually impaired users, can access the information provided. The most influential search engine itself, Google, describes the characteristics of its own web site-indexing algorithms ("GoogleBot") similar to those of a blind user. All the additional content elements introduced in the course of web accessibility implementation (e.g., detailed image or product descriptions in alt attributes) lead to a more context-loyal indexing of web page content by GoogleBot. An accessible web site will be found more often and with increased regularity by those users who will get exactly the information on a web site they want to find by the use of a search engine. This is commonly referred to as context loyalty.

As a consequence, accessible web sites are supposed to provoke an improvement of visitor behavior and an increase in web site traffic which can be measured by visitor statistics evaluation (e.g., bounce rate, conversion rate, and time on site). A framework for efficiency measurement of accessible web sites has been developed in a recent study (Leitner et al. 2009a). This framework has been applied to an organizational web site where the extant, inaccessible site has been analyzed, subsequently transferred to an accessible stage, and re-analyzed (Hartjes 2009). Results of this comparative analysis have yielded a significant improvement of all metrics (number of visits, keywords, time on site, bounce rate, number of returning visits). Hence, accessible web sites enable better search engine indexing of web sites which leads to an improved visitor behavior and web site traffic (Hartjes 2009).

2.4 Legal regulations

Most countries that have already considered web accessibility in their legislation have – at least indirectly – referenced to WCAG. Some countries even have already set up quality marks in order to judge web sites and make it possible for end users to identify and compare the level of accessible sites. But as the rather general design of WCAG allows some room for interpretation, these quality marks follow different inspection methods which already lead to some fragmentation in Europe.

Several legal regulations have been passed in the last decade on international and national level. On international level, the most important regulations are the Rights of People with Disabilities from August 2006, the European Charter of Fundamental Rights and the European Agreement for the Protection of Human Rights and Fundamental Freedom. In Austria, on national level, Article 7 of the Austrian Federal Constitution, the Austrian Equalization Act for People with Disabilities, and the Austrian E-Government Act of 2004 regulate the rights for the disabled, including the non-discriminative and equal right to access information. Although the WCAG 1.0 is a guideline, the EU considers it as de facto standard, and it is taken as reference by existing international laws (ENAT 2007). Sections 2.4.1 to 2.4.3 give an overview of existing laws and regulations in the European Union, the United States and Austria. The United States have taken over a pioneering role in terms of web accessibility which is the reason for their consideration in this book.

2.4.1 European Union

The subject of "web accessibility" has been an issue in the European Union since the launch of the "e-Europe – an Information Society for All" initiative in 1999. This initiative represented the starting point for a range of further communications, action plans and initiatives of the European Commission in this area. Latest developments of EU policy related to web accessibility will shortly be presented in this section.

Launched by the European Union, the initiative "i2010 – A European Information Society for Growth and Employment" foresees social and geographical measures to create an information society for all and to ensure a digital society that provides opportunities for everyone (Commission of the European Communities 2007). Inclusion and better public services make up an integral element of the i2010 initiative. Information and communication products and services – especially public services that account for 16% of the GDP – will be made more accessible (Commission of the European Communities 2007). Besides, at the conference "ICT for an Inclusive Society" in Riga in 2006, a ministerial declaration on e-inclusion was approved by 34 European countries in order to accelerate the accessibility of public web sites and to reduce digital divide by 2010 (European Commission 2006).

The declaration of web accessibility as a "European priority" was retained by the European commission in the Communication "Towards an Accessible Information Society" in 2008. This Communication calls upon stakeholders to increase their efforts in the area of web accessibility, explicitly refers to the importance of achievement of the objectives of the ministerial Riga declaration and encourages stakeholders to comply with mandate 376 on accessible procurement of ICT (Council of the European Union 2008). Mandate 376 has been issued in 2005 with two main objectives: (i) harmonization and facilitation of procurement of ICT products and services by definition of a set of European requirements and (ii) provision of an electronic toolkit for public procurers in order to make use of the harmonized requirements (European Commission 2005). European Standards organizations are mandated by the European Commission to provide solutions for common requirements and conformance assessment (i.e., assessment of testing and conformity schemes).

The rights of people with disabilities are protected by law in an increasing number of European Union member states. Some of these have adopted laws specifying that public web sites must be accessible by a certain point in time, others have issued guidelines and recommendations for accessible web site design.

Table 4 provides an overview of web accessibility laws (L) and guidelines or recommendations (G/R) in European member states. The column "National quality mark (QM)" shows which European Union member states have already established a web accessibility quality mark.

EU member state	Law on web accessiblity	National QM	EU member state	Law on web accessiblity	National QM	EU member state	Law on web accessiblity	National QM
Austria	L	no	Germany	L	yes	Netherlands	G/R	yes
Belgium	G/R	yes	Greece	-	no	Poland	G/R	no
Bulgaria	L	no	Hungary	L	no	Portugal	L	no
Cyprus	-	no	Ireland	L	no	Romania	G/R	no
Czech Rep.	L	no	Italy	L	yes	Slovakia	-	no
Denmark	G/R	no	Latvia	L	no	Slovenia	G/R	no
Estonia	G/R	no	Lithuania	G/R	no	Spain	L	yes
Finland	G/R	no	Luxembourg	G/R	no	Sweden	L	no
France	L	yes	Malta	G/R	no	UK	L	yes

Table 4: Overview of web accessibility in European Union countries (Leitner and Strauss 2008)

Table 4 indicates that 13 European Union member states have passed web accessibility laws and 11 EU countries have implemented guidelines or recommendations for web accessibility. In seven member states, national labels have been developed.

2.4.2 United States

The United States have taken over a pioneering role in terms of equal treatment for people with disabilities. Section 508, a law that regulates minimum accessibility requirements for information technologies, has been issued in 1998 (Section508 1998). Section 508 requirements approximately comply with priority 1 requirements of the WCAG 1.0 but are, in contrast to WCAG 1.0, focused on a broader area. The WCAG 1.0 places emphasis on the layout of accessible web sites whereas Section 508 can be applied to software applications, operating systems, telecommunications products, video and multimedia products, electronic devices, desktops, and portable computers. Section 508 is only of marginal interest for Europe, as it is specifically designed for the legal situation in the United States. Moreover, it reformulates and prioritizes the W3C criteria.

2.4.3 Austria

In Austria, Article 7 of the Austrian Federal Constitution (Austrian Federal Constitution 2008) states that no one should be discriminated against on account of his/her impairment. In addition, the Austrian Equalization Act for People with Disabilities indicates that people with impairments must be granted equal rights for participation in societal life (Austrian Equalization Act 2005). The Austrian E-Government Act of 2004 stipulates that public web sites have to meet international standards on web accessibility since January 2008 (Austrian E-Government Act 2004).

However, a recent study analyzed 50 Austrian governmental web presences in terms of their accessibility level. The study showed that only eight web sites (16%) met the conformity level AA and nine web sites (18%) reached single A conformance. The remaining web sites failed the accessibility criteria (Werner 2008). This is a surprising result in the light of the E-Government Act according to which these sites should have met accessibility standards since January 2008.

2.5 Business relevance

In addition to serving as a medium for communication (e.g., online communities), information (e.g., online news retrieval) and education (e.g., e-learning), the Internet can also serve to counterbalance discrimination by providing new opportunities for those who have been discriminated against. This is especially true for people who have been excluded from various activities in daily life because of their special needs (Darzentas and Miesenberger 2005). However, the Internet in its current status actually increases discrimination against people with impairments rather than compensating the disequilibrium, because too few web sites are constructed to be accessible and thus to unlock the potential benefits that the Internet holds for people with disabilities.

The new social model of disability that has developed in recent years has shifted the responsibility of reducing barriers away from the disabled and towards society. The social model of disability does not focus on an individual's limitations, but rather on society's failure to provide the requisite accommodations. This social model defines disability as a "rather complex social and environmental construct largely imposed by societal attitudes and the limitations of the human-made environment" (WHO 2001).

Individual citizens, non-profit organizations, corporations, and the public sector all have different ways of expressing their social responsibility and social awareness. Avoiding discrimination towards people with disabilities is a central characteristic of social responsibility and therefore constitutes a main issue in corporate social responsibility strategies (Moir 2001).

Organizations engage differently with corporate social responsibility. Different characterizations of organizations that deal with CSR have been developed: reactive, defensive, accommodative and proactive (Carroll 1979; Wartick and Cochran 1985; Clarkson 1995). Reactive companies do less than required, defensive companies do at least what is required, accommodative companies do what is required, and proactive companies do more than is required (Clarkson 1995).

Moreover, organizations behave differently in terms of social responsibility depending on the products they produce. According to Vitaliano and Siegel (2007), firms selling credence goods are "more likely to be socially responsible than firms selling search goods" (Vitaliano and Siegel 2007, p. 773).

Various studies on the relationship of corporate social responsibility with financial performance have discovered a positive link between these two components (Waddock and Graves 1997), which means that an increase in socially responsible actions will result in a rise in the overall financial performance of an organization ("doing well by doing good").

However, McWilliams and Siegel (2000) have criticized the Waddock and Graves (1997) model as it did not implicate a measure of firm-level investment in research & development (R&D). In their study, they detected a high correlation between corporate social performance and research & development. After implication of R&D in the model it resulted in corporate social performance having a neutral effect on profitability (McWilliams and Siegel 2000).

2.5.1 Web 2.0 impact

The notion of Web 2.0 has been introduced by Tim O'Reilly in 2005 who intended to describe the trend towards a new, more dynamic web. O'Reilly defines Web 2.0 as the "business revolution in the computer industry caused by the move to the Internet as platform, and an attempt to understand the rules for success on that new platform" (O'Reilly 2006). Moreover, Web 2.0 is characterized by an increase in user participation, openness, network effects, and the power to harness collective intelligence. Key Web 2.0 elements, such as the trend towards user generated content (Wikis, Blogs), social networks (Xing, Facebook), tagging and social bookmarking (Flickr, Delicious) provide the basis for Web 2.0. These technologies cause that the user turns from mere consumer to "prosumer", a term for Internet users who actively contribute to the web and therefore enrich the web's collective intelligence.

Hence, Web 2.0 offers new possibilities for individuals (e.g., social interaction, user involvement, knowledge acquisition) and organizations (e.g., knowledge management, user driven innovation). Individuals experience new ways of knowledge acquisition as they actively contribute to the web and, as a consequence, make their knowledge attainable for other users. Organizations may also profit from the ubiquitous character of the Web 2.0, especially given the fact that – under certain circumstances – knowledge of a group is regarded to be better than that of an individual (Surowiecki 2004). This concept of "wisdom of the crowds" is based on the idea that a group's knowledge may outperform that of an expert (Surowiecki 2004).

Several organizations have already adopted this idea. Google is a prominent example as its search algorithm "PageRank" is solely based on user experiences. The quality or relevance of the web pages is determined by the amount of links referring to them; the links referring to the pages that link to the ranked web page are also considered. The PageRank algorithm has adopted the system used in academic annotation and citation, where indications about the quality of a paper can be drawn from the number of times it is cited in other (high quality) papers. The result demonstrates that user experiences and individual decisions can classify and filter the vast amount of information on the web. In this case, collective intelligence of non-experts yields high quality and relevant results (Howe 2008).

However, the composition of the group is an indicator for the quality of the outcomes. Surowiecki (2004) suggest the diversity aspect as one of several group characteristics that have to be met in order to boost its wisdom. The more heterogeneous a group is the greater its wisdom. Lakhani et al. (2007) disclosed 166 different firm-specific and internally unsolved problems to a community of 80000 scientists with different backgrounds and got one third of them solved. Moreover, they discovered that successful solvers solved problems that were outside their field of expertise (Lakhani et al. 2007). This represents a knowledge transfer from one market to another that would not have been possible without disclosure of problems in the Web 2.0 environment.

Several organizations already use this open innovation concept which assumes that "firms can and should use external ideas as well as internal ideas, and internal and external paths to market, as they look to advance their technology" (Chesbrough et al. 2006). Open innovation platforms (e.g., InnoCentive) have been established in order to enable this paradigm to work. Organizations have the possibility to post their internal problems to the community in the form of innovation challenges and then reward the solver who provides the optimal solution.

The lead user concept suggests the inclusion of progressive consumers in the development of new products (Von Hippel 1986; Von Hippel 2005). Several organizations have integrated the lead user concept into their business model as they include users' ideas, experiences, and opinions in the development of a new product.

Diversity is crucial for wisdom of crowds. Radical ideas can only be generated when crowd is heterogeneous. Heterogeneous groups offer new perspectives. The composition of a group of different people leads to a better solution of problems (Surowiecki 2004).

Organizations which consider the lead user method and/or crowdsourcing techniques should therefore also find ways to guarantee heterogeneity. Companies such as *istockphoto, innocentive* or *threadless,* make significant contributions to the overall economy (Howe 2008), and it shall thus be in their interest to make their web sites accessible to everyone.

Given the fact that organizations depend on user involvement and that diversity is a crucial element for wisdom of the crowds, accessible web sites should be a prerequisite for such platforms and organizations. Harnessing collective intelligence is more likely if the access is not denied to a certain user group.

2.5.2 Business aspects

The term "web accessibility" is tied to several misconceptions, including the widespread idea that web accessibility does not pay off economically. This section demonstrates that, besides social responsibilities and legal obligations, economic advantages – especially in profit-oriented enterprises – also provide strong arguments for the implementation of accessible web sites. These economic advantages not only exist in increasing customers' positive perception of an organization and the resulting image ameliorations, but may also be found in the potential realization of augmented purchasing power and market potential.

Based on literature research, Figure 5 depicts the possible benefits of web accessibility and their relationships.

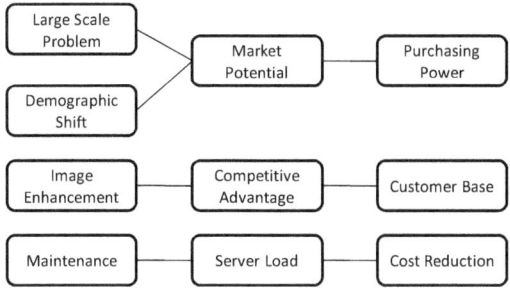

Figure 5: Business aspects of web accessibility

Many organizations are not aware of the fact that the accessibility of web sites represents a large scale problem that is not limited to people with impairments. Accessible web sites provide direct benefits for people with cognitive or physical disabilities, social, economic or educational constraints, as well as the aging population, people with out-dated modems, poor Internet connections (Mankoff et al. 2002), or with browsers on Personal Digital Assistants (PDAs) and mobile phones.

Elderly people may have comparable problems to those that people with physical disabilities face when performing tasks online (e.g., limitations of sight and hearing, arthritis, etc.) (Hanson 2001). Moreover, the ongoing demographic shift in Europe results in a significant increase of the aging population in the coming years: according to demographic trends, the proportion of the European population above the age of 65 will shift from 16.6% in 2005 to 24.7% in 2030 (VID 2006). The population forecast for Austria predicts a shift of people above the age of 60 from 22.6% in 2008 to 34.2% in 2050. This demographic shift (cf. Figure 6) and the electronic process will lead to a considerable increase in the number of elderly people using the web and therefore further emphasize the economic value of web accessibility in the coming years. Elderly customers therefore represent a considerable new market potential from an organization's economic viewpoint.

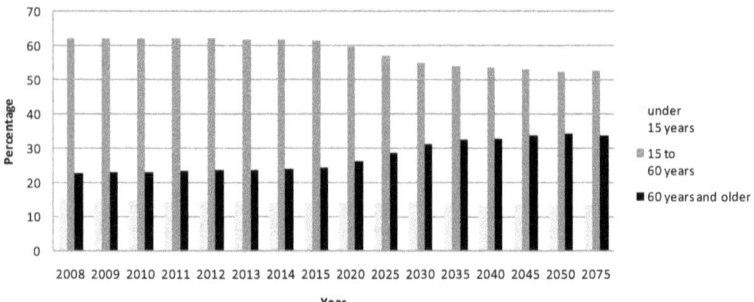

Figure 6: Population forecast for Austria (Statistik Austria 2008)

The UK government estimates that the combined spending power of impaired and elderly people is in excess of 297 billion Euros. This figure represents about 14% of disabled people in the UK with a combined spending power of about 60 billion Euros, and 33% of people over the age of 50 with a combined spending power of about 240 billion Euros (RNIB 2009).

Additionally, Figure 7 shows that in Austria there are hardly any income differences between people with and without disabilities. The results of an OECD study in 2003 demonstrate that in Austria, people with disabilities earn about 96% of the income of people without disabilities. By contrast, in the USA a 30% difference between the income of people with and without impairments can be observed (OECD 2003).

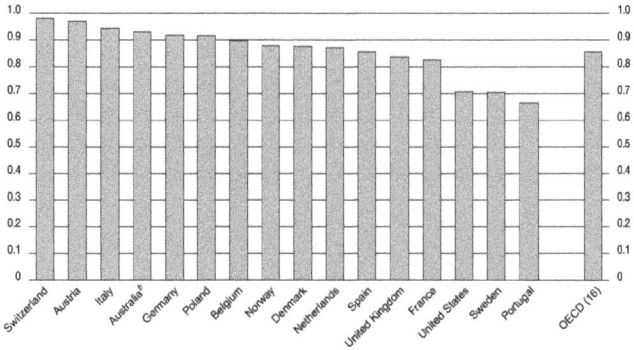

Figure 7: Income differences between people with and without impairments (OECD 2003)

Hence, it can be assumed that organizations with accessible web presences may gain image ameliorations due to their new social orientation and therefore obtain competitive advantage in their b2c business over their direct contenders due to an increase in the scope of their potential customers.

The transformation of existing, inaccessible web sites into accessible ones is a time-consuming task that requires specific know-how and therefore results in additional costs. However, these costs may be compensated by several advantages: e.g., a significant cost reduction in the maintenance of the less complex accessible web sites, a reduced server load, and/or a much quicker page reproduction.

A rough-cut cost-benefit analysis taking into account the total accessibility costs depending on the enterprise size and the complexity of the web site on the one hand and the audience increase on the other hand resulted in estimated relative savings for accessible web sites between 12% and 35% of the web site costs (Heerdt and Strauss 2004).

Web accessibility has become an issue in an increasing number of member states of the European Union. This general tendency will in the near future not only concern public web sites, but also become relevant for web presences of non-governmental organizations. Thus, web accessibility must be brought to the awareness of decision makers using the economic terminology and methods they are used to (e.g., ROI).

This section gives indications about possible business aspects and opportunities in connection with web accessibility implementation. Derived from literature, several theoretical business impacts have been identified (cf. Figure 5). However, an empirical substantiation for these business impacts may strengthen the theoretical findings. For these reasons, this work conducts case study research in three industry sectors in order to get insights into managerial experiences with and changes after web accessibility implementation. The methodology applied and the results of each case are discussed in chapters 3 and 4, followed by a cross-case analysis in chapter 5.

3 Case study research methodology

As already stated in section 1, the area of web accessibility has barely been analyzed from a business perspective so far. Apart from a lack of awareness for this issue, reasons may encompass difficulties in the confine of web accessibility from usability along with measurement troubles. Web accessibility as part of e-business, provokes measurement challenges due to this complex and rapidly changing research field. However, potential productivity impacts of ICT use on business functions turn measurement of e-business to a field of particular interest for policy makers (OECD 2005).

In order to gain insight into organizations' motives for and experiences with web accessibility implementation, as well as their reasons for a failure of implementation, exploratory qualitative research in the field of web accessibility is crucial and represents an important step towards its quantitative ascertainability. The need for provision of qualitative data in this research field has already been expressed by Frank who suggests the conduction of interviews with developers or designers in order to increase knowledge about factors promoting or deterring web accessibility implementation (Frank 2008).

This section analyzes web accessibility from an organizational perspective and determines business impacts of accessible web design with the help of exploratory case study research. Case studies in three industry sectors will give information about experiences with web accessibility implementation, identifying reasons for/against, incentives, benefits and problems with web accessibility implementation.

The main objective of this study is to give examples for successful and failed web accessibility implementation in different industries so that organizations intending to introduce web accessibility may profit from the experiences of others. Therefore, several contributions to research and organizational practice can be identified:

(i) Identification of reasons and incentives for and experiences with web accessibility implementation as well as changes after implementation, hereby filling an extant research gap and providing a basis for further quantitative ascertainability.
(ii) Provision of a knowledge base for other organizations, trying to turn the organizations' tacit, experiential knowledge to explicit, reproducible knowledge.
(iii) Rise of awareness for web accessibility through demonstration of its business impacts and thereby encouraging other organizations to adopt this concept.

(iv) Development of a process model for web accessibility implementation based on the experiences of organizations, hereby filling an extant research gap.

Case study research was chosen as an exploratory methodology for addressing this research problem. Several theories on case study as a research instrument have appeared in the literature (Eisenhardt 1989). Yin (2003) defines a case study as an empirical method of analysis of "a contemporary phenomenon within its real life context" (Yin 2003, p. 13). Eisenhardt (1998) considers a case study as a research strategy that focuses on "understanding the dynamics present within single settings" (Eisenhardt 1989, p. 534), where the case itself is the central point (Bryman 2008). A case study should therefore contain a real life analysis of a phenomenon, taking into account as many different sources of evidence as possible (triangulation) in order to be able to analyze a case in detail (Yin 2003).

The purpose of case study research is not the generalizability of its findings but rather an inductive approach, such as the development of theory out of the results (Bryman 2008). In the theory building process, the explanation of the "why" of a phenomenon needs to be considered additionally to "what" the phenomenon is, and "how" it works (Meredith 1998). Yin (2003) similarly defines "how" and "why" questions as appropriate research questions for an application of the case study method.

Eisenhardt considers Miles & Huberman's theories of qualitative research (Miles and Huberman 2005) as well as elements of grounded theory (Glaser and Strauss 1967), and further develops ideas for within-case and cross-case analyses or triangulation (Eisenhardt 1989). Moreover, the importance of triangulation is highlighted by Pettigrew (1990), as this strategy allows to combine the strengths of multiple data collection methods. However, the triangulation process requires multiple methods and tools which may result in difficulties in terms of cost, time and access hurdles (Meredith 1998).

Eisenhardt (1989) outlines a detailed process for theory building from case study research that is adopted in this contribution (cf. Table 5).

Step	Activity	Reason
Getting Started	Definition of research questions	Focuses efforts
	Possibly a priory constructs	Provides better grounding of construct measures
Selecting Cases	Neither theory, nor hypotheses	Retains theoretical flexibility
	Specified population	Sharpens external validity
	Theoretical, not random, sampling	Focuses efforts on theoretically useful cases
Crafting Instruments and Protocols	Multiple data collection methods	Strengthens grounding of theory by triangulation of evidence
	Qualitative and quantitative data combined	Synergistic view of evidence
	Multiple investigators	Fosters divergent perspectives and strengthens grounding
Entering the Field	Overlap data collection and analysis, including field notes	Speeds analyses and reveals helpful adjustments to data collection
Analyzing Data	Within-case analysis	Gains familiarity with data and preliminary theory generation
	Cross-case pattern search using divergent techniques	Forces investigators to look beyond initial impressions and see evidence through multiple lenses
Shaping Hypotheses	Iterative tabulation of evidence for each construct	Sharpens construct definition, validity and measurability
	Replication, not sampling, logic across cases	Confirms, extends and sharpens theory
	Search evidence for "why" behind relationships	Builds internal validity
Enfolding Literature	Comparison with conflicting literature	Builds internal validity, raises theoretical level and sharpens construct definitions
	Comparison with similar literature	Sharpens generalizability, improves construct definition and raises theoretical level
Reaching Closure	Theoretical saturation when possible	Ends process when marginal improvement becomes small

Table 5: Process of building theory from case study research (Eisenhardt 1989)

Eisenhardt's (1989) steps for theory building from case study research outlined in Table 5 are explained in further detail and simultaneously applied to the present case study in sections 3.1 to 3.6.

3.1 Research questions

Given the facts outlined in section 2.5.2, it is assumed that web accessibility implementation may lead to business benefits for organizations. Currently, few organizations have implemented accessible web sites which implies that little information is available concerning their experiences with implementation procedures, their incentives, or the direct benefits they obtained from an implementation of accessibility. Web accessibility implementation projects have been initiated in organizations but may have failed or been turned down due to various reasons. In this case, information about the reasons for project failure, for hesitation of web accessibility implementation, or required incentives can be useful. Derived from these considerations, the research questions for this case study can be formulated as follows:

(i) What is the **business impact** that can be obtained from web accessibility?
(ii) What are the **reasons** for web accessibility implementation?
(iii) What are the **changes** experienced after web accessibility implementation?
(iv) Why do organizations in the private sector **hesitate to adopt** web accessibility?
(v) Which **incentives** have to be initiated for private organizations to implement web accessibility?

The development of these research questions represents the starting point of case study research. The purpose of the development of research questions is to generate a well defined focus in order to avoid becoming overwhelmed by the volume of data. However, the research questions may change during research as they will be influenced by the case study findings. Despite a development of research questions, the field should be entered with as little preoccupation by the researcher as possible as this may bias the findings (Eisenhardt 1989).

3.2 Case selection

The literature on case study research does not stipulate a certain number of cases to be selected but suggests a number of four to ten cases for sound research results (Eisenhardt 1989). Ideally, in a comparative study design, cases should be chosen as to provide examples for extreme situations or polar types (Pettigrew 1990) in order to "maximize what we can learn" (Stake 1995, p. 4).

Yin (2003) distinguishes four types of case study designs: single-case, multiple-case, embedded, and holistic. These types can be combined among each other resulting in four case study possibilities: single holistic, single embedded, multiple holistic, and multiple embedded (cf. Figure 8). For reasons of validity and model robustness, the embedded, multiple-case design is chosen from these types as it addresses more than one case and permits multiple units of analysis within each case. Moreover, Yin distinguishes five case types (critical, extreme/unique, representative/typical, revelatory, longitudinal) that may be chosen for case study research (Yin 2003).

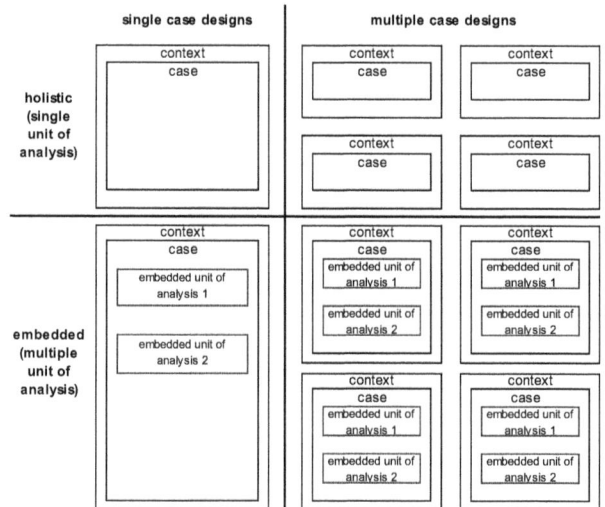

Figure 8: Case study design (Yin 2003)

The selection of cases is done though theoretical sampling which means that cases are deliberately chosen and not being sampled randomly. In case study research, random selection is not preferable as – due to the limited number of cases that can be studied – theoretical sampling offers the possibility to transparently observe the process under study, whereas with random sampling it is not guaranteed to obtain a sample containing this process (Pettigrew 1990). The main goal of theoretical sampling is to choose cases that are likely to extend emergent theory (Eisenhardt 1989) and not – as is the case with quantitative studies – to test existing theories.

Following these suggestions, our model comprises the analysis of private organizations in the b2c segment of three industry sectors with high relevance in electronic business (European Commission 2007): (i) financial services, (ii) information, and (iii) tourism.

Apart from their high e-business importance, these sectors were chosen as they represent organizations needed for day-to-day business, which implies that their accessibility is particularly relevant for people with disabilities Following Yin's distinction of cases, this research model comprises three "typical cases" that represent "conditions of an everyday or commonplace situation" (Yin 2003, p. 41). In each of the three sectors, the benefit of web accessibility is analyzed focusing on two extreme situations (Pettigrew 1990), namely organizations that have successfully implemented web accessibility and organizations that have failed web accessibility implementation.

Several determining factors for the choice of the financial services, the information, and the tourism sector for this case study have been considered:

Facilitation dimension: All three sectors provide day-to-day business services that are used on a frequent basis. Their online access represents an enormous facilitation for the average user as he/she becomes locally independent. For people with impairments, especially people with mobility constraints (sight disabled people, mobility disabled people), this facilitation dimension and the resulting locally independence are crucial. Alternatives to online service consumption may be tied to long range planning and/or complication. Online access alleviates the consumption of services which – in these three cases – represent day-to-day (news consumption, financial transactions) or frequent (hotel booking) necessities and therefore shall be equally accessible.

Relevance dimension: The three industry sectors have been chosen according to their relevance for electronic business. The tourism sector was one of the early adopters of ICT, high productivity gains in terms of online services are attained within the financial services and the information sector. These circumstances explain the high relevance of the three sectors for electronic business.

Awareness dimension: Literature review revealed a lack of accessibility in the tourism, financial services, and information sector. Further rise of awareness for the importance of web accessibility shall be attained by the consideration of these sectors in this case study.

Figure 9 shows the industry sectors investigated and their embedded units of analysis (UA).

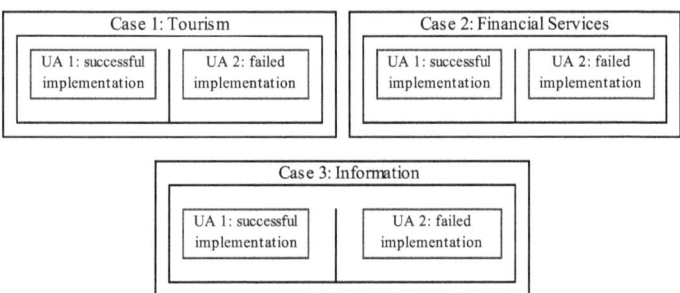

Figure 9: Embedded, multiple case study design for web site accessibility

The purpose of the case study design outlined in Figure 9 is to monitor the business impacts of web accessibility, the barriers of implementation, and possible incentives in order to overcome these barriers.

For reasons of internal validity, comparability, repeatability, and profound data analysis, the data collection methods used for this case study research (semi-structured interviews, questionnaires, observations, archives, etc.) have to follow a well structured framework. Furthermore, a consistent application of the same variables and issues in each case is required in order to ensure comparability. Following Miles and Huberman's suggestions for sound qualitative research, a conceptual framework has been established before entering the field. Despite the above mentioned reasons, a conceptual framework depicts the core areas of interest that can be changed and/or enriched during the research process (Miles and Huberman 2005). Figure 10 illustrates the conceptual framework with the relevant issues, variables, and their linkages. This framework will be applied to each of the three cases depicted in Figure 9.

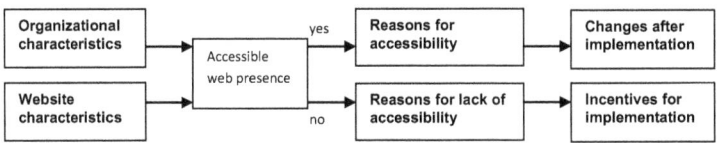

Figure 10: Conceptual framework for case study research on business impacts of web accessibility

The conceptual framework is split into two tracks depending on the units of analysis (cf. Figure 10). For organizations with accessible web presences, the interviews focus on the reasons for implementation and identify changes that occur after web accessibility implementation. For organizations which failed in web accessibility implementation, this research focuses on the determination of reasons for inaccessibility and derives possible incentives for an implementation. For each of the four categories developed in Figure 10 (reasons for accessibility, changes after implementation, reasons for lack of accessibility, incentives for implementation), an inductive approach is applied in order to find out about the subcategories and items. The application of this framework to the cases depicted in Figure 9 will lead to a first data collection that can be i) analyzed using within-case or cross-case analysis techniques and ii) progressively enriched and updated by additional new cases.

Given the case study design displayed in Figure 9, organizations representing the two polar types (successful vs. failed web accessibility implementation) have to be detected for each industry sector. In order to determine these organizations, an evaluation of their web presences had to be undertaken in the first place.

3.3 Research instruments

Typically, in case study research, multiple data collection methods are combined in a so called triangulation process in order to obtain stronger corroboration of hypotheses (Eisenhardt 1989). This may result in the combination of qualitative and quantitative data within a case study, profiting from advantages of both data types: (i) qualitative data sheds light on underlying relationships whereas (ii) quantitative data helps that the researcher is not misled in his interpretations (Eisenhardt 1989).

Yin suggests storing and structuring these different data types in a data base (Yin 2003). The data matrix in Table 6 gives an overview of the data collection methods used in this case study research and the type of information they provide (company specific or sector specific). Moreover, Table 6 indicates the overall number of documents used in each case study, and displays the corresponding data type.

Type of information	Type of evidence	Tourism	Financial Services	Information	Data type
company specific	In-depth interviews	2	6	4	qualitative
company specific	Personal documentation (interviewer's notes, meeting notes)	3	7	5	qualitative
company specific	Information about organizations interviewed (annual reports, website, press releases, Austrian Web Analysis data, Commercial Register data)	5	14	10	qualitative/ quantitative
sector specific	Quantitative website evaluation	52	19	18	quantitative
sector specific	Industry information (Internet, brochures, research)	10	6	3	qualitative
sector specific	Accessibility in the three industries (Internet, reports, studies, audiofiles)	16	3	7	qualitative
	Overall documents used	88	55	47	

Table 6: Data matrix

In this case study, both quantitative and qualitative data is involved. In every case, semi structured interviews have been conducted. The difference in sample size of the semi-structured interviews in each case (tourism: 2, financial services: 6, information: 4) is due to a small number of organizations which have implemented accessible web in these sectors. As a consequence, the number of interviews was limited and depended on the sectoral circumstances.

However, similarities between the results in each sector indicate that the number of interviews is appropriate. Further company specific data used for this case study included information about organizations interviewed (e.g., annual reports). The differences in the number of documents analyzed are due to a disparate availability of company information on the Internet. More information could be collected about large organizations than about small and medium organizations. However, information about every organization interviewed has been gathered beforehand. Interviewer's notes were taken in addition to each interview and meeting notes taken after discussion of each sector's interviews.

Sector specific information used for this case study included quantitative website evaluation, general industry information (Internet, research), and information about the accessibility in the three industries.

However, the focus is put on qualitative semi-structured interviews which capture – together with the interviewer's notes and the meeting minutes – a core part of the data analyzed. It can therefore be stated that this study mainly relies on qualitative data but uses quantitative data for reasons of corroboration of results. Apart from literature on industries and organizations interviewed, evaluations of web presences and semi-structured interviews represent the main research instruments in this case study research.

3.3.1 Evaluation of web presences

The web site evaluation that is conducted in an early stage of the analysis represents the largest quantitative data input into the case study. It is carried out in order to screen the three cases for the level of accessibility of their web sites. This way, the organizations which come into consideration for qualitative semi-structured interviews are identified. Following Yin's (2003) and Eisenhardt's (1989) recommendations, the complementary application of both data types (qualitative and quantitative) was chosen as the most reasonable and scientifically sound way for this case study.

The evaluation of web presences for the tourism, the financial services and the information and communications sector has been divided into three steps: (i) determination of relevant organizations, (ii) automated testing, and (iii) manual testing. Figure 11 displays the evaluation method for every web presence.

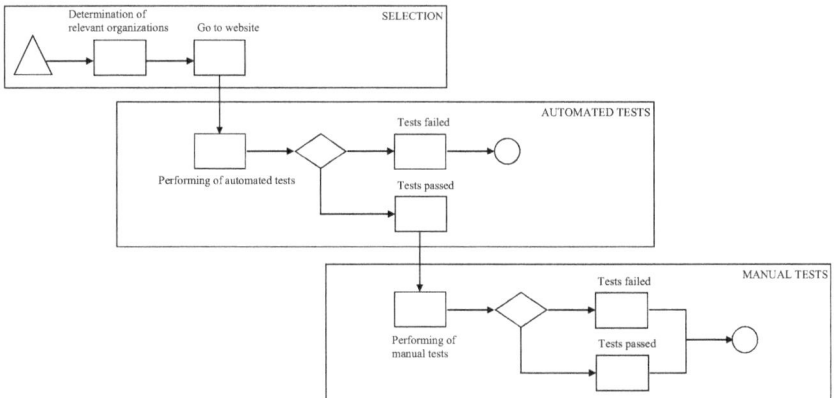

Figure 11: Evaluation method

Selection:
The identification of relevant organizations in every industry sector represents the first step in the evaluation process. In the tourism sector, hotels listed on one of Austria's largest portals on accessible tourism, the Information Portal for Accessible Tourism (IBFT), were evaluated. IBFT acts as an information platform for tourists with disabilities and – amongst others – lists hotels that provide physical accessibility. For this evaluation, 52 Austrian hotels from IBFT have been evaluated. After a sectoral research in the financial services sector, 17 Austrian, 1 German and 1 Swiss banking institution have been evaluated. The foreign banking institutions had to be added as the evaluation results for the Austrian banking institutions have not been positive. In the information & communication sector,

19 Austrian providers of information have been analyzed (e.g., online newspapers, television).

Automated Tests:
For 52 organizations in the tourism sector, 19 financial institutions, and 18 organizations in the information and communication sector, automated accessibility tests have been performed in May and June 2009. The main objective behind automated testing is to identify if the web presence disposes of the most essential accessibility features. Elaborate methods, such as the Unified Web Evaluation Methodology (UWEM) that requires long term professional experience in accessibility testing have therefore been avoided. Instead, the World Wide Web Consortium's "Preliminary Review" has been applied which offers a quick way to identify some basic accessibility problems and provides a sound impression of the web site's general accessibility (W3C 2008a). On each web site a random sample of three pages was chosen. For each of these pages, standard code validation was performed in order to check for markup errors. Correct markup application provides a prerequisite for web site accessibility. Currently, there are many tools for automated accessibility testing. For the evaluation in this contribution, the online software "Total Validator v. 5.3.0" was used as it has been recommended by the W3C (Vos and Ambrose 2007). The results found by the Total Validator tool consist of detailed error descriptions with indications of code lines and summarize parsing (correct syntax), HTML (correct application of HTML codes) and accessibility (correct application of web accessibility guidelines) problems. Moreover, warnings with manual check recommendations are issued. In case of accessibility errors, the web presences have not been considered for manual testing.

Manual Tests:
The warnings issued by Total Validator on WAI conformant web sites have been tested manually with the help of graphical and specialized browsers. Two different browsers have been used for the performing of multiple tests:
- Web Developer Plug-In on Firefox 3.0: disabling images, alt-text check, turning off sound, font sizes, resolutions, color display, navigation without the mouse;
- Lynx browser: text-only version of web presence;

Only web presences with positive automated and manual evaluation results were considered for the "successful implementation" sample.

3.3.2 Semi-structured interviews

Semi-structured interviews have been conducted in this case study research. This type of interview allows open questions and conversational style and therefore enables new viewpoints to emerge freely. The interviewee guides the conversation, whereas the interviewer listens actively and intervenes in case of breaks in the conversation or in case of major deviations of the interviewee in order to minimize the interview-induced bias (Thompson et al. 2006). For this purpose, two loose interview guidelines (see Annex A) have been developed on the basis of the conceptual framework (see Figure 10): one for organizations which successfully implemented web accessibility and one for organizations which failed in web accessibility implementation. These guidelines cover the main topics identified in the conceptual framework and ensure comparability across interviews. The interview guidelines start with a predetermined set of questions (personal background, description of work, description of organization). However, the core part of the interview was guided by participants. Interviewers only asked questions in case of breaks in the conversation in. Commonly, additional questions emerged out of the conversation.

The interviews have been conducted from January 2008 to March 2009. All semi-structured interviews lasted for about 60-90 minutes and were audio-taped and transcribed verbatim. Interview partners were informed beforehand (per e-mail or telephone) about the main topic of the interview. Moreover, anonymity for the participants and their organizations was insured.

In the literature, two possibilities of case study conduction have been applied: single investigators (Burgelman 1983; Gersick 1988) or research teams (Harris and Sutton 1986; Pettigrew 1990). In this case study, three researchers have conducted the semi-structured interviews although the author has covered a major part and instructed the two other researchers on interview techniques. Multiple advantages of research teams have been identified, e.g., the augmentation of creativity potential and the enhancement of confidence in the findings (Eisenhardt 1989). After each sector's interviews, discussions about interview outcomes have taken place in order to profit from differing insights of the other team members.

Table 7 shows the number of semi-structured interviews conducted in the three interview sectors and distinguishes between organizations with successful and failed web accessibility implementation.

Industry	Country	Employees	Function	Implementation
1 Financial Services	Germany	21000	Project manager IT	Successful
2 Financial Services	Switzerland	47800	Project manager	Successful
3 Financial Services	Austria	5358	Content manager	Successful
4 Financial Services	Austria	5351	Member of general secretariat	Failed
5 Financial Services	Austria	63376	Project manager IT	Failed
6 Financial Services	Austria	140	Content manager	Failed
7 Information	Austria	7	Marketing manager	Successful
8 Information	Austria	51	Technical manager	Successful
9 Information	Austria	9	Director	Successful
10 Information	Austria	12	Director	Failed
11 Tourism	Austria	19	Marketing manager	Successful
12 Tourism	Austria	140	Director	Failed

Table 7: Interview sample

Table 7 indicates the organization's industry and country of origin, the number of employees, the interview partner's function in the organization, and the success or failure of accessibility implementation. Considering the number of employees it becomes obvious that small, medium and large enterprises are among the sample. The reason for this heterogeneity of organizational sizes is to monitor possible differences with accessibility implementation.

The data collection process was divided into two phases. In the first phase, data was collected without simultaneous analysis. After six months, the available data was partly analyzed and integrated in the next collection phase of again six months. In the second phase, every new data was at least partly integrated in order to profit from above mentioned overlap between analysis and collection.

3.4 Field research

In the building process of theory from case study research, an overlap of data analysis and data collection is common. As the data collection process in qualitative studies may take over some time, the analysis and coding of data is recommended to be made simultaneously. This way, the learning effects from one case may be transferred to the next case. Moreover, the researcher is able to collect the data flexibly and make adjustments to the data and the conceptual framework while field research is ongoing (Eisenhardt 1989). In case of detection of new emergent themes from the data, these can be embedded in later data collection.

3.5 Data analysis

In qualitative research, the actual data analysis represents the core part for building theory but at the same time the least specified part in literature. Miles and Huberman identify several possibilities of qualitative data analysis and data display that were applied in this work (Miles and Huberman 2005). For every case, a within-case analysis was performed taking into account the multiple sources of data (cf. Table 6). After completion of within-case analyses of every case, a cross-case analysis was undertaken in order to detect possible patterns that emerge within all three cases.

3.5.1 Within-case analysis

In the beginning of every case analysis, a literature research is performed that provides indications about the sector's main organizations, it's relevance for electronic business and thus, for web accessibility. Moreover, based on the results of a web site evaluation, for each unit of analysis (successful vs. failed accessibility implementation) semi-structured interviews were conducted (12 interviews in total) that represent the main source of data for each case. The coding and analysis of the interview transcripts constitute the central element of within-case analysis. In total, 646 interview minutes (10.8 hours) were transcribed which resulted in a total amount of 181 transcription pages, single spaced font size 11. Atlas.ti software was used for coding and analysis of the interview transcripts.

In the literature on qualitative research, several different ways of data analysis have been developed. Glaser and Strauss suggest an inductive approach, where the researcher starts without any prefabricated start list of codes. The codes are generated freely during the analysis and – in a later stage – reviewed and summarized to categories. Grounded theory suggests to start by looking for conditions and consequences in the text with a special focus on the words "because", "since" and "as a result" (Glaser and Strauss 1967). Literature and data are iteratively consulted and analyzed simultaneously using open coding techniques (Goulding 2005). A diametrically opposed, deductive approach for the coding of qualitative data is suggested by Lofland who has developed a general accounting scheme for codes, where one predefined code list is supposed to fit for all studies (Lofland 1971).

In this contribution, an approach that is situated between Glaser and Strauss's (1967) inductive and Lofland's (1971) deductive suggestion is applied. Miles and Huberman (2005) take over the idea of a code master list with codes derived from the conceptual framework and the research questions. The resulting list is therefore not a general but a case-specific one and is developed before entering the field. However, during analysis, the codes are permanently revised, changed, added, or removed, so that after saturation the differences from the conceptual framework are clearly visible (Miles and Huberman 2005). Stake also suggests the preparation of pre-established codes and the subsequent data analysis in search for new emerging codes (Stake 1995). In either case, the iterative procedure of data analysis can be described as a "part-to whole movement" (Thompson 1997), starting at the first interview transcript and ending in pattern detection across all interviews. This way, the researcher is able to gain a holistic view of the whole case under study (Thompson 1997). In this case research, a code master list is developed beforehand that consists of the four main categories depicted in the conceptual framework (reasons for, incentives for, changes after, reasons for failure of implementation). Within these main categories, the codes are developed inductively. A grounded theory approach for each main category is applied. Code lists with the respective quotations can be found in appendix B.

Not only in the data collection but also in the data analysis stage, the existence of research teams is important. The validity of results increases if intercoder reliability is high[4]. Various quality criteria have been developed for measuring the intercoder reliability, e.g., Percentage Agreement, Cohen's Kappa (Brennan and Prediger 1981), Scott's Pi (Scott 1955), or Krippendorff's Alpha (Hayes and Krippendorff 2007). Differences between these reliability measures are discussed in Hayes and Krippendorff (2007). Additionally, the creation of intercoder consistency matrices for ensuring the appropriateness of category development is suggested (Srnka and Koeszegi 2007).

In this contribution, the coding process was undertaken by two coders. Intercoder reliability checks have been conducted by using the Krippendorff's Alpha measure. This measure can be applied regardless of the number of observers, levels of measurement, sample sizes, and presence or absence of missing data (Hayes and Krippendorff 2007). Additionally, Krippendorff's Alpha takes into account chance agreement, which, e.g., Percentage Agreement does not. Reliability is absent when units are categorized by chance; categories should have a relation to the units of analysis (Krippendorff 2009). For this purpose, two coders have coded 17 transcript pages independently. In total, 67 units have been coded independently by two coders who applied a total number of 35 categories (codes) to these units. Krippendorff's alpha yielded a value of 0.7065 (cf. Figure 12).

```
Krippendorff's Alpha Reliability Estimate

              Alpha    LL95%CI    UL95%CI     Units    Observrs      Pairs
Nominal       ,7065      ,5984      ,8147   67,0000      2,0000    67,0000

Probability (q) of failure to achieve an alpha of at least alphamin:
 alphamin         q
   ,9000      ,9999
   ,8000      ,9632
   ,7000      ,4401
   ,6700      ,2459
   ,6000      ,0424
   ,5000      ,0005

Number of bootstrap samples:
 10000

Judges used in these computations:
 o1        o2
```

Figure 12: Krippendorff alpha results

---

4 Hayes and Krippendorff (2007) suggest an ideal value of 80%.

Figure 12 displays the results obtained by the SPSS KALPHA macro[5]. This alpha measure means that about 70% of units of data are perfectly reliable, whereas 30% are the results of chance (Krippendorff 2009). Given a benchmark of 0.8, these results may be classified modest reliable (cf. Hayes and Krippendorff 2007). However, in case of complex data analyses, this moderate value is justified. Compared to a usual application of 3-5 categories per unit (Hayes and Krippendorff 2007), the data reliability matrix in this case is the result of an application of 35 categories and can therefore be classified as complex.

After first level coding, pattern or meta codes can be identified that explain possible emergent themes or configurations. For this purpose, codes are grouped into a smaller number of sets, themes or constructs. This procedure represents, on the one hand, an effective method for reduction of large amounts of data and, on the other hand, gives room for the elaboration of cognitive maps that may be visualized graphically. There is no standard format for data display; some researchers use data tables, others prefer graphs or tabular displays, others in turn prepare transcripts or case histories (Eisenhardt 1989). The findings of this pattern display process constitute the input for cross-case analysis.

3.5.2 Cross-case analysis

Due to information-processing biases that people usually tend to have (e.g., influence by vividness of respondents, ignorance of statistical properties, ignorance of evidence), Eisenhardt suggests to "look at the data in many divergent ways" (Eisenhardt 1989, p. 540) in order to avoid the drawing of false conclusions. This can be done either by selecting categories and then looking for within-group similarities and across-group differences or by selecting pairs of cases and then listing of analogies or discrepancies between each pair. A third approach is to analyze data from each data source independently. This way, researchers are forced to go beyond initial impressions and may therefore improve the probability of sound theory (Eisenhardt 1989).

In this case study, cross-case analysis is conducted following Eisenhardt's (1989) suggestions for paired selection of cases and categories and then searching for similarities and differences. The cross-case findings for this case study can be found in section 5.

3.6 Enfolding literature

The shaping of hypotheses in qualitative research involves two steps: (i) the iterative approach of data analysis that results in an emergence of themes, patterns and relationships that enable the definition and development of constructs and (ii) the

---

5 The Krippendorff alpha is not part of standard SPSS calculations. A SPSS KALPHA macro is available for download at http://www.asc.upenn.edu/usr/krippendorff/dogs.html.

replication of cases, using each of them for confirmation or disconfirmation of hypotheses (Eisenhardt 1989). In this context, transparency of results is a crucial element for researcher and reader. Due to the fact that no statistical tests (e.g., F-test) can be applied and the research team judges the construct relationships themselves, a detailed publication of research steps and findings is necessary.

The findings of case study research have to be combined with extant literature in order to strengthen the emergent theory. For this purpose, the consideration of both literature that conflicts and literature that is in line with the theory developed is crucial. In the first case, conflicting literature should not be ignored as the findings may be weakened or appear less credible. In the latter case, supporting literature may strengthen the internal validity of the findings. In case study research, findings are based on a small number of cases which makes the link to extant literature crucial (Eisenhardt 1989).

In the following sections, all three cases are analyzed in detail, beginning with a sectoral overview that is followed by the presentation of quantitative website evaluation results, qualitative interview outcomes, and a short summary and interpretation. In section 5, a cross-case analysis is performed across all three cases and the emerging patterns are presented.

4 Within case analyses: Empirical evidence and results

In chapter 4, the empirical evidence and results of the within-case analysis are presented for each case. After a brief overview of every sector analyzed and a clarification for its choice for this study, the results of both quantitative web site evaluation and qualitative analysis (semi-structured interviews) are introduced. In the qualitative analysis section, the quotations taken from the interview transcripts are highlighted in italics. Each category identified in the qualitative analysis was enfolded with extant concepts in academic research in order to corroborate the findings. The within-case analysis of each sector concludes with a brief summary and interpretation of the case's results.

4.1 Case 1: Tourism

4.1.1 Sector overview

The tourism sector has a significant importance in the economy. In Austria, the overall turnover in tourism reached 40 billion Euros in 2007, which represents over 16% of the gross domestic product (OECD 2008). Tourists are defined as people who "*travel to and stay in places outside their usual environment for not more than one consecutive year for leisure, business, and other purposes not related to the exercise of an activity remunerated from within the place visited*" (UNWTO 2007). Moreover, tourism is considered as a cross-sector industry that affects communication, transport, construction, training, human rights, etc. (Ambrose 2007) with accommodation as one of its core businesses (NatKo 2002). In Austria, 55% of accommodation is covered by the hotel sector (Federal Ministry of Economics and Labour 2007).

The tourism sector has been among the early adopters of the Internet technology (Williams et al. 2007) which led to the Internet being the top information source used by European travelers (OECD 2008). Over half of the European Internet users (108.6 million) have visited a travel related web site in March 2006. 17% of the European online travel market in 2007 (49.4 billion Euros) was spent in the hotel sector (Marcussen 2008).

In the hotel sector, electronic distribution channels are increasingly gaining in importance (O'Connor and Frew 2004). 89% of organizations in the accommodation sector with 10 or more employees have a web site, 39% of organizations are booked online. However, they are still below the average value with respect to integrated e-business solutions implemented (Knauth 2006). The number of guests who use online booking systems has increased by 34% since 2005, which resulted in an overall number of almost 50% in 2007 (JD Power and Associates 2007).

The main concept behind accessible tourism is the idea that *"everybody – regardless of whether they have any disabilities – should be able to travel to the country, within the country and to whatever place, attraction or event they should wish to visit"* (Neumann and Reuber 2004). The target group for accessible tourism and web accessibility are similar. People with reduced mobility represent 40% of the population 10% of which are people with disabilities. Therefore, accessibility in tourism can be claimed to be essential for 10% of the population, necessary for 40% and convenient for 100% (Ambrose 2007).

Based on previous research, it is assumed that 70% of the target group has the financial and physical condition to travel (Neumann and Reuber 2004). A recent fundamental study on the economic impact of accessible tourism in Germany has shown that more than half of the people with disabilities have been travelling, but a third of them have already renounced their travel due to inadequate conditions. However, half of the people with activity limitations would travel more if the circumstances were more favorable (Neumann and Reuber 2004).

In accessible tourism, a special emphasis is placed on the accessibility of information, as it constitutes a prerequisite for travelling. Disabled people are forced to plan their trips much longer ahead and with more attention to detail and would use the Internet to gather information to a larger extent than other travelers (Ray and Ryder 2003). Unfortunately, to a large extent, tourism stakeholders do not consider customers with disabilities and do not recognize their market potential. This underlines that although both web accessibility and accessible tourism have become a matter of concern in research and legislation. In reality, web accessibility in tourism is still in its infancy. The main reason for this is the lack of awareness, understanding, and/or an ignorance of the issue (Neumann and Reuber 2004; Pühretmair 2004; Williams et al. 2004; Williams et al. 2007).

In Austria, the following options are available for people with disabilities who search online for hotels that can accommodate their needs:

(i) Hotel web page
Few hotels provide information about the availability of accessible hotel rooms on their web presences.
(ii) Travel and booking platforms:
Travel and booking platforms generally do not provide information on accessibility beyond wheelchair accessibility. The largest platform in Austria is Tiscover[6] which offers only a limited search possibility on accessibility aspects. Furthermore, the web page itself is not accessible.

---

6 http://www.tiscover.com/ (last accessed: 19/11/09)

(iii) Information platforms for people with disabilities:
These platforms include a database on wheelchair accessible hotels and are maintained by interest groups, non-profit organizations, or private persons. To be listed, a hotel has to provide detailed information on hotel accessibility. The platforms offer an advanced search option, where every potential customer can search on their exact needs. Unfortunately, basically none of these platforms include the information if the hotel's web page is accessible. However, many of these platforms also lack basic web accessibility criteria
(iv) Designated sites of the regional tourist information systems:
These sites work on a principle similar to the information platform, collecting accessible accommodation regionally.

In cases, where no direct booking is offered on a platform, one can decide to contact the selected hotel by phone or e-mail. However, this causes a media disruption; the guest is forced to change media within the search process.

Similarly to other sectors in tourism (Neumann and Reuber 2004; Pühretmair 2004; Buhalis and Eichhorn 2005), accessibility in the hotel sector is a complex issue. The availability of an accessible web page is not sufficient. In order to really meet the needs of people with disabilities, the hotel itself has to be accessible and the guests have to be informed about the accessibility of the hotel[7].

The above argumentation clarifies the choice of the tourism sector as one case for this study:

(i) The planning and booking of touristic activities via the web entails enormous facilitations for people with disabilities (facilitation dimension).

(ii) The tourism sector is highly relevant for e-business and belongs to the early adopters of information technology (relevance dimension).

(iii) A lack of current web site accessibility in this sector needs further rise of awareness for its importance (awareness dimension).

4.1.2 Web site evaluation

In the tourism sector, 52 hotels listed on an Austrian platform for accessible tourism (IBFT[8]) have been evaluated in terms of web accessibility. This platform's listing is based on self evaluation of the hotels' (physical) accessibility. For this reason, it can be assumed that every hotel listed is familiar with accessible tour-

---

7   A recently developed hotel categorization model on accessibility enables benchmarking activities or current state evaluations of hotel accessibility (Erdey-Gruz et al. 2009).
8   The IBFT (www.ibft.at) is an information platform for accessible tourism in Austria where accessible hotels are listed.

ism and physical accessibility issues. The evaluation has been conducted following the methodology outlined in section 3.3.1.

Table 8 displays the web site evaluation results and uses three different colors that mark the status of the web site evaluated. White lines indicate that these web presences have passed both automated and manual tests (web sites number 1 to 3), web sites that have only passed automated tests are highlighted in light grey (web sites number 4 to 13), and dark grey lines show that these web presences have not passed automated tests (web sites number 14 to 52). Manual tests have not been performed on dark grey highlighted web presences. For reasons of data protection, the hotel names and web site URLs are not displayed. The organizations are ranked according to the number of their accessibility errors (WAI column). Moreover, the number of WAI, HTML, parsing and link errors are indicated in Table 8. If manual tests have failed, the reason for failure is given in the "manual testing results" column. In case manual tests have not been performed, the code "n/a" is entered.

Organization	Automated testing results					Manual testing results
	WAI errors	HTML errors	Parsing errors	Link errors	Total errors	
1	0	90	1	1	92	OK
2	0	1	3	1	5	OK
3	0	21	3	0	24	OK
4	0	0	0	0	0	Lynx
5	0	28	0	0	28	Lynx
6	0	38	0	3	41	Lynx
7	0	43	7	13	63	Lynx
8	0	2	0	0	2	Lynx
9	0	4	0	0	4	Lynx
10	0	9	2	2	13	Lynx
11	0	13	5	0	18	Lynx
12	0	33	0	0	33	Lynx
13	0	64	5	0	69	Lynx
14	1	12	1	0	14	n/a
15	1	3	0	0	4	n/a
16	1	27	18	0	46	n/a
17	1	28	5	0	34	n/a
18	1	29	11	0	41	n/a
19	1	96	0	1	98	n/a
20	1	114	8	1	124	n/a
21	2	5	0	0	7	n/a
22	2	5	0	0	7	n/a
23	2	8	0	0	10	n/a
24	2	30	5	0	37	n/a
25	2	31	1	0	34	n/a
26	2	78	1	0	81	n/a
27	3	5	0	0	8	n/a
28	3	8	0	0	11	n/a
29	3	9	0	0	12	n/a
30	3	16	0	0	19	n/a
31	3	18	2	1	24	n/a
32	3	38	0	0	41	n/a
33	3	42	18	0	63	n/a
34	3	66	12	0	81	n/a
35	3	68	4	4	79	n/a
36	4	10	0	0	14	n/a
37	4	11	0	0	15	n/a
38	5	4	0	0	9	n/a
39	5	9	1	0	15	n/a
40	5	15	0	0	20	n/a
41	5	108	1	1	115	n/a
42	6	7	0	0	13	n/a
43	6	10	0	0	16	n/a
44	8	135	1	0	144	n/a
45	9	138	2	1	150	n/a
46	12	33	3	0	48	n/a
47	15	69	15	0	99	n/a
48	20	61	42	0	123	n/a
49	22	47	0	0	69	n/a
50	46	89	5	1	141	n/a
51	111	305	1	6	423	n/a
52	298	402	57	0	757	n/a

Table 8: Web site evaluation results in the tourism sector

Table 8 indicates that 3 out of 52 evaluated web presences in the tourism sector have passed all tests, 10 sites have failed manual tests, because their content could not be displayed meaningfully on a text-only lynx browser.

The results of the evaluation were not surprising in the light of similar previously conducted studies. A three country hotel analysis (UK, USA, and Australia) showed that only 12% of the hotels passed even Priority 1 checkpoints of the WCAG (Williams et al. 2007). Another study on the German and UK tourist information sites showed that only 20% complied with Priority 1 checkpoints, and merely 3% with Priority 2 checkpoints (Williams et al. 2004).

In this evaluation, almost 90% of the web pages failed the automated tests, 80% failed both automated tests with more than a couple of errors. Many pages use rich Internet applications (i.e., Flash and JavaScript) that would have to meet special accessibility criteria. As a result, 3 out of 52 evaluated web pages passed both automated and manual tests. In other words, 3 out of 52 web presences fulfill the basic criteria of accessible web sites. However, recalling that every hotel evaluated has a focus on accessible tourism, it is rather surprising that web accessibility has only been taken into account by less than 10% of hotels.

4.1.3 Qualitative analysis

This section presents the results of the semi-structured interviews in the tourism sector. After a categorization of the hotels interviewed, the results identified in the four main areas under study (reasons for implementation, changes after implementation, and reasons for failure of implementation, incentives for implementation) are introduced. Each resulting category is documented by quotations from the interviews (in italics) and corroborated by extant literature.

4.1.3.1 Categorization

The tourism case is represented by two Austrian hotels in rural areas that were both listed on the IBFT platform. For both hotels, physical and web accessibility have been an issue which was – apart from the web site evaluation results they achieved – a major reason for considering them for this study. Web accessibility has been successfully implemented in hotel A which disposes of 118 rooms, 140 employees, and has wellness and conference guests as its main target group. Guests with impairments are below 1%. Hotel B has 82 rooms and 19 employees and focuses mainly on conference tourism (700-750 events per year). Individual tourists account for about 40% of business realized. Hotel two started a relaunch in 2008 that led to a significant decrease of accessibility as – when disabling JavaScript – essential procedures could not be conducted anymore (e.g., broken reservation request button). For this reason, the two sub cases represent the two units of analysis in this study: a successful and a failed web accessibility implementation.

The target group is split into conference and seminar guests and individual customers (wellness tourists, families) few of which have disabilities. People with disabilities do not represent a significant target group even if there have already been wheelchair users among the hotel guests. Wheelchair accessible hotel rooms are provided by both of the hotels.

4.1.3.2 Reasons for implementation

This section lists the reasons that led to an implementation of accessible web presences in organizations. These reasons have been identified in the course of the interviews. Examples in terms of quotations are given; the connection with extant phenomena in (other) scientific disciplines is provided in order to corroborate the findings.

Social commitment
Corporate social responsibility (CSR) has been identified to be an important aspect in the tourism sector with a special focus on sustainability and climate protection. The installation of wood chip heating and solar cells, the utilization of biological products, and the usage of regional products belongs to the CSR focus of both hotels.

> *"Sustainability and climate protection are parts of our organizational philosophy".*
>
> *"We try to use a lot of regional products. The wood comes from this region; the wood chips for our heating are bought from regional farmers. We try to work sustainably, especially in terms of food which we predominantly buy from local farmers".*
>
> *"We do not only sell our hotel but also the surroundings and the countryside. This is the reason why we have to demonstrate social responsibility".*

Academic literature suggests several drivers for corporate social responsibility which encompass economic, political, social and ethical motivations (Garriga and Melé 2004). One of the most cited definitions of CSR has been established by Carroll (1979) who characterizes organizations using corporate social responsibility as paying attention to "economic, legal, ethical, and discretionary (philanthropic) expectations that society has of organizations at a given point in time" (Carroll 1979, p. 499). Others claim that the only responsibility of an organization is the maximization of shareholder profit (Friedman 1970).

In the tourism industry, the trend towards CSR has emerged in the 1990s where hotels focused on environmental concerns for the first time (Kalisch 2002). Since then, other initiatives (i.e., Green Hotels) have fostered the environmental concern in this industry (Holcomb et al. 2007). A study on the leading world hotels revealed that hotels commonly consider charitable donations and diversity aspects in their CSR strategies (Holcomb et al. 2007). Surprisingly, environmental issues were not heavily reported in the study of Holcomb et al (2007). In this research, the hotels primarily focus on sustainability, environmental protection and the use of biological products. A reason for this may be that the hotels analyzed were situated in rural areas where the environment was part of their marketing. This may explain the special focus in the CSR strategy.

Apart from CSR, the social commitment of an organization can also be reflected by its organizational culture. Several definitions of organizational culture have appeared in the academic literature. Doppler defines organizational culture as the guidance system of an organization which regulates what is allowed, what is not allowed, what is good and what is not good (Doppler 1994). Another, more detailed approach to organizational culture is its decomposition into assumptions, values and artifacts (Schein 1990). Assumptions represent the beliefs about human nature and organizational environment, values stand for the shared beliefs that lead to the behavior of employees, and artifacts are an organization's symbols and visible language (Jones et al. 2005). From this definition, the extensive role of organizational culture in a company becomes obvious.

Besides other factors, organizational culture is influential on the readiness of employees for organizational change (Jones et al. 2005). As a consequence, it can be assumed that in organizational cultures, which focus on human relations and morale (cf. Quinn's four culture types in "The Competing Values Framework" (Quinn and Rohrbaugh 1983)), the readiness for change is rather distinct. Especially changes in social issues may be facilitated in cultures where social commitment is already anchored. Allocated to the case of web accessibility implementation it can therefore be assumed that if social commitment is present in an organizational culture, the enforcement of barrier-free web content can be made more easily.

Design for all
A major reason for web accessibility implementation is that the web presence entails advantages for every user.

> *"We learned that our new web site catches on all our customers – not just the ones with disabilities".*

> *"Elderly people appreciate if they do not have to climb steps – the same holds for web sites".*

> *"We wanted our web site to be simple and clear. The information should be quickly retrievable for everyone".*

The "design for all" argument therefore seems to be an issue in the hotel sector. However, the "design for all" aspect is much more distinct in terms of constructional implementation of accessibility than in terms of web accessibility. Interestingly, every hotel evaluated in section 4.1.2 disposed of wheelchair accessible rooms, ramps, or other facilities for people with disabilities.

"We have 8 accessible rooms where the beds are adjustable in height for wheelchair users; also some tables in our restaurant can be adjusted if necessary even if 90% of our customers do not have impairments".

From the results of the web site evaluation where almost 90% of the web sites failed automated tests, it can be seen that in the Austrian hotel sector the "design for all" aspect has not been transformed to the electronic environment yet.

Web site quality

An improvement of web site quality has been identified as a reason for web accessibility implementation. In this case, the focus is put on website quality enhancement and not on accessibility implementation in the first place. However, accessibility may represent a side effect of quality improvement.

"We stumbled across it [web accessibility] only because our old site was bad and poorly coded".

"That was just a feedback from many guests, some couldn't open the site at all, some had a very bad internet connection, for example especially in upper Italy, Southern Tyrol nearly any of our guests could view the site because the waiting times were too long and the system was overstrained, then it wasn't that well coded. But at that time we just thought that we must have a modern website, with flash animations, with a lot of moving pictures, with a lot of music, entertainment, and action. That was the former version".

In the course of a relaunch, organizations tend to improve the quality of their web presences and therefore often come across web accessibility. Therefore, it can be stated that web accessibility is implemented because of web site quality improvement objectives.

In the literature, different concepts on the factors relevant for web site quality determination have been established (e.g., Gehrke and Turban 1999; Olsina et al. 2001; Cox and Dale 2002; Loiacono et al. 2002; Webb and Webb 2004), but only some concepts identify accessibility as a distinct factor for web site quality (Olsina et al. 2001; Cox and Dale 2002). However, accessibility is hidden indirectly in every concept of web site quality. A closer look on the common factors across the various concepts shows strong parallels with the web accessibility guidelines. "Navigation efficiency" (Gehrke and Turban 1999) and "consistency of menus" (Cox and Dale 2002) for example, relate to checkpoint 13.4 ("Use navigation menus in a consistent manner") of WCAG 1.0 (W3C 1999). The importance of structural elements (headings, paragraphs) and the usage of clear and concise text also relate to WCAG 1.0. In other words, web accessibility represents – together with usability, correct markup and other factors – part of a bundle of measures that improve the quality of a web site.

Importance of web site
In the hotel sector, information gathering and booking activities are increasingly performed online. Almost 50% of hotel guests use the online booking possibilities on the hotel web site (JD Power and Associates 2007). For this reason, hotel web presences are of particular importance as they act as decision support for the customer. If the web site does not work or is not appealing to the prospective guest, he will probably hesitate to book (Cox and Dale 2002).

> *"Every new guest will see our web page first, judge it, and then decide if he wants to come or not."*

> *"Information retrieval and booking activities are increasingly done online. About 40% of our customers receive the information about our hotel by word of mouth (friends, relatives), and 38% get it online. Thus, the web site has to be designed in a way that people quickly find the information they search – at best within the first 30 to 40 seconds".*

Together with the quality improvement aspect mentioned above, the importance of a web site is a major reason for web accessibility implementation.

Key personality
People, who raise the issue of web accessibility, are committed to the idea, and initiate the project are called key personalities in this contribution. The existence of key personalities has been identified to be a crucial factor for web accessibility implementation in the hotel sector. Several characteristics of key personalities could be defined:

(i) They have friends and/or family with disabilities
   "My brother has a severe sight disability. He has to use magnification software when he uses the computer. He told me to take care for the magnification aspect when designing a new site".

(ii) They have friends and/or family with expert knowledge in this area
   "My friend is an expert, he told me to make the site accessible".

(iii) They cooperate with disability interest groups
   "We cooperate with the local representative of people with disabilities. He informed us about some accessibility problems".

A key personality's private surroundings have an important influence on his/her attitude. In psychology, the concept of reference groups shows the influence of "reference others", defined as "any actual or imaginary individual, group, social category, norm, or object that influences the individual's covert or overt behavior" (Schmitt 1972). This influence is cognitive which means that the reference others do not have to actively influence but remain passive and are being thought of by the person concerned (Richer 1976). The reason why an individual chooses a certain reference group depends on two components: (i) visibility and (ii) meaningfulness (Kelley 1955). Visibility encompasses the degree of observability of a reference group; meaningfulness relates to the prominence of a group in a person's awareness (Kelley 1955). Friends and family fulfill the visibility and meaningfulness criteria to a large extent and therefore play – according to the reference group concept – an important role in individual's attitudes.

4.1.3.3 Changes after implementation

This section lists the perceived changes after web accessibility implementation in organizations. These changes have been identified in the course of within-case analysis. Examples in terms of quotations are given in italics; the connection with extant phenomena in scientific disciplines is provided in order to corroborate the findings.

Cost efficiency

The long-term investment aspect of web accessibility has been identified as the web presence is not subject to short term trends anymore and therefore does not have to be recoded so often.

"The web site is much more cost efficient as we do not have to recode it so often. It is not subject to trends anymore. In the first programming phase we may have invested 500 or 1000 Euros more than for an inaccessible site. However, we have it for the third year now and it is unbelievably maintenance neutral and you can easily change the content".

The Web Accessibility Initiative (WAI) states in its business case that, in the long run, cost savings will occur, but the initial investments in acquiring knowledge, establishing processes, and increased development and testing time have to be taken into account when incorporating accessibility. However, when accessibility is considered from the beginning, this may be a small percentage of the overall web site costs (W3C 2009a).

For the hotels analyzed, initial accessibility investments did not seem to be an issue

"No, it does not cost more. Costs have never been an issue".

Accessibility was implemented in the course of a web site relaunch, which may be the reason for not considering additional accessibility costs. Moreover, the long term effects of web accessibility may have been the reason for its adoption.

Maintenance

The implementation of accessible web sites entails a reduction of site development and maintenance time in the long run (Darzentas and Miesenberger 2005; W3C 2009a).

> "We have the site for the 3rd year now and it is unbelievably maintenance neutral. New content can be easily inserted and the site is still well received".

This will result in decreasing personnel costs for site maintenance (W3C 2009a). The web site coding is regarded easier and long-lasting as it is not subject to trends. Due to the separation of content and layout, maintenance facilitations occur.

Simplicity/Usability

The implementation of an accessible web site leads to an increase in its simplicity and usability.

> "The web site has become more intuitive".

> "According to our experiences and customer feedback, the new web presence is well received also by customers without impairments because of the intuitive navigation".

Moreover, the loading times have decreased and customers do not report any broken links or broken buttons anymore. This is an indication for the "design for all aspect" discussed above.

Petrie and Kheir (2007) suggest the consideration of accessibility and usability as two overlapping sets with three categories: (i) pure accessibility problems, (ii) pure usability problems, and (iii) universal usability problems. Pure accessibility problems only affect people with disabilities (e.g., alternative texts for graphics), pure usability problems are only encountered by users without disabilities and universal usability problems affect both disabled and non-disabled users (Petrie and Kheir 2007). These universal usability problems are especially addressed by accessible web sites (for a more detailed explanation see section 2.1). As a consequence, the accessibility of a web site may also increase its usability.

Search engine ranking

As many other organizations, hotels are dependent on high search engine rankings.

> "To us, a high search engine ranking is very important".

> "The best website is of no importance when it is not found by search engines".

A recent study revealed that accessible web sites enable better search engine indexing which leads to an improved visitor behavior and web site traffic (Hartjes 2009).

However, concerning the issue of search engine optimization, different opinions have been expressed in the organizations analyzed. On the one hand, people experienced higher search engine rankings of accessible sites; on the other hand, they expected them to be ranked higher which did not turn out to be true.

> *"I have read about better search engine ranking through accessibility, but in practice, it does not seem to work".*

Reasons for invariant search engine rankings can be found in the nature of web accessibility implementation. A mere focus on technical criteria (that can be tested by automated evaluation tools) may render a site accessible but may not provoke a higher ranking. By contrast, a construction of relevant and simple alternative texts for graphics significantly contributes to better and more specific search engine results but represents a feature that cannot be verified by automated evaluation tools.

4.1.3.4 Reasons for failure of implementation

This section lists the reasons for failure of web accessibility implementation in organizations. These reasons have been identified in the course of the interviews in the tourism sector. Examples in terms of quotations are given in italics; the connection with extant phenomena in scientific disciplines is provided in order to corroborate the findings.

Lack of awareness
A wide-spread problem that has been encountered frequently during web accessibility research is the general lack of awareness about the subject. According to the interview partners, this is a major reason why the implementation of web accessibility failed or simply has not been considered

> *"If you conduct a survey about web accessibility in Austrian hotels, I am sure you would not get any reasonable answers, because they simply do not know what it means".*

The literature on organizational change offers a possible explanation for this issue. Poor (internal) communication is identified as a factor why projects of change in organizations may not succeed (Egan and Fjermestad 2005). However, the question remains why web accessibility efforts are not communicated accordingly. External communication (press releases, event organization, etc.) has been identified as an important driver for social and economic changes after web accessibility implementation.

4.1.3.5 Incentives for implementation

This section lists incentives for web accessibility implementation in organizations that resulted from the within-case analysis. Examples in terms of quotations are given; the connection with extant phenomena in scientific disciplines is provided in order to corroborate the findings.

Financial incentive
In order to raise the awareness for this issue, government aids for accessible web sites have been proposed.

> *"Money – in which form ever – is a big incentive".*

In this context, respondents have also mentioned tax advantages as an incentive for accessibility implementation.

Extrinsic motivation is usually controlled by financial incentives. Extrinsic motivation leads to the supply of a desire; but the activity to supply this desire is accomplished because of its consequences and not because of the activity itself (Döring-Katerkamp and Trojan 2002).

Financial incentives may therefore provoke an implementation of web accessibility which is executed because of money. These incentives may be the trigger for organizations to implement accessible web sites but in order to profit from the long term effects on web accessibility this has to be combined with intrinsic motivation. Intrinsic motivation entails a more stable motivation as activities are carried out because they are perceived to be meaningful and challenging (Bullinger 2001).

Hence, financial incentives may provoke short term motivation. Web accessibility implementation as a process requires changes in various organizational areas (e.g., corporate design, web site technique). It is doubtful that mere financial incentives can initiate and maintain this multifaceted process.

4.1.4 Summary and interpretation

The tourism sector as an important economic branch of business and an early adopter of information technology still holds a lack in the adoption of accessible web sites. Constructional accessibility in terms of ramps and wheelchair rooms are far more widespread than accessible web presences. A lack of awareness for the issue of web accessibility has been identified as a main reason why it has not been taken into consideration in the tourism sector. In order to foster awareness, financial incentives are suggested to be initiated by the government (e.g., tax advantages). Despite being a trigger for accessibility initiation, financial incentives are classified as extrinsic, short-term and unstable compared to immaterial incentives. Accessibility implementation represents a process and may therefore require a combination of material and immaterial incentives in order to entail more stable motivation.

Social commitment of an organization may provoke long-lasting motivation. The role of social commitment of an organization that is, amongst others, reflected to the external environment by its corporate social responsibilities and, to the internal environment, by its corporate culture, is likely to be an indication for the degree of difficulty of web accessibility implementation. Hotels, which have successfully implemented accessibility, focus on social values in their organizational culture and have an elaborate CSR strategy that mainly deals with environmental issues as integral part of their marketing strategy. If a company has a well pronounced social commitment, existing social values and norms facilitate the incorporation of another social measure, namely accessible web sites.

In the tourism sector, the quality of the web presence is crucial for attaining and retaining new customers and, as a consequence, is attached high importance to. Due to the fact that the web site purpose for every hotel interviewed encompasses communication, information, and service (booking) aspects, the quality of hotel web sites is fundamental for the success of the hotel. In an online environment, where the customer has low switching costs as the competitor's site often is just one click away, the importance of high-quality web presences becomes obvious. A site's overall quality improvement is identified as a reason for web accessibility implementation.

Several strongly interrelated changes after web accessibility have been discovered. Maintenance facilitations lead to a decrease in personnel costs (W3C 2009a) and therefore represent an indication for cost efficiency of accessible web sites. Simultaneously, maintenance facilitations together with an increase in simplicity and usability contribute to an improvement of the overall web site quality. Search engine ranking has been perceived differently by the interview partners. Both higher and invariant rankings have been reported as changes after implementation. The latter development may be due to different methods of web accessibility implementation.

Overall, the tourism sector holds high potential for an increase of accessible web presences. Awareness raising measures (e.g., accessibility related events, presentations) are crucial for triggering this process.

Table 9 summarizes the results in the tourism sector.

Reasons for implementation	Changes after implementation	Reasons for failure of implementation	Incentives for implementation
Social commitment	Cost efficiency	Lack of awareness	Financial support
Design for all	Maintenance		
Website quality	Simplicity/usability		
Importance of website	Search engine ranking		
Key personality			

Table 9: Overview of results in the tourism sector

Social commitment, design for all, website quality, importance of website, and key personality could be identified as reasons for accessibility implementation. Perceived changes after implementation were cost efficiency, maintenance, simplicity/usability, and search engine ranking. In the tourism sector, a lack of awareness led to failure of implementation; financial support was identified as incentive for web accessibility implementation.

4.2 Case 2: Financial services

4.2.1 Sector overview

The importance of the financial services sector for electronic business has increased tremendously, since the Internet has offered new opportunities for customers as well as new business areas for organizations. A recent European study indicates that 56% of banks provide online financial services to customers via the Internet, 46% offer online payment services. Financial services, such as electronic banking, are offered by 6 in 10 banks with the Nordic countries being front runners (European Commission 2008).

The financial services sector, especially the banking sector, together with retailing and telecommunication, belongs to the sectors, where the largest productivity growth effects have occurred within the ICT producing sectors (European Commission 2008).

According to a recent study, the Internet has provoked major changes in the banking sector and has become a critical element in the business strategy of banks (European Commission 2008). In particular, "the Internet has had a significant impact on banks operating with physical branches" (European Commission 2008, p. 8), whereby financial online services need to include all the stages and services of modern banking in order to be conducted online.

For people with disabilities, the execution of their banking transactions online provides an enormous facilitation of a day-to-day business for several reasons. First, they avoid the physical frequentation of banking institutions which may include several obstacles for people with mobility (e.g., people using a wheelchair) or visual impairments due to possible accessibility deficiencies of buildings (e.g., missing ramps, guidance systems). Then, the bank transfers in banking institutions are usually conducted by filling in forms and confirmed by the signature of the account holder. Both actions cannot be accomplished by blind or some physically impaired customers. The dependency on other people for such highly confidential tasks leads to a lack of control for blind people as regards the accuracy of their bank transfers. Accessible online banking overcomes such difficulties and facilitates these tasks for people with impairments.

In the Austrian banking sector, it can be distinguished between the traditional brick-and-mortar institutions known as affiliated banks and further so called direct banks, which provide their products and services mainly through the Internet. Direct banking led to a structural change in banking, which resulted in a rethinking and further strategic change of the majority of big affiliated institutions. Figure 13 emphasizes the significance of online-banking for each financial institution and additionally shows its popularity, indicating the number of customers of Austrian banks.

Company	Staff	Total Assets (in m.€)	Profit/Loss (in m.€)	Customers
Affiliated Bank				
Bank Austria AG Unicredit	6781	144168	1469,09	n/a
Bawag PSK	4514	42659	-71,11	n/a
BKS Bank AG	799	5509	29,39	n/a
Erste Bank AG	4315	91615	456,89	1000000
Hypo Alpe Adria Bank AG	568	6812	-15,78	n/a
Oberbank AG	1763	13912	73,65	n/a
Österreichische Volksbanken AG	401	29486	100,36	n/a
PSK	4514	42659	-71,11	n/a
Raiffeisenlandesbank NÖ-Wien AG	1213	18252	138,53	n/a
Raiffeisenlandesbank Oberösterreich AG	831	20350	105,51	n/a
Sparkasse	16226	150340	762,00	2944000
Wüstenrot Aktiengesellschaft	1223	5292	18,19	1800000
Direct Bank				
Allianz Investmentbank AG	53	312	9,38	30000
AutoBank AG	7	97	-5,83	45000
bankdirekt AG	10	132	0,62	150000
Boerse-Live.At	n/a	n/a	n/a	74000
DenizBank AG	160	1143	8,48	30000
direktanlage.at AG	125	518	14,64	51000
Easybank AG	68	458	4,05	245000
Generali Bank AG	71	599	-3,32	60000
ING-DiBa Direktbank Austria	130	76	469,00	357000

Figure 13: Overview of the banking sector in Austria (data based on Austrian Commercial Register)

Apart from these companies, dual combination banking was seen as another possibility to cope with the changes in the financial services sector. Thereby, customers perform traditional banking services online, whereas more specific financial affairs are performed in the banking institution (European Commission 2008).

The above argumentation clarifies the choice of the financial services sector as one case for this study:

(i) For people with disabilities, the online execution of their day-to-day banking transactions provides an enormous facilitation compared to the physical frequentation of the banking institution (facilitation dimension).

(ii) The banking sector is highly relevant for e-business as most productivity gains are attained within this sector (relevance dimension).

(iii) A lack of current web site accessibility in this sector needs further rise of awareness for its importance (awareness dimension).

4.2.2 Web site evaluation

Table 10 shows the web site evaluation results for the financial services sector. The organizations are ranked according to the number of their accessibility errors (WAI column). The best web presences in terms of accessibility are listed on top, the table ends with the least accessible sites. Furthermore, results of automated and manual tests are displayed in the tables. Automated test results consist of the number of WAI errors (indication for accessibility), HTML errors, parsing (syntax) errors, link errors (e.g., broken links) and the total number of errors detected in the automated testing process. Web presences without errors in the WAI column have been tested manually, for the remaining web sites the manual test was not applied (n/a).

Organization	Automated testing results					Manual testing results
	WAI errors	HTML errors	Parsing errors	Link errors	Total errors	
1	0	1	0	0	1	OK
2	0	40	11	0	51	OK
3	0	9	0	0	9	OK
4	0	9	1	0	10	OK
5	0	107	9	1	117	lynx
6	1	29	21	3	54	n/a
7	1	77	4	0	82	n/a
8	1	12	0	1	14	n/a
9	3	12	0	0	15	n/a
10	3	174	29	1	207	n/a
11	5	167	80	1	253	n/a
12	6	8	0	1	14	n/a
13	7	10	0	0	17	n/a
14	12	44	0	0	56	n/a
15	12	126	1	1	140	n/a
16	32	149	1	0	182	n/a
17	77	127	1	0	205	n/a
18	136	227	1	0	364	n/a
19	169	255	1	0	425	n/a

Table 10: Web site evaluation results in the financial services sector

Table 10 indicates that 4 web presences have passed manual and automated tests, one web site (line 5) has passed automated tests but failed the manual test, as it could not be displayed properly on the text-only lynx browser. 14 out of 19 web presences failed web site evaluation.

4.2.3 Qualitative analysis

This section presents the results of the semi-structured interviews in the financial services sector. After a categorization of the organizations interviewed, the results identified in the four main areas under study (reasons for implementation, changes after implementation, reasons for failure of implementation, and incentives for implementation) are introduced. Each resulting category is documented by quotations from the interviews (in italics) and corroborated by extant literature.

4.2.3.1 Categorization

The qualitative analysis in the financial services sector is based on semi-structured interviews with six organizations, four Austrian, one Swiss, and one German. Out of these institutions, three have successfully implemented web accessibility and three have failed in web accessibility implementation.

In terms of physical accessibility of the banking institutions, some efforts have been undertaken in the last years which range from simple ramps and door openers to account statements in Braille language or cash machines with speech output. The awareness for accessibility of buildings is more distinct than for web sites.

4.2.3.2 Reasons for accessibility implementation

This section lists the reasons that led to an implementation of accessible web presences in organizations. These reasons have been identified in the course of the within-case analysis. Examples in terms of quotations are given in italics; the connection with extant phenomena in scientific literature is provided in order to corroborate the findings.

Differentiation
The differentiation aspect encompasses the sum of attempts of organizations that have the objective to set themselves apart from their competitors. This aspect has been identified as a driver for web accessibility implementation.

The use of the Internet as a distribution channel in banking has become widespread in developed countries (Flavian et al. 2004). Still, the number of online customers is below the financial service institutions' expectations. A lack in differentiation has been identified as one of the reasons why people do not use online banking (Flavian et al. 2004). This may be an indication for the differentiation aspect that financial service institution declared as a major reason for web accessibility implementation.

Many interview partners specified that they wanted to set themselves apart from their competitors through web accessibility.

"We wanted to be different from other banks".

"We tried to be the first to implement accessibility in order to be different from our competitors".

For them, it was important to benefit from the first mover advantage. This differentiation aspect is accompanied by a certain market positioning intent of organizations with accessible web which, in turn, may lead to an improvement of image. However, first mover advantage represents a short-term advantage and only applies if no other organization has implemented web accessibility in that industry before. Moreover, imitators cannot reason with the differentiation aspect when justifying their web accessibility intentions. Therefore, this reason can be considered as transitory and only valid for industries, where accessible web sites have not been implemented before.

In the light of the ongoing financial crisis, banking institutions are especially intent on a good image.

"We want to be a decent bank; we roll up our sleeves and make an effort to do things properly".

The social commitment of organizations in the financial sector has been identified to play an important role and therefore constitutes a reason for web accessibility implementation.

"For us, it was a mix of social commitment and PR considerations".

Considering web accessibility as a long term investment, one interview partner said that the possibility that *"you can get indirect returns in terms of image"* caused his organization to take web accessibility into account.

Several studies have pointed out that strong corporate image contributes most effectively to a differentiation in banking (Morello 1986) and constitutes the initiation for customer loyalty-building (Nguyen and LeBlanc 1998).

Consumer consciousness

The socially conscious consumer takes into account "the public consequences of his/her private consumption or attempts to use his/her purchasing power to bring about social change" (Webster 1975). Additionally, the environmentally conscious or "green" customer pursues similar intents in terms of environmental change. According to a recent study, 87% of US-consumers are seriously concerned about the environment. Moreover, these green consumers consider a company's environmental practices as crucial for their purchase decisions (GfK Roper 2007). The 2007 monitoring report of the EU sustainable development strategy indicates that European businesses increasingly include social and environmental concerns in their business strategy which results in an increasing number of green products and services on the European market (Eurostat 2007). Thus, the increase in consumer consciousness leads to the fact that companies include environmentally friendly products in their product portfolio.

This study identifies the presence of the conscious consumer in the financial services sector.

> „The conscious consumer is a crucial factor for the disposal of products and services".

> "Ethical criteria are being more and more included in the purchase decision process".

The strong social connection attached to web accessibility may attract conscious consumers and influence their purchase decisions.

Social commitment

In the financial services sector, corporate social responsibility is attached importance to. Especially the areas social sponsoring and sustainability are pronounced.

> "Sustainability and climate protection are parts of our organizational philosophy".

Organizations analyzed dispose of corporate social responsibility strategies and especially focus on sustainability. Particularly, organizations with accessible web sites integrated the elements of social awareness and social commitment into their CSR strategies and corporate culture.

> "When I joined this organization in 1989, social awareness already existed. I have grown in this culture and I experience it every day".

An extant awareness for social commitment may facilitate the implementation of web accessibility.

> "We have always had awareness for social issues. In this case, implementation of web accessibility is easier; when the awareness already exists".

This means that in organizations, where certain awareness for social interests or environmental concerns is part of the corporate culture or corporate social responsibility strategy, the argumentation for web accessibility implementation is facilitated.

> „We have a strong social awareness in the bank that is grounded in former environmental and ecological measures".

Every organization in the financial services sector, which has implemented web accessibility, stated that the corporate culture within the organization has to be given beforehand.

> "The corporate culture has to be present; otherwise, such a project will fail".

The theory of employee resistance to change offers theoretical explanations for this process. Organizational culture is identified as one of the factors that influences the readiness of employees for organizational change (Jones et al. 2005). In addition, Quinn and Rohrbaugh (1983) state in their "Competing Values Framework" that the culture type focusing on human relations and morale has a higher readiness for change (Quinn and Rohrbaugh 1983). Regarding the implementation of web accessibility as a change process, it can therefore be facilitated in a culture focusing on social awareness.

In the financial services sector distinct customer needs occur. Apart from security, access, liquidity, and interest, social responsibility represents a typical customer need in this branch of business (Reifner 1997). A reason for this might be the responsibilities in society that financial institutions have in order to avoid financial exclusion. The financial services industry is not only seen as a vehicle for promoting economic performance but also for promoting social cohesion. As a consequence, financial institutions take over social commitment in terms of integration in the local environment (Kempson et al. 2000). In other words, the inclusion of socially responsible action may be a latent necessity in the financial services sector due to a certain responsibility in society.

Elderly customers
In many financial organizations, elderly people account for an important part of the customer group. Moreover, the so called "simple customer" who is interested in one single and simple product (e.g., bank account) represents a traditional customer for many banking institutions.

> "In our latest market research study we have discovered that we have a lot of simple customers who just want to have a bank account".

Elderly customers are an important target group of the financial services sector for several reasons:

(i) Market research has shown that elderly people increasingly use online banking tools. Seniors have been identified as a rapidly growing segment of the Internet economy (Trocchia and Janda 2000). They use the Internet mainly to stay in touch with friends and relatives, to stay current with news and events, for shopping or entertainment purposes or to access health and medical information (Iyer and Eastman 2006). However, in this case study analysis it becomes obvious that elderly customers increasingly perform online financial transactions.

> "Our web site is being used by elderly people above average".

This was one reason why financial services institutions considered accessible web sites.

"The fact that we have a lot of elderly customers has given a major reason for the initiation of the web accessibility project".

(ii) The demographic shift implies that this user group is becoming increasingly important in the years to come

"If you look at the demographic shift in the next ten years, accessibility will be an issue".

According to demographic trends, the proportion of the European population above the age of 65 will shift from 16.6% in 2005 to 24.7% in 2030 (VID 2006).

(iii) Elderly customers usually tend to be a wealthy customer group.

"The wealthy customers are the elderly, they have the money".

Elderly people dispose of a significant purchasing power. People over the age of 65 are estimated to account for about $200 billion of spending a year (Oumlil and Williams 2000) and control 70% of the net worth of U.S. households (Raymond 2000). Hence, the purchasing power of this segment justifies responding to needs of this customer group.

Fear of negative image

Some interview partners have also expressed a certain fear of negative image that may result out of a lack of web accessibility. Interestingly, this analysis has revealed that possible negative image in case organizations did not implement web accessibility was a much stronger reason for its consideration than image enhancements resulting from successful web accessibility implementation.

"We cannot afford negative headlines".

„We do not want to have the headline, 'this financial services institution does not care about the elderly'".

Negative publicity can seriously harm corporate image (Dean 2004). In psychology, the negativity effect offers a theoretical explanation for this process. In the evaluation of people, objects and ideas, more weight is put on negative than on positive information (Mizerski 1982). Computed with a formula for measuring the persuasiveness of media, negative publicity is given quadruple weight compared to positive news (Kroloff 1988). Negativity effect is likely to emerge when consumers are highly involved with the product category (Ahluwalia 2002), which means that they are aroused by and interested in the product category (Richins and Bloch 1986). However, a high number of loyal customers that have strong bonds with the product may soften or absorb this effect (Ahluwalia 2002).

Applied to the case of web accessibility in the banking sector, financial institutions with many loyal online banking users and a strong product image might experience the effect of negative publicity on corporate image in a less intense way.

Design for all

Due to several misconceptions about the subject of web accessibility, the "design for all" aspect is commonly not associated with accessibility. This means that organizations still do not know that web accessibility does not only concern people with impairments. One organization interviewed therefore completely left out the accessibility term in their argumentation. Instead, the notions of simplicity and design for all were the only reasons for the consideration of web accessibility.

"Our main reason was 'simple and for all'; the simpler the better and the more customers will understand and buy the product".

Other organizations used the "design for all" aspect as a side argument and reasoned that some accessibility features also provided advantages for the general audience.

"The convertibility of font sizes represents a benefit for everybody, not just for people with sight disabilities".

Others again discovered the "design for all" aspect that goes along with web accessibility only after its implementation.

"Everybody now profits from the new site; they have a faster site and can choose from where to read it".

Due to the nature of their service, financial institutions take over responsibilities in the marketplace. The importance of trust, customer knowledge, prudent management of funds, proximity and accessibility are identified as responsibilities of financial institutions (Decker 2004) in order to avoid financial exclusion. These recommendations recognize the importance of access to basic banking services to communities and society in general (Kempson et al. 2000).

Top management support

The experience of organizations in the financial services sector has shown that top management support in connection with a web accessibility implementation project is crucial.

"You need somebody from top management in order to succeed with this issue".

In every case of positive implementation, the top management favored the project either because they were personally involved with the subject or they disposed of exceeding interest in web technologies.

"I can completely understand you. My wife uses a wheelchair".

"We had the advantage that one member of the management board was 150% web affine; this made it easier to convince him".

The literature on organizational change supports these findings. A lack of top management support may lead to the fact that changes in organizations do not succeed (Egan and Fjermestad 2005). A reason for this may be that top management's beliefs influence organizational culture to a large part (Schneider et al. 1996). Additionally, top managers take over responsibility for strategic change in an organization and therefore have to identify with the nature of changes. As a consequence, top management represents the key to the effectiveness of a change process (Gioia and Chittipeddi 1991).

Key personality
In every organization interviewed, the initiation of the web accessibility project and therefore a main reason for its implementation was grounded in the existence of a key personality within the organization. Different key personalities could be identified in the financial services sector:

(i) Project managers that learned about web accessibility, were personally involved, or got inputs from colleagues.

"I have been at a lecture given by a sight disabled person. This has impressed me a lot".

"My grandmother uses a wheel chair. I know how inaccessible the town is. This all is a matter of awareness".

„A colleague from the technical department has a girlfriend with a hearing impairment. He had the first suggestions about this issue".

(ii) Interest groups that cooperated with the organization because of personal relationships.

"We have worked in cooperation with the institute of the blind; a former colleague now works with them".

(iii) Employees with impairments within the organization that raised awareness for the issue.

Strategies of organizations often reflect the top management's values (Gioia and Chittipeddi 1991). As a consequence, top management needs to identify with the proposed changes. It is crucial that the changes are understood and make sense to decision makers (Bartunek 1984). In the literature, the imitation of change has been conceptualized. Members of the top management initiate change and consequently pursue activities that represent sense making for them and sense giving for others. Top management can be seen as architect and facilitator of change in organizations (Gioia and Chittipeddi 1991).

4.2.3.3 Changes after web site implementation

This section lists the changes identified in organizations of the financial services sector after an implementation of accessible web presences. Examples in terms of quotations are given in italics; the connection with extant phenomena in scientific disciplines is provided in order to corroborate the findings.

Increase in awareness

Changes in awareness were identified to be both internal and external but to a varying degree. Within the organization, employees were informed about the issue which provoked a general raise of awareness. Some organizations arranged information days for their employees where they learned about disabilities and accessibility.

> *"We have organized the Disability Awareness Day, where we have worked with our 6000 employees".*

> *"We organize presentations and activities. We have planned to invite somebody from top management to take a wheelchair and try to do his work for one day".*

Other organizations communicated the changes in their internal newsletter. Either way, internal awareness increase was identified in every organization in the financial services sector.

> *"We have communicated web accessibility in our internal newsletter as this word has not been part of our vocabulary before".*

> *"I receive many requests from people who have some kind of sight disability and are dependent on special software. Or from people who suffer from multiple sclerosis that may also cause sight disabilities. The whole problematic begins to move. People begin to talk about it. It [web accessibility] has to be considered as something normal, something self-evident".*

However, differences in the external communication have been identified. Some organizations put a short note on a non-prominent place on their web site. Others performed extensive marketing which resulted in high media interest throughout the country. These organizations then experienced a first mover advantage and an increase in image due to their social commitment. A reason for these differences in the extent of communication may be that the perceived impact of accessible web sites is regarded differently by organizations. However, these findings are surprising, as changes in organizations that have an effect on the external environment are likely to be promoted by the organization itself.

It is identified that a notable increase in awareness after web accessibility implementation is realized by organizations that communicate their efforts to the public. Web sites will not be perceived as accessible by a layperson. As a consequence, marketing activities are crucial in order to provoke an increase in awareness for the issue. Additionally, companies can only profit from image enhancements when the new state is communicated.

Decker (2004) identified accessibility as one of the responsibilities of financial services institutions. Due to the social responsibility that financial institutions have in the marketplace, accessibility efforts will – especially in this sector – lead to positive perception by the customer. Increasing customer loyalty and better image are the consequences.

In-house knowledge exchange
Despite the existence of guidelines for web accessibility, their application may be a matter of discussion in some cases as it may be perceived differently by various users. For these reasons, a knowledge platform has been installed by some organizations, where employees can share information and experience concerning technical problems or also personal experiences.

> *"We have established the Disability Interest Forum, where persons concerned and other interested people can meet and exchange information and experience".*

The installation of a knowledge management tool both contributes to an increase of awareness for the issue and constitutes a valuable knowledge pool for the organization.

> *"I have made the experience that committed employees who work with the internet but come from different departments now talk about web accessibility. A knowledge exchange is happening".*

In the knowledge management literature, the process of knowledge creation has been addressed by Nonaka (1994). He distinguishes between tacit and explicit knowledge. Explicit knowledge can be transmitted and written down, tacit knowledge is a personal quality and cannot be formalized (Nonaka 1994). In his "Spiral of Knowledge Creation" he describes how explicit knowledge can be transformed to tacit knowledge so that it does not get lost within an organization. A knowledge platform as established by the organizations analyzed represents an important instrument for the knowledge creation process and enhances organizational learning as it represents a means to make tacit knowledge explicit.

Integration

An increase in integration and acceptance of people with disabilities was caused by web accessibility implementation.

> *"With our accessibility initiative, we contribute to the integration of people with disabilities".*

This applies to both employees with disabilities within the organization and customers with disabilities.

> *"A sudden sensitization has occurred for employees with disabilities. [...] They have been given motivation and self-confidence".*

Motivation has been identified as an important change that resulted from an increase of integration of employees with disabilities.

Motivation concerns aspects of activity and intention (Ryan and Deci 2000) and is defined as a set of "psychological processes that cause the arousal, direction, and persistence of voluntary actions that are goal oriented" (Mitchell 1982, p. 81). In more detail, motivation represents "the degree to which an individual wants and chooses to engage in a certain specified behavior" (Mitchell 1982, p. 82). From the latter definition it becomes clear that motivation causes some kind of behavior. Mitchell (1982) puts forth the relationship between motivation and job performance. In his study, he identifies that an increase in motivation (together with ability and other factors) causes higher job performance (Mitchell 1982). Integration of employees is identified as a change after web accessibility implementation which results in an increase in motivation. Applying Mitchell's findings to this case study, higher job performance will be the result of an increase in integration of employees with disabilities.

Additionally, motivation theories give explanations for the reasons for employee motivation. Several theories on motivation have been developed in the literature (e.g., Mazlow's hierarchy of needs (Mazlow 1943), Herzberg's two factor theory (Herzberg et al. 1959)). However, equity theory (Adams 1965) is identified to be most relevant for this case study. Equity theory states that people are motivated by fairness. Employees compare the ratio of outcomes over inputs with their colleagues. They seek equity between themselves and other workers. Equity is achieved when the outcome/input ratio between the individual and the other worker is perceived to be equal. If this is not the case, then inequity exists and distress of the individual occurs (Adams 1965). Carrell and Dittrich (1978) state that people in situations of inequity experience greater cognitive dissonance than in situations of equity. Additionally, they put forth that employees that are treated equitably are more content and less distressed than inequitably treated ones. As possible methods of coping with inequity, they identify quitting, transferring, and absenteeism (Carrell and Dittrich 1978).

In sum, equity theory states that perceived inequity leads to distress, discontent and may result in quitting the employment. The integration of people with disabilities represents a major contribution to fairness in an organization. The implementation of web accessibility reduces possible perceived inequities as people with disabilities are now granted equal possibilities than people without disabilities. As a consequence, people with disabilities may experience less distress and more contentment which may be a reason for an increase in job satisfaction and performance.

Corporate image

Corporate image is defined as the sum of public perceptions of the corporation's personality (Spector 1961). These perceptions may vary depending on the nature of different stakeholders: employees, consumers, suppliers, stockholders, and potential investors (Sethi 1979). Due to different relationships of these stakeholders to the organizations, they all have different images of the same organization (Riordan et al. 1997). Hence, an improvement in corporate image of an organization may affect employees' and customers' perceptions.

Corporate image has been found especially important for the services sector (Gronroos 1984). Moreover, it has been identified as essential for Internet banking to be perceived as a "reliable means of transaction, thus becoming a satisfactory option for the customer" (Flavian et al. 2004). In the services sector, image is determined by perceived quality of service, and thus updated every time the customer encounters the service (Nguyen and LeBlanc 1998). As a consequence, it is proposed in the literature to focus on the accessibility of services, as this may lead to a higher perceived quality of service and, in turn, to an enhancement of corporate image (Flavian et al. 2004).

In this study, image enhancements are among the perceived changes after web accessibility implementation.

> "This is a decent bank. I will rather go there and not to one that treats people badly".

Customer perceptions of the organizations may vary over time and be updated constantly and determine the degree of customer loyalty in the long run (Nguyen and LeBlanc 1998).

> "These days, where banks are associated with negative things, it is very important to show that we are doing positive things".

Employees' perceptions of corporate image have an influence on their action (Dutton and Dukerich 1991). Specifically, the better the image of an organization is perceived by employees, the higher is their job satisfaction and the lower their intention to quit the organization (Riordan et al. 1997). Hence, an improvement in corporate image may alter employee behavior and increase their job satisfaction.

In a nutshell, image enhancements due to web accessibility implementation may be caused by (i) a higher degree of constant service quality of accessible web sites and services and (ii) a better perception of the organizations by customers due to an increase in organization's social orientation. An increase in corporate image will affect both customers and employees. Customer effects may include a higher degree of customer loyalty (Nguyen and LeBlanc 1998), employees will react to image enhancement by an increase in job satisfaction (Riordan et al. 1997).

Customer loyalty

Organizations having implemented web accessibility announced that they received positive customer feedback. In some organizations, customers can post complaints if they come across accessibility problems or contact the call center, where the staff has been trained on accessibility issues. All these measures have been undertaken in order to strengthen customer loyalty. One interview partner has successfully realized these measures as he/she could claim a significant increase in loyal customers after the implementation of accessibility.

"Before the implementation of accessibility, 75% of the customers who wanted to open an account stayed with our bank; after the implementation this number increased to 95%".

E-loyalty is defined as the "customer's favorable attitude toward an electronic business resulting in repeat buying behavior" (Anderson and Srinivasan 2003, p. 125). This repeat buying behavior is of high importance in online environments (Ribbink et al. 2004). Due to low switching costs and fierce price competition in e-commerce, customer loyalty is both more difficult and more important than in brick-and-mortar businesses (Harris and Goode 2004). Customer loyalty ("lock-in"), represents the core part of any succeeding e-business model (Reichheld and Schefter 2000) as it is a key path to profitability (Srinivasan et al. 2002). The high costs of acquiring new customers lead to first unprofitable customer relationships which may last for up to three years (Reichheld and Schefter 2000). Profits are generated only after a certain number of transactions with already loyal customers (Srinivasan et al. 2002).

The factors influencing customer loyalty are manifold. In traditional and online marketing research, several different models of customer loyalty have been developed (Hallowell 1996; Sirdeshmukh et al. 2002; Srinivasan et al. 2002; Anderson and Srinivasan 2003; Harris and Goode 2004; Ribbink et al. 2004) and different antecedents have been proposed. However, three key factors that have an important influence on customer loyalty could be identified across the literature: (i) trust, (ii) satisfaction, (iii) and quality.

Firstly, trust, defined as the "degree of confidence consumers have in the online exchange channel" (Ribbink et al. 2004, p. 447), represents an important variable in human interaction and exchange. In online environments, a lack of physical contact even intensifies the role of trust (Reichheld and Schefter 2000) compared to offline environments. In the banking sector, the use of online banking is considered to be risky, since customers have to hand over sensitive information in order to complete transactions. Trust significantly influences customer's attitude towards Internet banking. Consequently, interaction with online environments that are processing sensitive information requires a relationship of trust (Suh and Han 2002).

Secondly, e-satisfaction influences customer loyalty. Anderson and Srinivasan (2003) define e-satisfaction as the "contentment of the customer with respect to his or her prior purchasing experience with a given electronic commerce firm" (Anderson and Srinivasan 2003, p. 125). Satisfaction is closely related to trust. Satisfied customers are likely to increase their purchases with the online company (loyalty) and also their trust in the online medium (Ribbink et al. 2004).

Thirdly, service quality has an influence on customer loyalty. Ribbnik et al. (2004) define five dimensions of service quality: ease of use, web site design, customization, responsiveness, and assurance. These dimensions include some aspects of accessible web design and are therefore considered especially relevant for this study. Ease of use refers amongst others to web site functionality and accessibility of information. Additionally, good web design influences service quality. The personalization of web sites (customization), the promptness of answering to consumer requests (responsiveness), and the degree of security and privacy of an online medium (assurance) cause service quality.

Having identified and analyzed the most important factors that have an influence on customer loyalty, namely trust, satisfaction, and service quality, the reason why accessibility may provoke an increase in customer loyalty becomes clear. Accessibility may have an impact on each of the three influencing factors and therefore increase customer loyalty towards the online company. The stability of accessible web pages, for example, can increase trust towards the web site, because transactions and forms can be completed without errors, broken links, unclear definitions, broken buttons, etc. At the same time, stable web pages can increase customer satisfaction. Every time the customer encounters the service, independently of the device he/she uses, he/she will be able to successfully complete the transaction which may lead to increased satisfaction. The service quality factor is especially influenced by web accessibility. By definition, accessibility of information represents a dimension of service quality. Additionally, the contribution of web accessibility to the improvement of overall web site quality has already been discussed in section 4.1.3.2. As a consequence, service quality may also be improved by accessible web sites.

Simplicity/Usability
Common changes after accessibility implementation are increases in usability and simplicity of the web presence. The relationship between usability and accessibility has already been addressed in section 2.1, where it became obvious that a clear confine between these two terms is not possible. Instead, besides pure accessibility and pure usability problems, an overlapping set has been defined that contains elements of both approaches. This overlapping set explains why accessibility also causes increases in web site usability (Petrie and Kheir 2007).

Furthermore, the structure of each page is clearly defined and consistent throughout the web site. This was the reason for fewer negotiations within the organization about text placements etc. and therefore also for a certain economy of time

> *"We used to have disputations within the organizations, because some people wanted their text to be positioned above right, others below left, and others again in bigger letters, etc. These conversations do not exist anymore as the structure is now predetermined. This also means an economy of time".*

However, an economy of time due to clear web site structures is more likely to emerge in organizations with voluminous web presences where many departments contribute to content generation. For small and medium organizations, this criterion may not apply to the same extent.

Maintenance
Due to an increase in web site simplicity (as mentioned above), maintenance facilitations can be observed.

> *"Maintenance has become much easier".*

Moreover, the training of new employees can be executed faster due to structural consistencies throughout the web presence.

> *"We can train new employees much faster because every web page has the same structure now".*

These findings are in line with the WAI business case, where a reduction of site development and maintenance time is claimed in the long run. As a result, a decrease in personnel costs for site maintenance is observed (W3C 2009a).

However, maintenance problems have been identified primarily by organizations with voluminous web presences and a high number of web site editors. The retention of the accessibility status with many editors involved has caused problems because of a lack of time and resources for accessibility checks on every accessibility feature.

> *"The web site editors do not understand why some fields are now obligatory. [...] This is difficult to check, because we have about 50 editors in our organization and we cannot check on every alt attribute inserted".*

In other words, voluminous web presences face the problem of quality assurance. Despite employee trainings, guideline documents, and CMS adaption (e.g., the definition of the alt-attribute as mandatory for images), the compliance with web accessibility standards is difficult to maintain over time, especially with a high number of web site editors. Daily checks on every accessibility feature are not feasible. The use of automatic evaluation tools (e.g., Total Validator) may help to detect some accessibility problems. However, many features need manual evaluation. For instance, an automated tool can detect the existence of alt attributes but cannot check on the meaningfulness of the alt texts. Following example illustrates the meaningfulness of alt texts: In an online store, visually disabled consumers who want to complete a purchasing process are dependent on the existence of alternative texts because they need to distinguish at least between the "delete" and the "buy" button. In case of existence of alternative texts, the meaningfulness of these texts is also required. Two buttons with the same text but different functions (e.g., two buttons that say "buy" or two buttons that say "delete") will not be helpful. This leads to the fact that visually impaired customers may have to interrupt a purchasing process.

The definition of quality assurance processes may constitute a possible resolution for this problem. However, time and resource scarcity may hamper its implementation. The outsourcing of quality assurance to an external web agency may represent another possibility. Lastly, a quality mark on web accessibility can act as means of quality assurance.

Search engine ranking

An accessible web site is ranked higher in search engine results than an inaccessible site.

> *"Google ranked us on top".*

The alt attributes as product descriptions lead to a higher number of keywords that search engines can use for index creation.

"Our web site is found more easily by search engines now because of the higher number of keywords in the code".

The impact of accessible web sites on search engine ranking has already been addressed in section 2.3.3. The development of a framework for web site evaluation (Leitner et al. 2009a) and the subsequent application on a business case yielded better search engine ranking for accessible web sites (Hartjes 2009).

Long-term investment
Every organization interviewed indicated that the direct effects of accessibility on customer increase and turnover cannot be measured.

"Accessibility is not something, where I can say, that I have invested the amount of x today and have saved the amount of y tomorrow".

Moreover, they characterized accessibility as a long term investment that had positive effects on organizations in the long run.

"I think that the money invested (in accessibility) will draw long term profit".

The WAI business case supports this finding as it specifies cost savings in the long run for accessible web sites. However, initial investments (e.g., knowledge acquisition, process establishment) have to be taken into account (W3C 2009a). Anyhow, this business case is not based on empirical grounds but reflects the experiences of the Web Accessibility Initiative. To date, measurement models of web accessibility have not been developed.

4.2.3.4 Reasons for failure of accessibility

Several reasons could be identified why implementation efforts for web accessibility have failed in organizations. These reasons only refer to organizations that started initiatives for web accessibility implementation and failed. The reasons identified show the possible obstacles for web accessibility implementation and may therefore constitute a collection of experiences for organizations intending to make their web presence accessible.

Misconceptions
Due to a lack of awareness and understanding for the issue, several misconceptions have got into circulation. Some people still believe that only blind people benefit from accessible web sites. In case of an insurance company, the web accessibility attempt was turned down with the words:

"Blind people don't buy cars".

Clarification of the "design for all" aspect of accessible web may be an adequate strategy to refute the objection so that the response one interview partner faced may have been disproved.

> "We do not have blind customers; this would not be profitable".

Moreover, misconceptions concerning the web site's look are widespread.
> "Accessible web sites are ugly".

Section 2 specifies the social, economic and technical dimensions of web accessibility that refute each of the myths mentioned above. Reasons why they still represent a reason for the failure of a web accessibility project may be due to several circumstances: (i) a lack of argumentation of the project initiator (cf. "lack of arguments" section below), since it may be the case that the person presenting the project is not aware of all the facts about web accessibility and cannot refute the misconceptions put forth by decision makers; (ii) power of decision makers, since despite argumentation of project initiators, decision makers might not be convinced, not want to implement or simply not be interested in the project.

Research on organizational change supports these findings. The resistance to organizational change can be grounded on three reasons: (i) people lack the skills to use the technology and gain benefits, (ii) people do not understand the "big picture" of how this technology may ease or change their daily processes, and (iii) upper management fears the changes of business models, redefinition of organizational structures and power bases (Wargin and Dobiey 2001).

Lack of arguments
In almost every case of failed implementation, a lack of arguments for web accessibility was among the main reasons.

> "If I had had a plan on how to present the subject to decision makers, I would not have been turned down so easily"; "I have only pointed out the social argument, which was the reason why it has not been considered further".

Due to these facts it can be assumed that the initiators of such a project have not considered the number of obstacles they could face and therefore have not planned their strategy well enough beforehand. They possibly were not aware of the fact that – apart from technical considerations – web accessibility also entails business and management aspects. Moreover, the way of presentation seemed to be a problem.

> "I did not succeed in presenting the subject in a way the others could follow".

People who are not familiar with technical terms should be given understandable arguments and not technical details.

Lack of top management support

In section 4.2.3.2 the importance of top management support turned out to be a reason for web accessibility implementation. On the other hand, a lack of top management support constitutes a big obstacle for project success.

> *"We had numbers, statistics, arguments, but it was of no use; it was completely illegitimate".*

They did not succeed because the top management did not provide support. The marketing department also seems to play an important role with this issue.

> *"The marketing department turned my effort down with the words: "We do not have many sight-disabled customers. As long as this is not stated in the law, we do not implement it".*

Corporate design requirements

Several times, the interview partners have issued concerns about the up-to-dateness or appeal of an accessible web page.

> *"In my opinion, accessible web sites do not look 'up-to-date'; it is a matter of taste".*

It can be concluded that people who initiated the web accessibility project do not feel confident about the project themselves and may therefore not have been able to convince others.

> *"If we had implemented accessibility, our web site would be worse compared to our competitors' sites".*

However, it has become clear that accessible sites may limit the design possibilities as they require certain color contrasts and font sizes.

> *"From a design perspective, you do not have as many possibilities as with non-accessible sites".*

Especially in international organizations, corporate design requirements predetermine the design of web presences including color contrasts or font sizes. This turned out to be an obstacle, especially when web accessibility efforts do not come from the headquarters but are a local initiative.

> *"The headquarters issued requirements on how a web presence had to look like that were contrary to our accessible web site proposal. It was completely impossible for us to succeed".*

This obstacle may either result in a failure of the whole project or in a compromise as regards design or color contrast.

> "We had to compromise with the corporate design department as regards several design elements".

Reasons for this aspect can be found in the research on organizational change. Organizations are subject to strong inertial forces which leads to the fact that they may respond slowly to opportunities in their environment (Hannan and Freeman 1984). Organizational inertia represents a key concern of management and a common reason for the failure of organizational change (Fincham and Rhodes 2005). Inertia is likely to emerge in complex organizations when change is incremental (Keen 1981). The organizations which declared corporate design requirements as a reason for failure of web accessibility implementation were complex, partly multinational organizations.

4.2.3.5 Incentives for implementation

Several incentives could be identified that may possibly motivate organizations to take into account web accessibility considerations. These incentives refer to organizations with and without successful implementation.

Competition

The competition aspect has been identified as an incentive for web accessibility implementation.

> "If 90 % of organizations in our sector had implemented web accessibility and we had not, it would be an absolute must for us".

One interview partner reported that in his/her country three other banking institutions have now started accessibility projects. A major reason for these initiatives was the big success of their accessibility implementation. One other banking institution – a direct competitor – gave the following feedback,

> "We would have liked to implement it as well, but our internal structures do not let us".

Law

The role of law as an incentive is considered differently by the respondents. Some are convinced that law is not a good incentive. Others regard law as the best incentive for web accessibility implementation.

> "Law as an incentive is always bad. Something that is regulated by law will always result in compromises". "Law is the top incentive".

4.2.4 Summary and interpretation

The financial services sector partly disposes of knowledge about the need for accessibility as most of the financial service institutions have undertaken attempts to make their buildings accessible (e.g., construction of ramps, decrease of assembly level of cash machines). However, the results of the web site evaluation (cf. section 4.2.2) show that there is still a lack in web accessibility implementation. Organizations which succeeded in web accessibility implementation conducted more elaborate constructional accessibility attempts (cash machines with speech output, account statement in Braille) than those who did not succeed. The awareness for the issue facilitates its implementation.

Several factors have been identified to be particularly relevant in the light of with web accessibility implementation in the financial services sector. Firstly, the exchange of sensitive information in online banking requires a certain degree of trust in the online exchange channel. The role of trust is crucial for attaining customer loyalty ("lock-in") which represents a core part of any succeeding business model (Reichheld and Schefter 2000). Secondly, a social orientation has been identified which is visible in corporate culture and corporate social responsibility strategies of financial services institutions. This may be due to the responsibility in society that financial services institutions take over in order to avoid financial exclusion. Thirdly, differentiation and image enhancement play an important role because of an ongoing tendency of associating financial services institutions with negative characteristics. In this context, a fear of negative image has been identified to be more influential than possible image enhancements. These three factors represent the main triggers for web accessibility implementation in the financial services sector.

However, obstacles for web accessibility implementation have been identified. Incompatibilities with corporate design and argumentation problems led to a lack of top management support and subsequently to a failure of web accessibility implementation.

Table 11 summarizes the results in the financial services sector.

Reasons for implementation	Changes after implementation	Reasons for failure of implementation	Incentives for implementation
Differentiation	Increase in awareness	Misconceptions	Competition
Consumer consciousness	In-house knowledge exchange	Lack of arguments	Law
Social commitment	Integration	Lack of top management support	
Elderly customers	Corporate image	Corporate design requirements	
Fear of negative image	Customer loyalty		
Design for all	Simplicity/usability		
Top management support	Maintenance		
Key personality	Search engine ranking		
	Long-term investment		

Table 11: Overview of results in the financial services sector

Differentiation, consumer consciousness, social commitment, elderly customers, fear of negative image, design for all, top management support, and key personalities could be identified as reasons for accessibility implementation. Perceived changes after implementation were increase in awareness, in-house knowledge exchange, integration, corporate image, customer loyalty, simplicity/usability, maintenance, search engine ranking, and long-term investment. In the financial services sector, misconceptions, a lack of arguments, a lack of top management support, and corporate design requirements led to failure of implementation; financial support was identified as incentive for web accessibility implementation.

4.3 Case 3: Information

4.3.1 Sector overview

Over the years, the Internet has become a powerful information source. In order to avoid information overflow, the vast amount of information is currently being filtered and structured by several portals and platforms on the Internet.

Information in that sense seems to be a very elastic term. Different kinds of portals and platforms have been established providing divers content information. The U.S. Census Bureau defines the information sector as comprising establishments engaged in the following processes: "producing and distributing information and cultural products, providing the means to transmit or distribute these products as well as data or communications, and processing data" (U.S. Census Bureau 2001, p. 1). From this definition it becomes obvious that the information sector is very broadly defined. Therefore, the evaluation of organizations in this sector is based on a study conducted by the Austrian Web Analysis (ÖWA) in 2008 where Austrian Online Media organizations were analyzed.

An extract of this study's results is depicted in Table 12. This study differentiates between single offers, which refer to user access to a single web site and umbrella brand offers, consisting of multiple web sites. Table 12 depicts one umbrella brand offer (ORF[9] network) and 45 single offers. The market leadership of the *orf.at* network, disposing of a range of 38.5% of the Austrian online population is clearly visible. This means that 1.9 million users have visited this web site in the fourth quarter of 2008 (ÖWA 2008). The top five single offers encompass *herold.at* (25.7%), *krone.at* (15.9%), *derstandard.at* (14.7%), *sms.at* (10%), and *kurier.at* (9.7%). By contrast, the top five umbrella brand offers include the *orf.at* network (38.5%), *gmx.at* (28.8%), *herold.at* (25.7%), the *Microsoft Advertising Network* (25.1%), and *oe24.at* (16.1%) (ÖWA 2008).

In addition to the number of users, measures like page impressions, sum of visits or the length of the session time have been surveyed and analyzed. A closer look at the online offers of traditional publishing companies reveals that the *oe24 network* with a range of 16.1% is number one followed by *derstandard.at,* a newspaper that has the seventh highest number of printed copies in Austria (Verband österreichischer Zeitungen 2008). On the contrary, the newspaper with the highest number of printed copies, *Kronen Zeitung* reaches the first place in the single offer category (15.9%) and outperforms *derstandard.at* by 1.2% with 14.7% range followed by *Kurier* and *diepresse.com*. These numbers again highlight the difference between bricks and clicks. Furthermore, the variety of different offers is reflected in the "description" column.

---

9   Austrian Broadcasting Institution

Organization	Unique Clients	Sum of Visits	Sum of Page Impressions	Description
netlog.com (netlog.com)	834946	9205003	359131355	Community
MyVideo (myvideo.at)	339318	909503	14193269	Community
Puls4.com (puls4.com)	328956	1255411	7748844	Community
meinbezirk.at (meinbezirk.at)	83677	136844	1483576	Community
fratz.at	27964	35313	93796	Community
ORF Network (orf.at)	4048787	34346067	259323744	Information
derStandard.at (derstandard.at)	1525250	7540959	53236497	Information
krone.at (krone.at)	1277368	7408179	141118125	Information
diepresse.com (diepresse.com)	1108934	2825036	15919651	Information
KURIER (kurier.at)	872834	3502994	23911274	Information
ÖAMTC.at (oeamtc.at)	678896	1249560	8979781	Information
NetDoktor.at (netdoktor.at)	593683	919343	6422001	Information
Vorarlberg Online (vol.at)	587194	4559463	33617088	Information
VIENNA ONLINE (vienna.at)	532221	1021031	7752915	Information
ProSieben.at (prosieben.at)	408518	728417	8103701	Information
Salzburger Nachrichten (salzburg.com)	397678	846679	15857129	Information
HELP.gv.at (help.gv.at)	373584	524657	2409431	Information
Wirtschaftsblatt.at (wirtschaftsblatt.at)	346750	1011460	3374393	Information
krone.tv (krone.tv)	313353	753404	1839007	Information
ichkoche.at (ichkoche.at)	195439	268411	2093089	Information
Salzburg24.at (salzburg24.at)	150680	303989	3684444	Information
dieStandard.at (diestandard.at)	110699	228639	546403	Information
Mamilade Ausflugstipps Österreich (mamilade.at)	102686	118870	394986	Information
tvheute.at	93214	276842	1436120	Information
Seitenblicke.at (seitenblicke.at)	86673	233571	1966016	Information
wienweb.at (wienweb.at)	61898	111474	545862	Information
rundschau.co.at (rundschau.co.at)	39607	67313	729107	Information
FONDS professionell (fondsprofessionell.at)	29286	101915	526605	Information
GENUSS.online (genuss-magazin.eu)	10827	14606	44052	Information
Economy (economyaustria.at)	3991	4517	9554	Information
Herold.at (herold.at)	1966944	5684599	47881453	Service
123people.at (123people.at)	1420908	2244640	7444489	Service
willhaben.at (willhaben.at)	945370	2888371	89477372	Service
sms.at (sms.at)	723984	4254146	102004201	Service
Szene1 (szene1.at)	651835	5615151	264193311	Service
drei.at (drei.at)	355141	1126157	7015813	Service
landwirt.com - das Agrarportal (landwirt.com)	311000	1037350	16513343	Service
car4you.at	258508	649599	16013617	Service
1000ps.at - Die stärkste Motorradseite (1000ps.at)	252252	678079	8168298	Service
tele.at	180028	509604	2899613	Service
ATV (atv.at)	163527	315718	3475709	Service
immodirekt.at (immodirekt.at)	148607	341913	12896936	Service
EVENTSZENE.at (eventszene.at)	113278	141541	689888	Service
Love.at (love.at)	110231	459628	10064912	Service
compnet.at (compnet.at)	98184	121042	381310	Service

Table 12: Online media in Austria (ÖWA 2008)

Organizations listed in Table 12 are grouped to community, information, and service providers. The ranking per group is based on the number of unique clients on every site. The information providing organizations (cf. description column) are considered for web site evaluation in this study.
Especially online media organizations live on the popularity of their web presences. Switching costs in every online business are low which is especially true for the information sector. Given media contents of comparable quality, the web site appearance (design, usability, simplicity, accessibility) may be the crucial factor for customer loyalty. In order to reduce customer switching, it is recommended to make marketer generated content more accessible (Keaveney and Parthasarathy 2001).

Moreover, media generation gap is an issue in the information sector. A forth of the age group of 18-29 year old adults have shifted to online news consumption (Ahlers 2006). This age cohort represents an important user group that may be affected by disabilities or handicaps in their middle ages. Web accessibility in the online media sector will therefore be of importance in the years to come.

For some people, online retrieval sometimes is the only way to access daily news and information at a point in time chosen by the user. Visually impaired people, for example, are dependent on online media and television news in order to be informed about current happenings. Online information retrieval represents the only possibility, where the blind user can chose the point in time. The accessibility of online media web presences constitutes a prerequisite for the access by people with disabilities.

The above argumentation clarifies the choice of the information sector as one case for this study:
(i) For people with disabilities, the online information retrieval is a day-to-day business and provides much facilitation (facilitation dimension).
(ii) The information sector is highly relevant for e-business as most productivity gains are attained within this sector (relevance dimension).
(iii) A lack of current web site accessibility in this sector needs further rise of awareness for its importance (awareness dimension).

4.3.2 Web site evaluation

Table 13 shows the web site evaluation results for the information sector. The organizations are ranked according to the number of their accessibility errors (WAI column). The best web presences in terms of accessibility are listed on top, the table ends with the least accessible sites. Furthermore, results of automated and manual tests are displayed in the tables. Automated test results consist of the number of WAI errors (indication for accessibility), HTML errors, Parsing (syntax) errors, Link errors (e.g., broken links) and the total number of errors detected in the automated testing process. Web presences without errors in the WAI column have been tested manually, for the remaining web sites the manual test was not applied (n/a).

Organization	Automated testing results					Manual testing results
	WAI errors	HTML errors	Parsing errors	Link errors	Total errors	
1	0	23	10	0	33	OK
2	0	3	0	1	4	OK
3	0	0	0	3	3	OK
4	0	1	0	10	11	OK
5	1	130	1	21	153	n/a
6	1	151	16	0	168	n/a
7	1	156	0	129	286	n/a
8	1	2	0	0	3	n/a
9	2	125	4	3	134	n/a
10	3	47	0	1	51	n/a
11	3	22	1	1	27	n/a
12	3	5	0	0	8	n/a
13	13	42	14	1	70	n/a
14	16	59	11	2	88	n/a
15	21	417	44	12	494	n/a
16	28	116	875	171	1190	n/a
17	76	852	4	0	932	n/a
18	87	1102	421	31	1641	n/a

Table 13: Web site evaluation results in the information sector

In the information sector, 18 web presences were evaluated in terms of accessibility, four of which passed automated and manual tests (cf. Table 13). The remaining web sites (numbers 5 to 18) failed both automated and manual tests. In this analysis, almost 78% of the web pages failed both automated and manual tests. Many pages use rich Internet applications (i.e. Flash and JavaScript) that would have to meet special accessibility criteria. As a result, 4 out of 18 evaluated web pages passed both automated and manual tests.

4.3.3 Qualitative analysis

This section presents the results of the qualitative analysis in the information sector. After a categorization of the organizations interviewed, the results identified in the four main areas under study (reasons for implementation, changes after implementation, reasons for failure of implementation, and incentives for implementation) are introduced. Each resulting category is documented by quotations from the interviews (in italics) and corroborated by extant literature.

4.3.3.1 Categorization

In the information sector, semi-structured interviews were conducted with four organizations, three of which have successfully implemented web accessibility. One organization failed in accessibility implementation. All four organizations represent online media and service providers, and can be classified as small and medium organizations.

Similarly to other business sectors, corporate social responsibility strategies in the information sector are implemented in large organizations; small and medium sized enterprises do not attribute high importance to this issue. As a consequence, organizations analyzed in this sector did not focus on corporate social responsibility strategies.

4.3.3.2 Reasons for implementation

This section lists the reasons that led to an implementation of accessible web presences in organizations. Examples in terms of quotations are given in italics; the connection with extant phenomena in scientific disciplines is provided in order to corroborate the findings.

Web site quality
A reason for web accessibility implementation was the bad quality of the existent web site.

> *"Nobody was satisfied with the old web site. It did not look good, did not work satisfyingly, and did not have enough traffic".*

> *"We also changed the background of the architecture completely. A second not unimportant reason was also that we wanted to get away from the former table layout".*

Moreover, some interview partners claim the existence of technological limits of the extant web site.

> *"With our old web site we finally reached our limits. This is why we decided to start from scratch".*

Usability considerations often are one of the reasons for web site relaunch.

> *"Users change the web site if it is better usable than another one".*

As already discussed in section 2.1, the confine of usability and accessibility is not always obvious. However, the "web accessibility package" entails higher quality, simplicity, and usability. These features significantly contribute to the consideration of web accessibility.

> *"We wanted a top-quality web site that conforms to standards, is usable and accessible".*

In the information sector, web accessibility considerations were undertaken in the course of a relaunch. The relaunch decision was undertaken beforehand, due to poor quality or technological limits of the extant web site. Therefore, the decision on accessibility implementation was made in a second stage and did not represent the main driving force. However, it was considered as an additional feature to enhance web site quality.

Social commitment
The meaningfulness of the own work and its sense and impact on society has been identified as a reason for web accessibility implementation.

> *"For me, it has always been important to bring in social and user-centered aspects in my technical work. Technical work should comply with ethical standards".*

The Corporate Social Responsibility strategies that have been implemented in the organizations interviewed are focused on relief operations for disadvantaged countries. However, especially small organizations cannot afford to establish a CSR strategy.

> *"Small organizations like us do not think in CSR terms".*

One interview partner said that CSR was not a driving force for web accessibility but its absence would be one.

> *"CSR is not an important driving force for web accessibility because, as a layperson, you would not notice the difference between an accessible and an inaccessible site. However, somebody complaining about an inaccessible web site of an organization may represent a huge problem from CSR point of view".*

The negativity effect of media offers a theoretical explanation for this statement. In the evaluation of people, objects, and ideas, negative information is weighted higher than positive information (Mizerski 1982). According to Kroloff, negative publicity is even given quadruple weight compared to positive news (Kroloff 1988). However, a weakening of this effect can be attained by organizations which dispose of a high number of loyal customers who have strong bonds with the product (Ahluwalia 2002). In other words, organizations with many loyal customers might experience the effect of negative media in a less intense way.

All the same, complaints that cause negative media will harm the organization in some way or the other. Therefore, organizations tend to avoid being subject to customer complaints. This is especially true for big organization with elaborate CSR strategies that may be questioned in terms of their credibility.

Elderly customers
The importance of elderly customers is referred to in the information sector. Organizations are aware of the future potential of elderly customers that results from the ongoing demographic shift.

"We have realized a platform for a senior community, where accessibility was a big issue".

Similarly to the financial services sector, the importance of elderly customers, being the fastest growing segment of the Internet economy (Trocchia and Janda 2000), is also true for the information sector. One of the main areas of online usage of elderly people is to stay current with news and events (Iyer and Eastman 2006). Iyer and Eastman's survey was based on the responses of 190 people over the age of 65 and resulted in 83% using the Internet approximately 9 hours per week, 37% of which did this for information gathering purpose.

Key personality
In the information sector, key personalities are the initiators of web accessibility projects. Following types of key personalities can be identified:

(i) Web developers interested in web accessibility
"According to my opinion, you can pique web developers' interest in accessibility. Sometimes they then implement it proactively without the management forcing it".

(ii) Project managers
"The project manager took over the initiative for web accessibility implementation".

(iii) Web developers interested in standards
"The discussion about WAI standards, HTML standards, and usability issues has led to our interest in accessibility and the involvement with the institute of the blind".

(iv) Disability organizations
"We have worked together with disability associations in the development process".

4.3.3.3 Changes after implementation

This section lists the perceived changes after implementation of accessible web presences in organizations that have been identified in the course of this case study. Examples in terms of quotations (in italics) are given; the connection with extant phenomena is provided in order to corroborate the findings.

Cost efficiency
There are two ways of implementing accessible sites: changing an existing site into an accessible one or creating a completely new site. The operating expenses are significantly higher in the first case.

> "If you want to change an existing site to an accessible one, this means high operating expenses".

One interview partner gives a comparison that illustrates this fact quite well.

> "Changing an existing site into an accessible site is like changing a motorbus to a Porsche".

Moreover, the additional expenses which accrue for an accessible site can hardly be quantified. Estimations about cost saving potential are mentioned by one interview partner.

> "If you code negligently you may perhaps save 3% of the web site costs".

Others admit, on the one hand, an increase in complication as regards accessible coding of several elements but on the other hand, state that the facilitations that go along with web accessibility lead to a fast amortization of these costs.

> "I cannot number the additional costs. I admit that some issues are more complicated to implement, but maintenance facilitations cause a fast amortization of these costs".

Due to a lack of measurement, web accessibility changes in terms of costs are subject to estimations and experiences and cannot be quantified. However, several conclusions can be drawn out of the findings of this study: (i) the implementation of web accessibility in course of a relaunch is less costly than the adaptation of an extant site, (ii) additional costs will occur in the initial phase of web accessibility implementation, and (iii) maintenance facilitations and learning effects accelerate the amortization of these initial costs.

Awareness

Another reported change after web accessibility implementation is the increase of awareness for the issue.

> "For those who were not familiar with the issue, it has activated a thinking process".

Web accessibility is regarded as a constant learning process that takes place within the organization.

> "We are in a constant learning process as regards web accessibility".

The process of awareness rising predominantly took place within the organization. Employee awareness for the issue of accessible web sites rose and provoked a learning process.

Web site quality
Another change is represented by an increase of web site quality.

> *"In terms of quality, the accessible site is not comparable to the old version".*

Another quality aspect is the better structuring of the site that is – especially at online media organizations – a complex issue. One organization interviewed solved this problem as follows:

> *"The sequence in the code now complies with the journalistic weight of the article. The further up, the more important".*

The contribution of web accessibility to the overall quality of a web site has already been addressed several times in this contribution. For online media companies, the aspect of web site quality is identified to be of high relevance due to several reasons: (i) the web site represents the medium that enables consumers to access the service, (ii) the service consumption takes place directly on the web site, and (iii) the web site requires permanent update.

Search engine ranking
Due to an increase in specific keywords in the code, accessible web sites reach better search engine rankings than inaccessible web sites.

> *"You cannot be as clumsy as to not attain a better search engine ranking with accessible sites".*

Accessible web sites dispose of a more context-loyal indexing of web site content. It is believed that an accessible web site will be found more often and with increased regularity by those users, who will get exactly the information on a web site they want to find by the use of a search engine.

> *"The most influential blind user is still Google".*

A study on user interaction of results pages of search engines analyzed the eye movements of users before the selection of links. Findings of this study showed that despite similar fixation times of the links ranked first and second, the first link is predominantly chosen. Fixation times drop off sharply after rank 2 (Granka et al. 2004). Top rankings in search engines are crucial for attaining web site traffic, which is the reason why organizations invest large amounts of money in search engine optimization. A recent study showed an increase in search engine ranking and web site traffic with accessible web sites (Hartjes 2009). However, the generalizability of the results has to be questioned as the web site traffic of one single organization was analyzed.

Web site traffic

An increase of web site traffic is reported as a notable change after web accessibility implementation. This fact is especially caused by the search engine optimization potential of accessible web sites.

> *"Our accessible site has become a traffic driver. 94% of our web site visits come from search engines".*

Higher web site traffic may also deploy economic advantages for the web site owner.

> *"We have experienced economic advantages, since the web site is technically better found".*

Competitive advantage

Accessible sites may provoke competitive advantage due to several reasons: better search engine ranking, better web site quality, and higher level of usability.

> *"With our accessible web site we have definitely gained advantage in the market".*

However, competitors in the market imitate and cause this advantage to be short-term. Hence, the lack of awareness about accessible web and the lack of implementation of barrier-free web content, entails that organizations with accessible web sites may profit from competitive advantage.

Maintenance

The maintenance of accessible web site is easier and less time consuming than the maintenance of inaccessible sites.

> *"Changes and maintenance of our site have become considerably easier".*

Especially, certain tasks (i.e., changes of the navigation menu), can be effectuated faster.

> *"With accessible sites I can rename my navigation menu without having to phone a designer".*

With inaccessible sites, a serious problem were new browser releases because they entailed that whole sites had to be recoded or new browser specific sites had to be produced.

> *"The release of a new browser used to provoke a crisis because we had to recode almost all the web sites. This is no longer the case".*

These maintenance costs drop out as accessible web sites are compatible with every browser.

"We now have lower expenses concerning browser optimization".

This argument is also true for mobile portals.

"The optimization for mobile portals is much less expensive with accessible sites".

The increasing mobile use is currently forcing organizations to change their web sites as to be compatible with mobile browsers so that it does not make a difference for customers if they access the site with a personal computer or with a mobile device.

4.3.3.4 Reasons for failure of implementation

This section lists the reasons that led to a failure of web accessibility implementation in organizations. These reasons have been identified in the course of this case study. Examples in terms of quotations are given in italics; the connection with extant phenomena is provided in order to corroborate the findings.

Corporate design requirements

Corporate design requirements of organizations are quite strict and do not allow variations. This causes conflicts of accessibility and corporate design principles.

"It would be necessary that organizations adapt their corporate design guidelines to accessibility standards. But unfortunately, they do not do that".

This is predominantly caused by a lack of awareness of web accessibility and its effects. Moreover, especially in complex or multinational organizations, these structures are predetermined by the headquarters and cannot be changed easily. The recognition aspect can also influence decisions in this area. If a company colors do not conform to web accessibility standards (e.g., due to insufficient color contrast), a change may cause a lack of recognition by the customers. This aspect can lead to web accessibility implementation failure due to non-negligible side-effects.

Lack of awareness

Most interview partners indicated that a lack of awareness is the reason for a failure of accessibility implementation.

"The basic understanding of accessibility is not available".

Web site evaluations in this industry sector (cf. section 4.3.2) have shown that 78% of organizations evaluated failed both automated and manual tests. Lack of awareness may constitute a reason for this situation.

4.3.3.5 Incentives for implementation

This section lists the incentives for web accessibility implementation in organizations which have been identified in the course of this case study. Examples in terms of quotations are given in italics; the connection with extant phenomena in scientific disciplines is provided in order to corroborate the findings.

Internal Drivers
Besides external influences such as market regulations, government or legal incentives, internal drivers are claimed to be better incentives for web accessibility implementation.

> *"This organization has such a dominating position in radio, TV and Internet, but I still do not think the market will regulate web accessibility implementation on its own. The initiation has to come from internal driving forces".*

In this case, internal drivers represent the organizational settings, in which changes or innovations may be facilitated. In an organizational culture where social commitment is anchored, incentives for web accessibility implementation may emerge internally.

Law
Law is considered as an incentive for web accessibility implementation, because it forces organizations to consider social aspects.

> *"Legal incentives and public sponsorship shall provoke a more charitable thinking of organizations".*

However, it is doubtful that profound and long term changes can occur under such circumstances. The Austrian Equalization Act for People with Disabilities foresees a compulsory arbitration process before filing a lawsuit. In other words, in case of complaints by consumers due to inaccessibility of web presences, an arbitration process has to be conducted by the Federal Ministry of Social Affairs in order to achieve a settlement out of court. This arbitration process is for free which offers the opportunity for every consumer to make use of it. In Austria, several arbitration processes have already been executed most of them with positive outcome[10]. This mechanism may support accessibility considerations in organizations because of possible negative media in connection with arbitration processes.

---

10 An overview of arbitration processes in Austria is available on an arbitration database at: http://www.bizeps.or.at/gleichstellung/schlichtungen/.

4.3.4 Summary and interpretation

The information sector and especially online newspapers are exposed to a short-time window as regards data actualization. The whole web presence is subject to a constant changing process as news articles have to be permanently updated. For these reasons, compared to social and business aspects, the technical aspects of web accessibility implementation take over a dominant role in this sector. High web site quality and ease of technical maintenance are therefore among the main triggers for web accessibility. Maintenance facilitations gain in importance when having to deal with a huge amount of data (e.g., the production of between 100 and 200 articles a day in case of one interview partner's organization). However, the data load may entail quality assurance problems, especially in case of big organizations with many employees involved in content generation.

Social commitment is not the main trigger for accessibility implementation in this sector. This finding may be due to the fact that small and medium sized organizations do not apply corporate social responsibility measures to the same extent than complex organizations.

The background to accessibility implementation has been identified to be decisive for cost efficiencies. Changing extant sites into accessible web presences is more costly than implementing accessibility in the course of a relaunch. In the information sector, predominantly technical impacts of web accessibility implementation (web site quality, search engine ranking, and maintenance) have been identified. The web presence constitutes a means to enable service consumption by the customer which takes place directly on the web site. The importance of the web presence and its quality, stability and device independency becomes a crucial element for the information sector.

Table 14 summarizes the results obtained in the information sector.

Reasons for implementation	Changes after implementation	Reasons for failure of implementation	Incentives for implementation
Website quality	Cost efficiency	Corporate design requirements	Internal drivers
Social commitment	Awareness	Lack of awareness	Law
Elderly customers	Website quality		
Key personality	Search engine ranking		
	Website traffic		
	Competitive advantage		
	Maintenance		

Table 14: Overview of results in the information sector

Website quality, social commitment, elderly customers, and key personalities could be identified as reasons for accessibility implementation. Perceived changes after implementation were cost efficiency, awareness, website quality, search engine ranking, website traffic, competitive advantage and maintenance. In the information sector, corporate design requirements and a lack of awareness led to failure of implementation; internal drivers and law were identified as incentives for web accessibility implementation.

Section 4 analyzed three industry sectors in terms of their experiences with web accessibility implementation. The findings discussed in this section are distinct for the relevant sector and therefore constitute a valuable knowledge pool and decision support for other organizations in the three sectors intending to implement accessible web sites.

However, cross-case analysis reveals common patterns across all three sectors and substantiates these patterns by analogous concepts from academic literature. Section 5 gives an overview of the findings of cross-case analysis which may be of importance for organizations in other branches of business as they reflect common experiences with web accessibility implementation.

5 Cross-case analysis

5.1 Purpose

In cases 1, 2 and 3, three different organizational sectors have been analyzed. A comparison of these sectors reveals similar patterns of circumstances under which accessible web sites have been implemented. The purpose of conducting cross-case analysis is to point out the similarities and differences across the three sectors analyzed. The application of a conceptual framework in each sector (cf. Figure 10) enables their comparability in terms of reasons for, changes after, reasons for failure of, and incentives for web accessibility implementation. Thus, the conduction of cross-case analysis had three different objectives:

(i) The scientific procedure of case study research foresees within-case and cross-case analyses for reasons of full exploitation of the findings.
(ii) Cross-case analysis represents the basis for development of a general framework.
(iii) The patterns detected are substantiated by established management science concepts in order to corroborate the findings.

Literature of organizational change has partly been used to explain these patterns and their outcomes. Additionally, innovation research offers concepts and theories that may be applied to explain reasons for web accessibility implementation. Before taking these concepts as an analogy, the definition of innovation and its applicability for accessible web sites needs to be highlighted.

In the literature, manifold definitions of innovation can be found, ranging from very general to specific, some focusing on innovation as a novelty, others on innovation as a process. An innovation is an "idea, practice, or object perceived as new by an individual or other unit of adoption" (Rogers et al. 1996). Rickards (1985) describes an innovation as "a process whereby new ideas are put into practice" (Rickards 1985, p. 10). The novelty of the idea is perceived by the relevant unit of adaption which can vary from a single individual to a business firm, a city, or a state legislature (Zaltman et al. 1973). Brockhoff (1999) adds the element of profitability to the innovation definition and states that any invention which is promising in terms of profitability and introduced on the market or implemented in a process is defined as a product or process innovation respectively (Brockhoff 1999).

Moreover, Rogers (1995) defines several characteristics of innovations that explain the rate of their adoption, (i) perceived advantage, (ii) compatibility with extant values and norms of a social system, (iii) complexity of innovations, (iv) trialability and experimentation, and (v) observability of the innovation results for individuals. Innovations with perceived higher relative advantage, compatibility, trialability, observability and less complexity will be adopted more likely than other innovations (Rogers 1995).

Innovations can be categorized by means of several criteria[11]. In this section, only the categorizations relevant for this contribution are explained in further detail. Radical innovations represent fundamental, revolutionary changes in technology, whereas incremental innovations are minor, evolutionary improvements or adjustments to current technology (Dewar and Dutton 1986). The degree of new knowledge embedded in the innovation is the main difference between radical and incremental innovations (Dewar and Dutton 1986). Innovations can also be classified according to their dimension. An innovation that has not been existent before represents an objective innovation (e.g., invention of the wheel), subjective innovations are only new to a certain group of people (Hübner 2002). An idea, product, process or service that is perceived as new by an individual can therefore be an innovation (Rogers et al. 1996).

Applying these definitions to web accessibility implementation in organizations, its innovation character becomes obvious. Web accessibility represents a process that is perceived as new by organizations and their employees, has already been introduced onto the market, and therefore constitutes an innovation.

The implementation of accessible web in an organization represents an incremental innovation because changes are evolutionary improvements of current technology. The technology itself is not the innovation but its application. Additionally, web accessibility is not a new concept to the world[12] but to the organization which wants to adopt it. This is why, from an organizational point of view, it can also be classified as a subjective innovation. Having defined web accessibility as an incremental, subjective innovation the application of theories in the innovation literature to the case of web accessibility implementation is justified.

Subsequent sections 5.2 to 5.6 provide a cross-case comparison of the common patterns detected across the three industry sectors. Innovation concepts are referred to for reasons of explanation and clarification of certain patterns.

---

11 A detailed overview of categorizations of innovations is given in Stummer et al. (2008).
12 The Web Content Accessibility Guidelines 1.0 have been developed in 1999 (W3C 1999).

5.2 Reasons for accessibility implementation

The reasons for web accessibility implementation of all three cases analyzed are summarized in Table 15. The indication of the sector is given where the respective reason has been identified (T=tourism, F=financial services, I=information). Moreover, the reasons are classified into three different categories (economic, social, and technical motivations) and substantiated by selected quotations. Detailed explanation and background to every reason specified can be found in the analyses of cases one to three (sections 4.1.3, 4.2.3, and 4.3.3).

Motivation	Reasons for implementation	Sector	Selected quotation
Economic	Differentiation	F	"We tried to be the first to implement accessibility in order to be different from our competitors".
	Elderly Customers	F,I	"Our website is being used by elderly people above average".
	Fear of negative image	F	"We cannot afford negative headlines".
	Importance of website	T	"Every guest will see our web page first, judge it, and then decide if he wants to come or not".
Social	Consumer consciousness	F	"Ethical criteria are more and more being included in the purchase decision process".
	Design for all	T,F	"Our main reason was 'simple and for all'; the simpler the better and the more customers will understand and buy the product".
	Key personality	T,F,I	"The technical department colleague's girlfriend has a hearing impairment; he had first suggestions about the issue".
	Social commitment	T,F,I	"We have always had awareness for social issues. In this case, implementation of web accessibility is easier; when the awareness already exists".
	Top management support	F	"We had the advantage that one member of the management board was 150% web affine; this made it easier to convince him".
Technical	Website quality	T,I	"Nobody was satisfied with the old website. It did not look good, did not work satisfyingly, and did not have enough traffic".

T=tourism, F=financial services, I=information

Table 15: Reasons for web accessibility implementation

Patterns across all three sectors can be derived as some of the reasons appear in every case analyzed (key personality, social commitment). Others are mentioned in two of the cases (e.g., web site quality, design for all, elderly customers) and others again turn out to be specific to one certain case (e.g., consumer consciousness, importance of web site).

A closer look on the reasons for web accessibility implementation results in their classification in social, economic and technical motivations.

5.2.1 Economic motivations

The implementation of web accessibility in an organization can be initiated out of economic motivations. In this case, organizations focus on customer orientation and customer satisfaction and implement an accessible web site as a means to increase turnover, image, and customer base. Organizations with Internet presence (both "click and mortar" companies with an additional offline presence and pure online companies) face the problem of lower switching costs of customers compared to traditional ("brick and mortar") companies. Thus, the importance of customer satisfaction and loyalty increases tremendously (Cox and Dale 2002). At the same time and out of similar reasons, competition and, thus, the need of differentiation gains in importance. Web accessibility implementation can provoke competitive advantage due to differentiation from direct competitors which is mentioned as one of the economic reasons for its implementation.

The ongoing demographic shift (cf. section 2.5.2) and the continuing trend of elderly people using the Internet constitute other economic motivations for web accessibility implementation. Elderly people are a rapidly growing segment of the Internet economy (Trocchia and Janda 2000) with significant purchasing power (Reisenwitz et al. 2007) and may dispose of mobility limitations similar to people with disabilities. Thus, for organizations with accessible web presences elderly people represent a new customer group.

The "design for all aspect" of accessible web presences implies not only the consideration of people with disabilities and elderly people, but the inclusion of any Internet user group. Simplicity, usability, and high web site quality of accessible web presences entail advantages for every user. Design for all has been identified as a major economic reason for accessible web presences.

Prospective image amelioration through web accessibility is a major motivation for organizations. This aspect is closely linked to the differentiation aspect and has also a strong relationship to the social reasons for web accessibility implementation (e.g., social commitment). The way how an organization is perceived by its customers influences customer loyalty which is, in turn, strongly related to a firm's profitability (Reichheld 1995). As a consequence, image enhancement due to web accessibility implementation may result in an increase of a company's profitability.

5.2.2 Social motivations

The implementation of web accessibility can be result from social motivations. In this case, web accessibility efforts are merely targeted to people with disabilities. Social aspects, such as equality, ethical behavior, social commitment, and responsible attitude towards society represent the main drivers for web accessibility implementation.

The degree of social commitment of an organization is closely linked to its corporate culture. A study shows that social responsibility of organizations represents one of the central motives for corporate culture (Schmid 1995). The important role of corporate culture in conjunction with web accessibility implementation out of social motivations becomes obvious. In the innovation literature, corporate culture is identified as the most important reason for driving innovation (Yu 2007).

Besides other factors, organizational culture is influential on the readiness of employees for organizational change (Jones et al. 2005). In their "Competing Values Framework", Quinn and Rohrbaugh (1983) put forth four culture types and conclude that the culture focusing on human relations and morale has a higher readiness for change (Quinn and Rohrbaugh 1983). Drawing on these assumptions, the change process of web accessibility implementation can be facilitated in a culture based on social commitment.

Therefore, the organizational background may play an important role in the implementation of web accessibility. An extensive social commitment of an organization and a corporate culture that includes social values may facilitate web accessibility implementation. The awareness for social issues is present in organizations with an elaborate corporate social responsibility strategy. Thus, the need for web accessibility as a social instrument is perceived important in organizations that dispose of such a background.

Moreover, consumer consciousness can be added to this classification as the deliberate choice of organizations according to their social responsibility clearly reflects social motivations from both the customer's and the organization's side.

The importance of the meaningfulness of own work has been expressed by one organization as a major reason for their commitment to web accessibility and can also be classified as a social motivation. In addition, employees having discovered the meaningfulness of their own work are intrinsically motivated and therefore more satisfied with their work.

Social commitment as a reason for web accessibility implementation has been identified across all three sectors. However, traditionally, mostly large organizations dispose of a clearly defined corporate social responsibility strategy. Jenkins points out that "the power and resources of large companies produces responsibility to use that power and develop those resources responsibly" (Jenkins 2006, p. 242). Despite recent trends of CSR for small and medium enterprises (Jenkins 2006; Murillo and Lozano 2006), large organizations are more likely to define and implement CSR strategies than SMEs (Perrini et al. 2007).

Moreover, some business sectors seem to be especially concerned for their reputation towards customers. In the financial services sector, this has particularly become obvious. The ongoing financial crisis led to the fact that banking institutions are eyed on suspiciously which – in turn – has forced them to focus on social issues. Many interview partners have expressed the need to be perceived as a "decent bank" that "cares for others" as a reason for web accessibility consideration.

In a nutshell, organizations that dispose of elaborate social values due to a corporate social responsibility strategy and corporate culture will rather implement web accessibility out of social reasons. Additionally, organizations in crisis-ridden business sectors (e.g., financial services sector in times of the economic crisis) especially focus on image amelioration by social instruments. These reasons may especially be the case for large organizations which usually dispose of corporate social responsibility strategies.

Individuals who initiate the project are called "key personalities" in this contribution and can be characterized as the initiators who are sufficiently committed to the subject.

Similar phenomena emerged in the literature on innovation management where the existence and importance of "product champions" has been identified. The notion has been described for the first time in 1963 (Schon 1963) and is still valid and part of ongoing innovation research. Schon (1963) identified product champions as crucial for innovation processes as they help to overcome organizational barriers and resistance (Roure 2001). In his opinion, "a new idea either finds a champion or dies" (Schon 1963, p. 84).

One of the core characteristics of such a product champion is that he/she recognizes a new market opportunity as having a significant potential and commits personally to the project (Markham and Aiman-Smith 2001). The product champion is the key individual who sells the idea to the management or at least gets it sufficiently interested (Chakrabarti 1974). For successful product innovation in large corporations, the presence of product champions is especially important as systems, procedures and the hierarchy are more elaborate than in small organizations (Schon 1967). The importance of product champions in the area of innovation can be compared with the importance of key personalities when initiating a web accessibility project.

Across all three cases, different key personalities can be identified that either come from personal relationships of the project manager or stem from their business backgrounds. Table 16 displays the key personality characteristics identified in the respective organizational sectors. These characteristics are categorized according to their background (personal and business) and documented by selected quotations.

Background	Key Personality Characteristics	Sector	Selected quotation
Personal	Disability	F	"I initiated the project, because the bank's website was not accessible with my screenreader".
	Friends and family with disabilities	T	"My brother has a severe sight disability. He uses magnification software and told me to take care for the magnification aspect when designing a new site".
	Friends with expert knowledge in the field of web accessibility	T	"My friend is an expert. He told me about accessibility".
Business	Colleagues with impairments	F	"A colleague from the technical department has a girlfriend with a hearing impairment. He had the first suggestions about this issue".
	Colleagues with technical interest	I	"According to my opinion, you can pique web developers' interest in accessibility. Sometimes they then implement it proactively without the management forcing it".
	Interest groups/disability organizations	F	"We have worked in cooperation with the institute of the blind".
	Former colleagues with impairments	F	"A former colleague has a sight disability and works for the institute of the blind".
	Other inputs (presentations, events)	F	"I have been at a lecture given by a sight disabled person. This has impressed me a lot".

T=tourism, F=financial services, I=information

Table 16: Key personality characteristics

The personal commitment necessary for product champions (Markham and Aiman-Smith 2001) can also be identified for the key personalities in the three sectors. They either have a disability, have friends and family with disabilities, or friends and family with expert knowledge about web accessibility. Their personal commitment can also stem from business background (e.g., colleagues with impairments/technical interest, cooperation with interest groups) and accessibility events or presentations. Committed and empowered key personalities are crucial for the efficiency of innovations (Rothwell 1994).

Besides the presence of key personalities, top management support has also been identified as crucial for the success of web accessibility implementation. In the literature, top management support for the success of a project or an innovation has been highlighted by various researchers (Maidique and Zirger 1984; Pinto and Slevin 1988). Additionally, top management commitment and support have been found out to be among other factors relevant for increasing development speed and efficiency of innovations (Rothwell 1994).

5.2.3 Technical motivations

Web accessibility implementation can be initiated out of technical motivations. The poor web site quality of existing sites is a major reason for the consideration of accessibility, as it comprises several elements that lead to an increase in simplicity, clarity, usability, download speed, and web site quality. The usage of structural elements (e.g., headings, lists) contributes to a clearly arranged web presence, the separation of content and layout reduces code and provokes a reduction of download times, and the consistent navigation and layout for the whole web presence causes an increase in usability. In short, accessible web sites dispose of a higher web site quality than inaccessible sites.

The mere focus on the aesthetic design of a web site goes at the expense of its usability and may therefore cause frustration by the customer (Cox and Dale 2002). Moreover, web sites with many design elements tend to be more voluminous and thus slower in their download times. This is a crucial issue, given the fact that convenience and speed are the main reasons why customers prefer the Internet over traditional "offline" firms. Fast download times of a web site are therefore decisive for the success of the firm. Cox and Dale (2002) identify six key quality factors for web sites: clarity of purpose, design, accessibility and speed, content, customer service, and customer relationships (Cox and Dale 2002). Additionally, they classify accessibility as the "most critical factor for any web site" (Cox and Dale 2002, p. 867). The increasing use of mobile devices for Internet access further enforces the use of accessible web sites which provide device independency.

Technical motivations for web accessibility implementation encompass the intention of an organization to improve the web site from its technical point of view in order to obtain a stable, secure, high quality site. This is the reason why the implementation of web accessibility out of technical motives is often initiated by IT experts who know about the advantages of accessibility in terms of quality of web pages.

Compared to the tourism and financial services sector, the information sector was more concerned about the stability and quality of their web sites. Technical reasons were among the major motivations for web accessibility implementation in this sector because of a high fluctuation of web site contents especially in the online media branch.

The improvement of web site quality may concern every sector analyzed. However, its importance increases with the importance of the web presence for the organization. Additionally, web sites where content is subject to high fluctuations will be more interested in web accessibility implementation.

5.3 Changes after accessibility implementation

The changes after web accessibility implementation of all three cases analyzed are summarized in Table 17. The indication of the sector is given where the respective change has been identified (T=tourism, F=financial services, I=information). Moreover, the changes are categorized into economic, social and technical changes and documented by selected quotations.

Category	Changes after implementation	Sector	Selected quotation
Economic	Competitive advantage	I	"With our accessible website we have definitely gained advantage in the market".
	Cost efficiency	T,I	"The website is much more cost efficient as we do not have to recode it so often".
	Customer loyalty	F	"Before the implementation of accessibility, 75% of the customers who wanted to open an account stayed with our bank, after the implementation this number increased to 95%".
	Corporate image	F	"These days where banks are associated with negative things, it is very important to show that we are doing positive things".
	Website traffic	I	"Our accessible site has become a traffic driver. 94% of our website visits come from search engines".
Social	In-house knowledge exchange	F	"I have made the experience that commited employees who work with the internet but come from different departments now talk about web accessibility. A knowledge exchange is happening".
	Awareness	F, I	"For those who were not familiar with the issue, it has activated a thinking process".
	Integration	F	"A sudden sensitization has occurred for employees with disabilities. [...] They have been given motivation and self-confidence".
Technical	Maintenance	T,F,I	"The website editors do not understand why some fields are now obligatory. [...] This is difficult to check because we have about 50 editors in our organization and we cannot check on every alt attribute inserted".
	Search engine ranking	T,F,I	"Our website is found more easily by search engines now because of the higher amount of keywords in the code".
	Simplicity/Usability	T,F	"We used to have disputations within the organizations because some people wanted their text to be positioned above right, others below left and others again in bigger letters, etc. These conversations do not exist anymore as the structure is now predetermined. This also means an economy of time".
	Website quality	I	"It has shown that accessibility entails better structure of websites".

T=tourism, F=financial services, I=information

Table 17: Changes after implementation

5.3.1 Economic changes

Economic changes after web accessibility implementation are multifaceted. In terms of costs, the widespread assumption that accessibility is costly cannot be supported. Organizations having implemented accessible web sites regard this project as a long term investment. Due to the fact that accessible web sites are persistent, their implementation leads to cost efficiencies in the long run. These, in turn, may create advantage over the direct competitors. The dependencies and relationships of the indicators of changes after web accessibility implementation listed in Figure 14 have been identified in the course of this cross-case analysis. The relationship between differentiation, corporate image and customer loyalty has already been discussed (cf. section 4.2.3.2). Strong corporate image contributes to differentiation (Morello 1986) and initiates customer loyalty building (Nguyen and LeBlanc 1998). Moreover, the effect of negative publicity on an organization may be weakened by a high amount of loyal customers (Ahluwalia 2002). Competitive advantage is caused by differentiation (better service than competitor) and cost leadership (cheaper products) (Porter 1998).

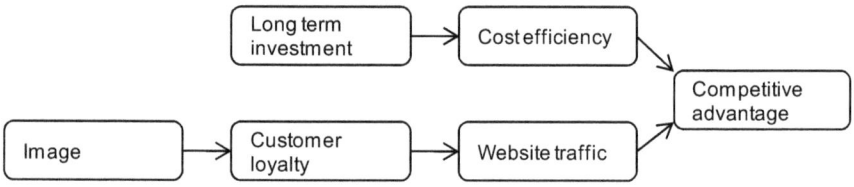

Figure 14: Economic changes after web accessibility implementation

However, organizations are unable to quantify their cost savings due to problems of confine in this field. Nevertheless, the cost criterion has not been an issue for most organizations in the course of web accessibility implementation.

The raise of awareness among customers and employees about web accessibility (cf. social changes in Figure 15) has provoked image enhancement for the respective organization. The communication of accessibility efforts to the public remains a prerequisite. Competitive advantage is the consequence, providing organizations with a first mover advantage in terms of web accessibility. They play the leading role and force competitors to imitate.

5.3.2 Social changes

After successful implementation of accessible web sites, several indicators for social changes have been observed. Employees with disabilities experience a higher degree of integration into the company. The fact that their handicap is suddenly taken seriously and respected by the organization leads to a higher degree of motivation of employees with special needs which, in turn, provokes an intrinsic incentive and therefore a higher motivation for their work. The implementation of web accessibility is observed to be a learning process. Some organizations have established knowledge management tools that foster knowledge exchange among employees about the subject (e.g., internal knowledge platforms); these tools enable knowledge exchange and contribute to the transfer from tacit to explicit knowledge. Moreover, an increase in awareness among both customers and employees is created. An overview of the social changes after web accessibility implementation and their relationships is depicted in Figure 15.

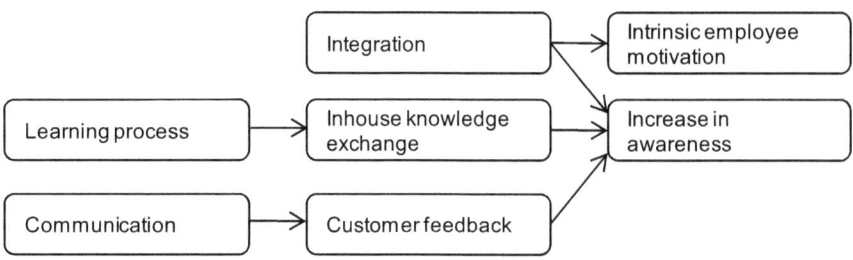
Figure 15: Social changes after web accessibility implementation

Given the fact that the accessibility of web pages is not visible for the layperson, communication about accessibility is a prerequisite for a rise of awareness (cf. Figure 15). Moreover, positive customer feedback results from communication about accessible web sites. Some organizations have indicated their status of accessibility on the web site, others have had their sites certified and labeled[13], and again others have not communicated their efforts to the public. It can be observed that the organization which had a quality mark on their web site, provoked the most effective rise in awareness in society (awards, organization of awareness days, press communications, competitors as imitators) compared to the other organizations. This may be an indication that it does not only matter to communicate web accessibility, but also the way of communication is essential; the more impartial the better and the more credible. Quality marks are issued when the web presence is regarded accessible by a third party. This impartial evaluation may provoke higher credibility than the organization claiming their efforts.

5.3.3 Technical changes

Several technical changes after web accessibility implementation have been observed. In terms of maintenance, considerable facilitation is reported and specified by following items:

- Faster effectuation of changes and update of web site content
- Faster training of new employees
- Device and browser independence (different versions of browsers, mobile portal optimization)

This ease of maintenance is mentioned in every sector analyzed but may be especially important for organizations with a high fluctuation of web site content. However, limitations are reported by these organizations in terms of quality as-

---

13 Currently, in Austria, no accessibility quality mark exists. The organization the author refers to is located in Switzerland where accessible websites can be certified (www.label4all.ch).

surance. Despite well trained staff, checks on every alt-attribute are crucial but impossible with voluminous web presences (e.g., online newspaper).
Across all three cases, a higher ranking in search engine results and, as a consequence, higher web site traffic is attained by accessible web presences. An empirical study yielded similar results, attaining significant increases in web site traffic (visits, time on site, returning visits) through search engine optimization of accessible web presences (Hartjes 2009).

Moreover, an increase in simplicity and usability are among the technical changes of web accessibility implementation. These have a strong relationship with web site maintenance, and again with web site traffic. Web sites with a high level of usability will attain more web site visits than sites with a low level of usability. As already analyzed in section 2.1, accessible sites contribute to a site's usability.

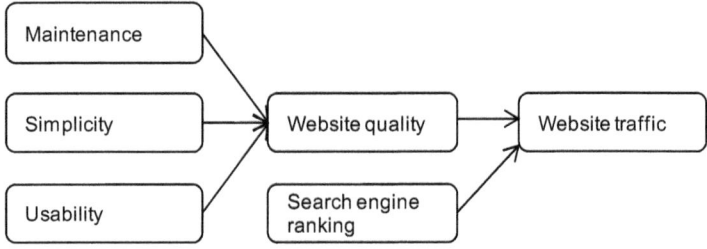

Figure 16: Technical changes after web accessibility implementation

The changes mentioned in this section all contribute to a better web site quality (cf. Figure 16). In the back end, quality improvements in terms of maintenance facilitations and in the front end, usability and simplicity increases provoke a higher web site quality. As a consequence, web site quality and search engine optimization result in an increase of web site traffic of accessible web presences.
Figure 17 displays an overview of social, economic, and technical changes after web accessibility implementation and shows the relationships of their elements.

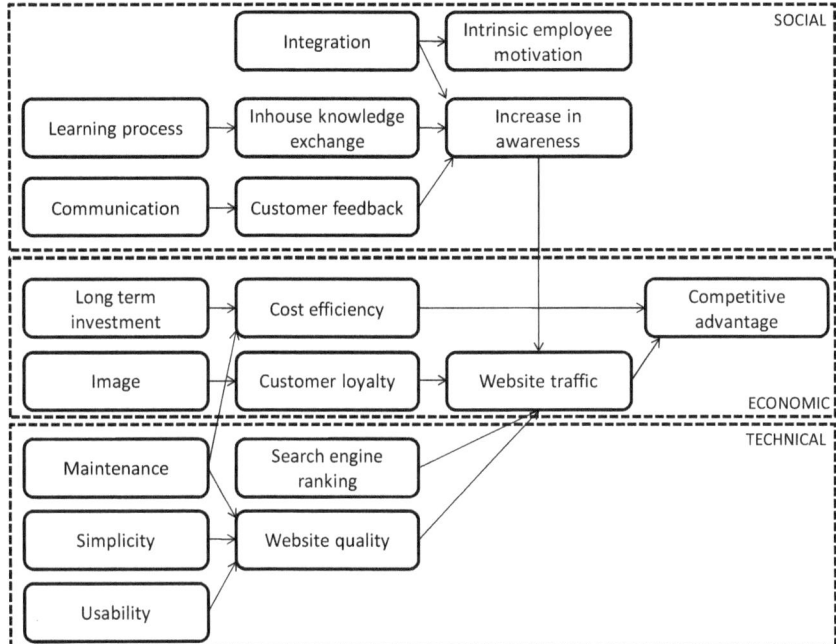

Figure 17: Perceived changes of web accessibility implementation: overview and relationships

It is clearly visible that social and economic changes are interrelated as well as technical and economic changes.

Figure 17 displays perceived positive changes after web accessibility implementation. However, in some cases, problems have been identified in the social, economic and technical areas:

Quality assurance
A high number of web site editors may provoke problems in terms of quality assurance. Despite employee trainings on accessibility, human errors or negligence are difficult to check in case of a high frequency of web content actualization and a high number of people changing content. Additionally, time and resources for quality assurance checks are not available.

Awareness
The more organizations invest in accessibility promotion, the more effective the awareness increase. Depending on the web accessibility status in the organization, marketing efforts were conducted differently. A lack of awareness and media echo has been identified in organizations which rather focused on technical than on social or economic reasons in the course of web accessibility implementation.

Cost efficiency

In case of adaptations of extant web presences, high initial costs are reported. Additionally, complex web presences entail coding difficulties that provoke high costs and time effort.

Search engine ranking

Predominantly, a better search engine ranking of accessible web sites has been identified across all sectors. However, a mere focus on technical criteria (that can be tested by automated evaluation tools) may render a site accessible but may not provoke a higher ranking. This may be a reason why in some cases search engine rankings have not improved.

5.4 Reasons for failure of implementation

The findings of this section are based on interviews with organizations that failed web accessibility implementation and give indications about their reasons for failure. Table 18 categorizes the reasons into argumentation based and design/layout based reasons and lists the sector where the respective reason has been identified. Moreover, selected quotations are indicated in order to provide evidence for the reasons identified.

Category	Reasons for failure of implementation	Sector	Selected quotation
Argumentation	Lack of arguments	F	"I have only pointed out the social argument which was the reason why it has not been considered further".
	Lack of awareness	T,I	"The basic understanding of accessibility is not available".
	Lack of top management support	F	"The marketing department turned my effort down with the words: We do not have many sight-disabled customers. As long as this is not stated by law, we do not implement it".
	Misconceptions	F	"We do not have blind customers. This would not be profitable".
Design/ Layout	Corporate design requirements	F,I	"The headquarters issued requirements on how a web presence had to look like that were contrary to our accessible website proposal. It was completely impossible for us to succeed".
	Differences in accessible layout	F	"If we had implemented accessibility, our website would be worse compared to our competitors' sites".

T=tourism, F=financial services, I=information

Table 18: Reasons for lack of implementation

The reasons why accessibility implementation has failed can be divided into two categories: design/layout and argumentation.

5.4.1 Design and layout

Especially in multinationals and big organizations, strict corporate design requirements are issued which include detailed definitions for consistent web site layout. In very few cases, these requirements conform to web accessibility guidelines. As a consequence, local web accessibility initiatives fail because of the company-wide corporate design that does not conform. To give an example, insufficient contrasts of company colors may constitute a first obstacle for accessible web sites. The effort of changing inaccessible corporate design to an accessible one requires approval of many internal decision makers and is claimed to be unrealistic. Additionally, accessibility initiators state that accessibility deteriorates the web site layout as the design possibilities are limited. These reasons for web accessibility implementation failure have been observed in complex organizations; for small and medium organizations, corporate design adjustments can be made more easily.

However, in organizations where social values are part of the company culture and the awareness for accessibility is prioritized, these obstacles may become conquerable. If organizational change alters existing values within an organizational culture, resistance can be expected (Trader-Leigh 2002). Therefore, the resistance may be lower or not present at all if the values of the existing culture are not changed.

5.4.2 Argumentation

A main reason for the lack of implementation is the absence of awareness for web accessibility that has also been observed in other contexts (Schmetzke 2001). This absence may cause misconceptions and myths (e.g., *"web accessibility only concerns blind people"*) that need clear and concise presentation of web accessibility facts. Additionally, a lack of knowledge of the project initiator of the social, business, and technical benefits of web accessibility implementation has been a reason for its failure. Lack of awareness, existence of misconceptions and lack of argumentation are three major reasons that separately and even more in common may cause a failure of web accessibility implementation. Moreover, each of these reasons will lead to a lack of management support which, as already indicated in section 4.2.3.2, constitutes a prerequisite for successful project implementation. In cases where a lack of argumentation was identified, accessibility projects have been subject to "ad hoc" implementation. This means that elaborate project preparation and planning was omitted beforehand.

Across all cases, organizations which failed web accessibility implementation disposed of several characteristics: (i) no or poor indication of elaborate corporate social responsibility strategies or social values anchored in their corporate culture; (ii) project initiators were highly frustrated and not totally convinced of the issue; (iii) project initiators were not well prepared and were not aware of the full range of argumentation at the time of project presentation; (iv) web accessibility implementation was conducted as an "ad hoc" attempt.

5.5 Incentives for accessibility implementation

The incentives for web accessibility implementation of all three cases analyzed are summarized in Table 19. The indication of the sector is given where the respective reason has been identified and selected quotations are indicated.

Category	Incentives for implementation	Sector	Selected quotation
External	Competition	F	"*If 90% of organizations in our sector had implemented web accessibility and we had not, it would be an absolute must for us*".
	Financial Incentive	T	"*Money – in which form ever – is a big incentive but it is not the solution. The basic attitude cannot be changed by financial incentives*".
	Law	F,I	"*Legal incentives and public sponsorship shall provoke a more charitable thinking of organizations*".
Internal	Internal Drivers	I	"*This organization has such a dominating position in radio, TV, and Internet but I still do not think the market will regulate web accessibility implementation on its own. The initiation has to come from internal driving forces*".

T=tourism, F=financial services, I=information

Table 19: Incentives for implementation

Organizations with and without accessible web presence have given suggestions about incentives that could win over organizations to implement web accessibility. These incentives may either stem from the government (external incentive) or the organization (internal incentive).

5.5.1 External incentives

External incentives can be realized in order to raise the awareness for accessible web pages. As already stated in section 2.4.3, legal regulations about web accessibility only concern public web pages. The web presences of private organizations, especially of those which are concerned by the consumer protection law, can only be legally forced to implement web accessibility in case of complaints of users who feel discriminated against. These users may invoke the Austrian Equalization Act for People with Disabilities. However, these so called "negative incentives" do not entail long term motivation. As one interview partner put it, *"law always results in compromises"*. Incentives by the government may rather include privileges (e.g., monetary, tax) for organizations with accessible web sites.

5.5.2 Internal incentives

On the contrary, internal incentives can only be realized when awareness for the issue of web accessibility is present within the organization. These internal incentives can either be caused by competitive pressure and the intention to profit from a first-mover advantage which leads to an outperformance of the direct competitors or they can be issued internally as part of the corporate design or social responsibility.

5.6 The web accessibility implementation process model

The analysis of organizations which failed in accessibility implementation has shown that this failure frequently resulted out of "ad-hoc" implementation attempts. A lack of systematic preparation and planning of the whole implementation process led to a failure of its adoption in the first place. One of the factors for development speed and efficiency of innovations is an adequate preparation that encompasses careful planning and project evaluation (Rothwell 1994). A review of relevant literature has shown that web accessibility implementation processes have been identified sparsely so far. The WAI has issued considerations for the web accessibility planning process (W3C 2002), some other suggestions for possible processes in web accessibility implementation have been expressed but are not based on empirical evidence (e.g., Puhl 2008). As a consequence, a main contribution of this work represents the development of a web accessibility implementation process model that is based on the empirical data of three industry sectors.

In the analysis of organizations which have successfully implemented web accessibility, similar implementation patterns regarding their implementation processes have emerged. These patterns are assembled to an implementation process model for accessible web sites in organizations (cf. Figure 18). The process model aggregates findings of all three sectors and organizations with different sizes and structures. Therefore, a general process model is depicted in Figure 18 that can be applied to every organization in every sector. However, differences in the application emerge within the respective stages and are highlighted in the subsequent analysis.

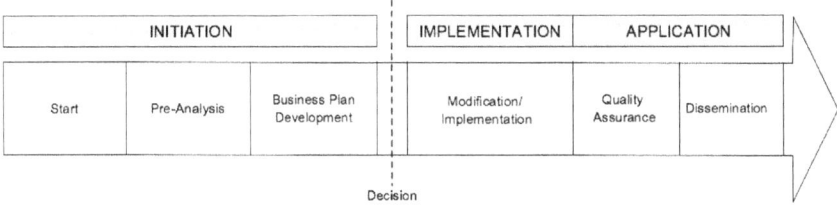

Figure 18: Web accessibility implementation process (WAIP) model

The web accessibility implementation process (WAIP) is divided into three phases: (1) initiation, (2) implementation, and (3) application. Each of these three phases consists of several stages which are explained in further detail in sections 5.6.1.1 to 5.6.3.2.

5.6.1 Initiation

The *Initiation* phase encompasses the first three stages that have to be passed through before decision making can take place: the *Start* stage, the *Pre-analysis* stage, and the *Business plan development* stage. Each of these stages is explained in more detail in sections 5.6.1.1 to 5.6.1.3.

5.6.1.1 Start

In the *Start* stage the necessity of web accessibility implementation in an organization is created. Either an individual or a group of individuals learn about the issue of web accessibility and connect this issue to the organization. The awareness creation process is often part of this stage but can also happen before. The important aspect is that an individual establishes a connection between the innovation web accessibility and the organization, which causes the development of an idea and subsequently a project.

Individuals who launch such a project have been identified as key personalities. They either have a disability themselves or have friends and family with disabilities or with expert knowledge about web accessibility. Their personal commitment can also stem from business background (e.g., colleagues with impairments/technical interest, cooperation with interest groups/agencies) and accessibility events or presentations (for further details see Table 16). These key personalities act as initiators, or people who spread the virus (Gladwell 2000). Gladwell (2000) describes three types of *initiators*: (i) connectors who have a tight network, (ii) *mavens* who are experts in a field and who love to share information, (iii) and *salesmen* who can convince others. An initiator can have characteristics of one or more types defined.

> *"The stimulation was set by the agency. The agency stated that there are these rules and that it would be nice, if we fulfill them anyway to a great extent, if we would then again refinish there and we say that we fulfill them completely".*

> *"The issue encourages a lot of people, especially in the technical sector. You can really excite web developers with the topic accessibility which is interesting. I have already experienced this. They pick this up and often they do it on their own initiative also without their management and bosses forcing it".*

In the *Start* stage, several factors cause the initiation of a web accessibility implementation. The extension of the current customer base includes a company's focus on elderly customers or the intention to build a web presence that is designed for all. Moreover, current efforts in terms of constructional accessibility (e.g., ramps) may lead to web accessibility considerations. Additionally, the motivation can be due to quality enhancement of the extant web presence or the endeavor for standard compliant web presences (e.g., in course of a relaunch). Finally, external agencies consulted for relaunch purposes may dispose of accessibility knowledge and initiate the project.

> *"The best way is to pick a person who has impairments and works with this tool. One should without any doubt pick someone who is concerned. And then explain how he or she works, what the difficulties and what the barriers are respectively. And this wakes a light bulb moment – this is what I also experienced over and over again. People are very impressed. I often do this for IT project managers, for the management. This is something I have heard about often, that people are impressed. I think one has to approach this in a practical way. Go there yourself and absolutely show with a demo so that people experience it live".*

The result of the *Start* stage should be the development of a heterogeneous coordination team with at least one key personality. The use of cross-functional and integrated teams during development and prototyping has been identified as one of the factors for efficient innovation (Rothwell 1994).

5.6.1.2 Pre-analysis

In the *Pre-analysis* stage, the web accessibility level of the current web presence is determined in order to get a feeling and understanding for the status quo of the web presence.

> *"At first, we had an analysis made by a firm [...] to find out what is not in line with the accessibility guidelines. We received a suggestion and support by the company's subsidiary which also implemented the system. That means that following questions have been worked out: What are we doing? What are we capable of doing? What stages are necessary?"*

The outcome of this initial assessment is influential for the decision if a relaunch has to be done or if an adaptation of the extant web presence is sufficient. Relaunch decisions may have an effect on the costs of the accessible site.

> *"The development process will not become more expensive, if we focus on the accessibility from the beginning of a website development".*

In the latter case, this analysis also gives indication about current accessibility errors that have to be fixed when modifying the site. Figure 19 depicts the implementation alternatives of an organization. In case of a start-up organization, a completely new web presence would have to be built. This process is similar to web site relaunch and is therefore not described in further detail. In both cases (relaunch and adaptation), the realization can either be accomplished in-house or can be outsourced.

> *"We charged an external company with the adjustment, which took six months".*

"The Content Management System is an in-house development".

Usually, the current policy is retained, which means that if the current web site development and maintenance is performed by an external agency, the new development is likely to be outsourced. In some organizations, even a specific Content Management System (CMS) has been developed in-house which is why the accessible web site will rather be developed in-house even if this involves major CMS adaptations.

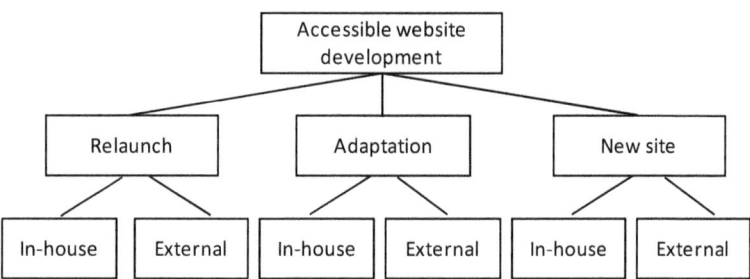

Figure 19: Web accessibility implementation alternatives

The initial assessment can be conducted using the W3C's Preliminary Review method which is a way to quickly identify the problems' extent (W3C 2008a). However, expert consultation in this stage is crucial and has been identified as one of the factors for the efficiency of innovations (Rothwell 1994). Web developers with specialization in the field of accessibility or disability interest groups can give important input and consulting about the current level of accessibility, the priority of errors to be fixed, the relaunch or modification decision, the future level of accessibility, the authoring tools to be used, the applicability of current software and CMS, and the estimation of resources for the whole accessibility implementation process. Moreover, user testing by people with disabilities or screen reader tests will identify the extant site's main problems.

"At that time we acquired the homepage-reader, which helped me to read it by showing the structure of the site".

Another process in the *Pre-analysis* stage is the determination of web developers' and web editors' knowledge about web accessibility in order to better estimate the training costs. Depending on the number of editors/developers, this can be done either by personal communication or by a self-assessment questionnaire.

At the end of the *Pre-analysis* stage, the coordination team is aware of the following aspects: current accessibility level of web presence, technology adaptations/modifications necessary for accessibility, future level of accessibility, web developers' current level of expertise, and relaunch or modification of current site.

5.6.1.3 Business plan development

The *Business plan development* stage encompasses all research steps for generation of a business plan. The main objective of the *Business plan development* stage is to create a business plan that can be presented to decision makers. The decision about the project will happen after this stage. Decision makers need to be convinced about the necessity of the project. It has been identified that the marketing department usually has a strong influence on web site project decisions. This stage is crucial for the further development of the web accessibility project as it represents the basis for decision making on top management level.

> *"This may be due to the fact that we had to provide a precise business plan. When we relaunched a web site during the Easy One Project last year, we discovered an increase in sales due to the 'clear and simple' definitions of our business plan. Our plan worked out and we can proof it now".*

The degree of precision of the business plan varies according to the organizational size, the business sector, and organizational climate for innovation and change. Due to more argumentation efforts, complex organizations with a low level of readiness for change need a more elaborate business plan than small, innovative organizations. However, the basic elements of a business plan must be considered by every organization. These are: specification of a business idea, products and services, cooperation network, industry analysis, marketing plan, operational strategy, and financial strategy.

Business idea

Differences in the development of a business idea for web accessibility implementation could be identified across all sectors. One organization exchanged accessibility by simplicity and called their project "simple and for all", another used the accessibility aspect as the main business idea.

> *"Easy for all - that is how we marketed the relaunch. Not accessibility - we just called it 'Easy for all'".*

> *"Our goal is accessibility, and the idea that I mentioned was to introduce accessibility sort of reversely. Because with accessibility itself, you don't get through or at least we didn't get through with it. If I now go the other way and say "We keep on working normally and implement accessibility gradually", but I don't start right away with accessibility, with some probably technical expressions and explanation,. [...] I then have more likely a foot in the door, at least according to my opinion".*

"The basic starting position was, actually the story with 50-plus, that has been en vogue back then. And as we are a bank that has a lot of elderly people as customers, we also have strong relationships to the retiree association. This was actually the reason to rebuild this into an accessible site".

The development of the business idea is a delicate aspect; the organizational culture, the climate for organizational change and the organizational sector have to be taken into account. In the simplicity approach, accessibility is a side effect which may not be fruitful in terms of awareness rising. However, the notion "simple and for all" is clear for everybody and does not contain any unknown terms. As a consequence, the degree of reference to accessibility in the business idea is a situational decision. In every case, it should encompass the benefit and uniqueness of the intention.

Products and services
In this section, the results of the initial assessment in the *Pre-Analysis* stage are detailed. The current web presence's accessibility level and the corresponding problems are specified. Additionally, the intended future level of accessibility is indicated and a procedure of how to reach and maintain this level is proposed. In this section technical details have to be specified. These will differ according to the procedure chosen: in-house vs. external accomplishment, relaunch vs. modification of extant site. For instance, in case of in-house accomplishment, the CMS system will have to be adapted; in case of relaunch, a different authoring tool may be chosen.

Cooperation network
The specification of the cooperation partners is necessary. In case of in-house development, the intended cooperation with external consultants (disability interest groups, web developers) is specified. Additionally, their tasks are defined. These may range from consultancy with the creation of accessible web presences to training of employees. In case of outsourcing, web developers are specified.

Industry analysis
An analysis of the industry in terms of web accessibility implementation is given. The specification of competitor behavior in conjunction with accessibility leads to important arguments either for the first-mover advantage (competitive advantage), or, in case of competitors having implemented accessibility it enforces the necessity to imitate. Additionally, target customers for the accessible web presence are identified.

Marketing plan
Due to the fact that the accessibility of a web site is not detectable by the inexperienced user, a marketing concept has to be issued. In the analysis, organizations with elaborate marketing and PR activity have profited from image enhance-

ments. Some organizations have indicated their efforts on the web site, others have issued press releases and organized events (e.g., a disability awareness day). Promotion activities are crucial for the media response to accessibility implementation.

Operational strategy
The operational strategy encompasses human resources necessary for the realization of the project. In this case, the amount of training necessary for employees (web editors) has to be specified. Additionally, a rough project plan of the whole implementation process (duration, manpower, tasks) has to be made.

Financial strategy
A cost benefit analysis and estimations about web accessibility investment is specified in the financial strategy. This section will differ across organizations and depends on the implementation procedure chosen (in-house vs. external; relaunch vs. modification). Modification of extant sites is more expensive than the construction of a new site (one interview partner compared these efforts to *"changing a motorbus to a Porsche"*). Details on reasons (economic, social, and technical) for and changes after web accessibility implementation that are either corroborated by research literature or qualitative study results can be found in sections 4 and 5 respectively.

5.6.2 Implementation

After decision making, the *Implementation* phase starts. This phase consists of the *Modification/Implementation* stage which is explained in more detail in section 5.6.2.1.

5.6.2.1 Modification/Implementation

After a positive decision and commitment by the top management, the *Modification/Implementation* stage commences. The basic requirements for the new web site should be known from the *Pre-analysis* stage. However, a detailed web site assessment shall reveal the prerequisites for accessibility implementation. In case of an external accomplishment, external web developers create the accessible site. The timeframe for this task depends on the complexity, technology, and current accessibility level of the web presence. In-house realization usually involves technical adjustments. Either CMS systems have to be adapted for accessibility reasons or new authoring tools have to be chosen.

> *"We had the problem of an already existing Content Management System. Therefore we had to adjust our websites to the accessibility requirements. In order to do so, we cooperated with an organization that even evaluated our websites and the assessment results".*

"We adapted the CMS in terms of accessibility. For example, if the alt-text is not defined with the WYSIWYG-tool, this is visible to the authors. Furthermore, introducing help-comments clarifies the meaning of the alt-text and its usability to the users".

Both processes can be tedious given the fact that staff must be trained both on the use of the adapted or new CMS and on the correct application of accessibility. Moreover, compromises in corporate design can occur and may threaten accessibility. The importance of extant layout in some organizations has been a problem in this stage. However, the *Pre-analysis* stage may weaken these problems, as they should already emerge after an initial assessment of the web presence and can therefore be taken into account in an earlier stage. Detailed technical implementation procedures have been developed by the W3C and the WAB Cluster (Nietzio et al. 2008; W3C 2008c) that are mentioned for reasons of completeness but will not be discussed in further detail in this context.

In the *Modification/Implementation* stage, training of web site editors has to be performed both in case of in-house and outsourced accomplishment. Additionally, in case of CMS adaptations or new authoring tools, employees need to be trained on the use of these tools.

"A web editorial team and the members of staff are of course trained and informed, for example "How do I have to handle this, if I create something new?" and so on, in order to keep it accessible also in the future".

"First there was an editor training, because it was another CMS than before - just from the handling point of view - for all editors. During this training we have hardly ever mentioned the term accessibility".

"Sure, I did two trainings, but this is just half the way".

After successful accessibility implementation, the level of accessibility has to be verified. In this stage, experts are consulted in order to evaluate the web presence. Usually, tests with users with disabilities and screen reader evaluations are executed in order to detect possible accessibility errors that need to be fixed.

"We cooperated with an organization that evaluated our websites and even the assessment results. A blind woman was very helpful in this matter".

"We have been working there with disabled persons, with visually handicapped, and took a look at it together with them, tested the websites together, and took a close look on what they were actually doing".

The results of the *Modification/Implementation* stage are a successfully implemented and evaluated accessible web presence and web site editors, developers and technical staff being trained on web accessibility guidelines and techniques.

5.6.3 Application

The *Application* phase starts after successful implementation of the accessible web site and encompasses the *Quality assurance* and the *Dissemination* stages which are explained in further details in sections 5.6.3.1 and 5.6.3.2.

5.6.3.1 Quality assurance

The *Quality assurance* stage is the most important and simultaneously the most difficult one. Web pages are dynamic and change constantly. In order to guarantee long term accessible web pages, a quality assurance methodology is crucial. Accessibility is a constant learning process which is why employee training on accessibility features constitutes a first step to quality assurance (see *Modification/Implementation* stage).

> "Basic improvements have been accomplished for the last two years. This is even a constant process within our company".

> "The other thing is that you organize trainings - especially in the IT Accessibility Training sector - we did this in an academy and organized an 'accessible web design' course. Accessibility then was mandatory. We wrote guidelines which people had to stick to. In this way we can guarantee that accessibility doesn't get lost overnight. I am in some sense an accessibility motor in order to assure this. But I think that with certification we have a good mechanism to control web accessibility".

Moreover, knowledge management tools such as Wikis or knowledge platforms have been utilized by some organizations in order to exchange experiences and expert knowledge about specific web accessibility problems.

> "When the guidelines were put into action we opened a Wiki at our company, there the editors could get all the material".

For web site users, a feedback and complaints channel is commonly implemented where accessibility errors can be reported.

> "We provide an email-address for customers in case of difficulties with downloading files or comprehension difficulties".

In addition, guidelines for accessible web site development have been issued by the organization.

"We developed guidelines for accessible websites, which became the company standard for our web sites".

However, it is recommended to stick to the guidelines issued by the W3C that have become a de-facto standard in Europe.

In some European countries, quality marks for accessible web presences have been established (cf. Table 4). Quality marks would foster quality assurance processes as they entail regular checks of the awarded web presence (section 6 develops a business model for a web accessibility quality mark and provides alternatives about quality mark issuing and compliance processes).

"Another measure is that as soon as the website is certificated, the process starts all over again in order to be certificated next year. In case of failures, measures of troubleshooting and correction have to be taken".

However, in Austria web sites cannot be certified in terms of web accessibility yet. Given the constantly changing medium Internet, discussions about the up-to-dateness of certificates or quality marks have emerged. However, the request for a quality mark or certificate by an independent party has been expressed by some organizations.

The result of the *Quality assurance* stage should be the evaluation of the new, accessible web presence, at best by an independent third party. Ongoing modifications of the accessible web presence should undergo the *Evaluation* and *Quality assurance* stages (cf. Figure 18).

5.6.3.2 Dissemination

In the last stage, the accessibility efforts of an organization have to be communicated to the public and within the organization. This process of internal and external rise of awareness provokes image enhancements for the organization.

"There has actually just been a press release. It has been announced popularly on the homepage for a certain period of time. I think there has also been an attachment to the account statement, where it has been referenced to this fact".

"If you click on the menu item "accessible" on the website, this press release can be found. But it actually had, I have to say, not that echo than we had initially expected. But obviously journalists aren't interested in this or it is simply not a prominent topic".

This can be done by press releases, awards, organization of in-house disability awareness days, statements on the web presence, presentations on conferences, or web site certification. In the latter case, a third party certifies the accessibility of the web presence and issues a quality mark. The *Dissemination* stage is crucial for the organization because some of the organizational web accessibility benefits can only be obtained after elaborate communication to the internal and external environment. Both organizational and public awareness for the issue of web accessibility have to be promoted. Benefits such as competitive advantage and image enhancements are based on a communication process. In case of one organization, press releases and organization of events provoked a media response that now led to competitors implementing accessible web presences. Moreover, employee motivation and understanding can be fostered by adequate internal communication. The communication within the organization may also be facilitated by the creation of a knowledge database about internal experiences with web accessibility. At the same time, knowledge exchange is promoted which may accelerate future accessibility related implementation processes. The extension of such a database to a knowledge management library can be an important contribution to overall knowledge management processes in an organization[14].

The findings of this section indicate that web accessibility implementation entails benefits for the organization but is still subject to risk. Section 5.1 has already clarified the definition of web accessibility implementation as an innovation process in an organization. Rogers et al. (1995) have developed an innovation process model (cf. Figure 20) that is considered for reasons of corroboration of the WAIP model developed in this contribution.

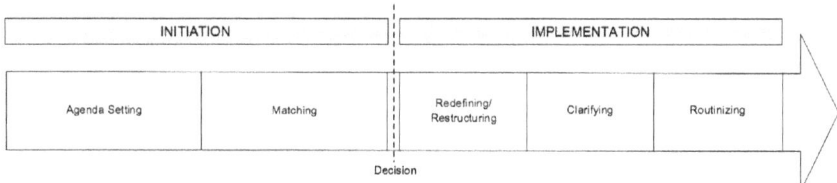

Figure 20: The innovation process in organizations (Rogers 1995)

Figure 20 depicts the innovation process in organizations. Rogers et al. (1995) divide the innovation process into two sub-processes (i) initiation and (ii) implementation. The initiation process encompasses the whole information gathering and planning process and leads to the decision to adopt or reject the innovation. The implementation process consists of actions and decisions in putting an innovation into use (Rogers 1995). Each of these two processes is divided into different sub-stages each of which is briefly explained. In the agenda setting stage organizational problems are defined and innovations are searched for to meet these problems. In the matching stage, an organizational problem is matched with an

---

14 This work draws on similar considerations. The findings of case study research represent a knowledge base that may be transferred to a knowledge management tool in terms of a case study library.

innovation. This new combination is planned and designed. After decision making, the redefining/restructuring phase begins where the innovation is adapted to satisfy the organization's needs. The organization may also modify its structures to fit with the innovation. The importance of product champions for the success of innovations is highlighted in this stage. In the clarifying stage, the innovation is communicated to the employees and embedded in the organizational structure. The end of the innovation process is marked by the routinizing stage where the innovation is incorporated in organizational structure and loses its separate identity.

Figure 21 gives an immediate phase-by-phase comparison of the innovation process defined by Rogers (1995) and the web accessibility implementation process developed in this contribution.

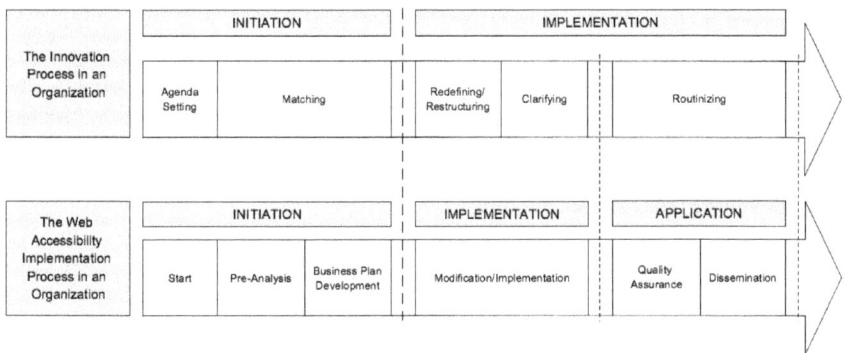

Figure 21: Innovation process model (Rogers 1995) vs. WAIP model (own approach)

Figure 21 shows the parallels of the web accessibility implementation process developed in this work with the innovation process model by Rogers. The dotted lines indicate which stages of the web accessibility implementation process (WAIP) model correspond to the innovation process model. The *Agenda Setting* stage and the *Launch* stage are equal as in both stages an organizational problem is defined and innovations are searched for to meet this problem. The *Matching* stage comprises the planning and design of the innovation. In the WAIP model, two stages have been developed (*Pre-analysis, Business plan development*) as the planning and design represents an elaborate and essential process in web accessibility implementation. After decision making, Rogers defined the *Restructuring/Redefining* stage where both innovation and organizational structures are adapted in order to fit with one another. The *Clarifying* stage occurs when the innovation is put into widespread use within the organization. These two stages are comparable with the *Modification/Implementation* stage in the WAIP model where both implementation and subsequent use of the web presence occurs. Once implemented, the accessible web presence is immediately used by employees due to a lack of other options. This is the reason why a *Clarifying* stage has not been developed but incorporated in the *Modification/Implementation* stage. Finally, the innovation becomes part of the organization and loses its innovative status in the *Routinizing* stage. The WAIP model defines two stages for routinizing purpose: quality assurance and dissemination. *Quality assurance* reflects the process of checking the accessible web presence on compliance with the underlying criteria. This process has to be undertaken after every modification of the site and represents the most difficult and time-consuming process in the WAIP model. Additionally, dissemination efforts are crucial for the success of web accessibility and therefore represent a distinct stage.

In summary, great analogy between the WAIP model and the innovation process model is identified. This similarity further strengthens the assumption that web accessibility implementation represents an innovation process in an organization as it follows similar steps. Additionally, the comparability of the WAIP model with an elaborate model of innovation literature signifies a validity of underlying data, and sound research process in the course of the inductive development of the WAIP model.

Web accessibility in the light of an innovation process has been considered mainly referring to the qualitative data analyzed in this case study. In addition, quantitative web site evaluations conducted in each sector may further strengthen this innovation perspective. Section 5.7 recalls the findings of the web site evaluations, compares them across all cases and gives further insights based on the literature on innovation diffusion.

5.7 Web site evaluation

Web site evaluations have been conducted in all sectors analyzed. Section 3.3.1 gives a detailed explanation about the evaluation method applied for this purpose. Table 20 displays a summary of the web site evaluation results. In the tourism sector, 45 out of 52 web presences (87%) failed automated tests, 4 out of 7 (8%) failed manual tests and 3 web presences (6%) passed all tests. In the financial services sector, 15 out of 19 web presences (79%) failed automated tests; the 4 remaining web sites passed manual tests (21%). In the information sector, 14 out of 18 web presences (78%) failed automated tests; the 4 remaining web sites (22%) passed all tests.

	Tourism		Financial Services		Information		Total	
	abs.	rel.	abs.	rel.	abs.	rel.	abs.	rel.
Pages checked	52	100%	19	100%	18	100%	89	100%
Failed automated tests	45	87%	15	79%	14	78%	74	83%
Failed manual tests	4	7%	0	0%	0	0%	4	5%
Passed all tests	**3**	**6%**	**4**	**21%**	**4**	**22%**	**11**	**12%**

Table 20: Web accessibility evaluation results

Most common errors on all web sites tested are HTML markup mistakes (71% in the tourism sector, 79% in the financial services sector, 94% in the information sector). A reason for this high number of markup mistakes may be that new graphical browsers commonly tend to "pardon" markup errors and still display the text correctly. This is not the case with text-only browsers (e.g., Lynx), Braille displays or screen readers. Additionally, missing alt-attributes and the usage of unlabeled frames or flash and JavaScript in a non accessible way represent frequent accessibility errors.

Overall, only 12% (every 6th web site) of 89 web sites analyzed passed this evaluation. As already stated in section 3.3.1, this evaluation does not guarantee entire accessibility of the site analyzed as no elaborate methodologies of accessibility evaluation (e.g., UWEM) have been applied. A site that passed the evaluation can be characterized as "on the right way" towards web accessibility. Consequently, the application of a more detailed evaluation method may presumably have resulted in even fewer web presences passing the test. In short, about 12% of the web sites tested passed; the vast majority of 88% failed the evaluation. As previously conducted studies on web accessibility evaluation have shown, these results are not surprising (Petrie et al. 2006). Assumptions about the reasons for this lack of implementation circulate within the scientific community and range from "lack of awareness for the issue" to "high expenses of web accessibility implementation". However, these myths and speculations have neither been proved nor refuted yet. Additionally, the minority of organizations having implemented accessible sites have not been questioned about their motives and reasons for doing so.

The web site evaluation results reflect the low tendency towards web accessibility in the respective sector. In all three sectors, a minority of organizations has successfully implemented web accessibility. These results lead to the conclusion that there must be effects that hamper accessibility implementation. Moreover, the findings underline that web accessibility does not seem to be widespread in the private sector which, in turn, justifies further examination of this development.

The concept of innovation diffusion offers a means to further examine the findings of the web site evaluation. Diffusion is the "process by which an innovation is communicated through certain channels over time among the members of a social system" (Rogers 2003, p. 5). Diffusion means the communication of new ideas and is therefore tied to some degree of uncertainty. After diffusion, these ideas are adopted or rejected (Rogers 1995). The adoption of an innovation does not happen simultaneously but is based on the innovativeness of an individual or other unit of adoption. In turn, innovativeness means "the degree to which an individual or other unit of adoption is relatively earlier in adopting new ideas than the other members of a system" (Rogers 1995, p. 22). In short, the diffusion concept draws on the time element to classify different innovation adopters. Figure 22 shows the adoption of innovations that follows a normal, bell shaped curve when plotted over time on a frequency basis.

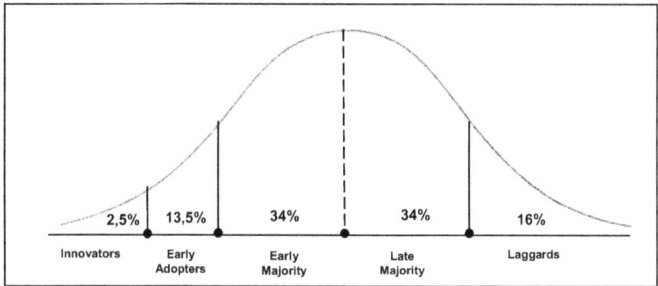

Figure 22: Adopter categorization (Rogers 2003, p. 262)

The dotted line in Figure 22 indicates the mean of the normal distribution. *Innovators* represent the first 2.5% of individuals in a system to adopt an innovation. *Innovators* are characterized as venturesome and able to cope with a high degree of uncertainty and play a gate keeping role for innovations. The *Early Adopters* are the next 13.5% of individuals to adopt an innovation. *Early Adopters* usually are opinion leaders and serve as a role model for potential adopters. Before the average member of a system adopts the innovation, the *Early Majority* (34%) does which makes it a crucial link in the diffusion process. Their innovation decision process is longer than that of their predecessors. The next 34% to the right of the mean is represented by the *Late Majority*. For them, adoption may be either caused by economic necessity or network pressure which is why they are usually cautious and skeptical. The last 16% to adopt an innovation are called *Laggards*. They tend to have traditional values, and are suspicious about innovations unless they are certain that these innovations will not fail (Rogers 1995).

The adoption of innovations can also be plotted cumulatively which results in an s-shaped curve with the time factor on the horizontal and the rate of adoption on the vertical axis. In the beginning, few adopters provoke a slow rise of the s-curve; then it accelerates until half of the individuals have adopted the innovation which is followed again by a slower rate of increase as fewer individuals are left to adopt the innovation. The "take-off" of an innovation takes place when interpersonal networks are activated and spread the innovation so that the diffusion of the innovation can often not be stopped, even if desired (usually at about 20% of adoption) (Rogers 1995).

In this work, web site evaluations in terms of accessibility have been conducted for 89 web sites in three business sectors. From these, only 12% passed the evaluations. Considering (1) the process of web accessibility implementation as an innovation process, (2) the adopter categorization in Figure 22, and (3) the diffusion s-curve, it becomes obvious that in Austria, in the tourism, financial services and information sector, those web sites which passed the evaluations (12%) may be categorized as Early Adopters of the innovation web accessibility. According to these findings, the innovation web accessibility has not taken off yet. Given the fact that the concept of web accessibility has already existed for at least ten years[15], and that still take-off has not occurred, two alternatives can be assumed: (i) the web accessibility diffusion s-curve is flatter and needs a longer time to take off or (ii) the innovation will not take off at all.

The most important success factors of innovations are market suitability, time, and costs (Stummer et al. 2008). The market factor relates to expectations of the user in terms of quality, security, and market demand. Timely innovations are launched at the economically right time. In case of an early introduction of the product, the acceptance of the customers may not be given. The cost factor encompasses a minimization of the R&D and production and service costs of a product or service (Stummer et al. 2008).

The time and market factor may give indications why the innovation web accessibility has not taken off yet. Ten years ago, the web looked completely different. HTML and CSS were the prevalent techniques, static web presences dominated; neither diversity of browsers nor of devices was an issue. At that time, the economic benefits of web accessibility for an organization of the private sector were considerably smaller compared to today. Moreover, the benefits of the average user (device independency, mobile use) were not given. In short, the market[16] was not ready for the adoption of the innovation. Due to an increase of complexity of the web, an increase in the number of browsers, a variety of different output devices, and a development of a range of new technologies that hamper the accessibility of web sites, this situation has considerably changed. Additionally, external

---

15 The year of development of the Web Content Accessibility Guidelines 1.0 (1999) is taken as reference.
16 The market in the context of this work is represented by the organizations of the private sector.

factors such as laws and regulations have been developed that further trigger the adoption of the innovation web accessibility[17].

In a nutshell, the innovation web accessibility may take a longer time to take off because of unfavorable market conditions at the time of its launch. A change in these conditions provokes a higher probability that web accessibility will spread. Additionally, the findings of this case study give evidence of business benefits based on empirical data and thus support the assumption that the innovation web accessibility has not failed.

5.8 Discussion

This section shows the results of a qualitative study across three industrial sectors (tourism, financial services, information) and gives information about (i) the level of accessibility of 89 web presences in these sectors, (ii) the reasons for and changes after web accessibility implementation, (iii) the incentives for and reasons for failure of web accessibility implementation, and (iv) develops a consolidated web accessibility implementation process (WAIP) model for accessible web pages in organizations.

Organizations implement accessible web presences out of social, economic, and/or technical motivations. The kind of motivation depends on the size and complexity of organizations, the organizational sector, the corporate culture and degree of readiness for change, the purpose and degree of complexity of the web presence.

Complex organizations in the financial services sector rather implement web accessibility out of social motivations. This is caused by several factors: a certain social responsibility of the financial services sector, an adoption of CSR strategies of complex organizations, and negative image associations with financial services institutions that are intended to be solved by a focus on socially responsible action.

By contrast, small organizations in the information sector rather draw on technical motivations. Reasons for this development are: a technology-affinity of the information sector, a high importance of web site quality as the service is consumed directly on the site, a high fluctuation of web site content, and a low adoption tendency of CSR strategies of small organizations.

In general, organizations likely to implement web accessibility dispose of several characteristics: (i) elaborate corporate culture with commitment to social values and corporate social responsibility strategies, (ii) high importance of extant web

---

17 An overview of laws concerning web accessibility can be found in section 2.4.

presence for core business, (iii) web site content subject to frequent changes, (iv) relevance of elderly customers for core business, and (v) existence of key personalities. The more of these characteristics are met, the higher the probability for an organization to implement accessible web presences.

Perceived changes after successful implementation of web accessibility also vary across organizational sectors, sizes, and web site characteristics. Analogously to the reasons for web accessibility implementation, social, technical, and economic changes are identified. Organizations experience a higher degree of employee integration, knowledge exchange, and awareness for the issue. In terms of economic changes, an increase in image, customer loyalty, and web site traffic are determined. Additionally, quality improvements of web presences are the outcome.

However, several problems with web accessibility implementation are identified. Organizations with a high number of web site editors and a high fluctuation of web site content face difficulties in terms of quality assurance. The negligence or error of one web site editor can render a site inaccessible. A high number of editors involved and a high frequency of content subject to change may provoke errors that remain undetected. Daily quality checks on a big amount of data are not feasible. A lack of automated evaluation tools and a lack of time and resources for quality checks aggravate this situation. By now, the enduring quality of accessible web presences can only be fostered by measures such as routine check-up and regular staff training. Organizations which focused on technical reasons for implementation experienced a lack of media attention. This is due to the fact that the quality improvement of web presences was paid more attention to than the social or economic aspects of accessible web. In these cases, accessibility was regarded as a side effect of quality improvement and did not constitute the main reason for implementation. In order to profit from business benefits (e.g., image enhancement), accessibility has to be promoted accordingly. Organizations with complex web presences face high initial costs in case of adaptations of extant web presences. Coding difficulties rise with the degree of complexity of a web presence and thus result in increasing time effort.

Despite the problems identified with web accessibility implementation, a considerably higher potential of advantages are detected. Thus, the question remains why only few organizations in the private sector have adopted accessibility so far.

The attempts of web accessibility implementation have sometimes been realized in a professional way. In other cases, especially the ones which failed, it seems that the initiators have not had a strategic plan in mind but just proceeded on a trial and error basis. These "ad hoc" implementation decisions led to corporate design incompatibilities or argumentation problems and consequently to a failure of implementation. A web accessibility implementation process (WAIP) model developed in this work gives an explicit guideline to overcome such implementation failures. A major portion of reasons for failure can be omitted considering the WAIP model because it foresees a web site pre-analysis and a detailed business plan development as one of the first stages which enables a well grounded structure of the project. Argumentation problems should then become eliminated. Still, corporate culture, climate and values have influence on employee's resistance to change and management decision making. These influence factors cannot easily be changed. Thus, cultures with social values and commitment to socially responsible action will facilitate web accessibility implementation.

The lack of implementation is not only based on argumentation problems or corporate design incompatibilities. Very often, the awareness for the issue of web accessibility is not present in organizations of the private sector. Additionally, the extent of web accessibility impact for the average, non disabled customer is not known. Web site evaluation results show that only 12% out of 89 web sites evaluated are accessible. However, the constructional accessibility of these organizations is much more widespread. Almost every banking institution has ramps, every hotel considered for evaluation has wheelchair accessible rooms but few have accessible web sites. The adaptation of buildings undoubtedly requires a higher investment than accessible web presences do which once again raises the question why web presences are not rendered accessible.

The diffusion of innovations concept shows that the innovation web accessibility has not taken off yet. Organizations which have adopted web accessibility can be classified as Early Adopters. Assumptions about future take-off would be audacious. However, external factors (e.g., laws and regulations) may influence the success of innovations. Legal forces and government aid have been identified as perceived incentives for web accessibility implementation.

Web accessibility is a large scale issue. It encompasses interdisciplinary aspects and is therefore difficult to confine. However, this very characteristic distinguishes the web accessibility concept and enables its examination from different viewpoints. This cross-case comparison has identified that organizations implement web accessibility out of different motivations. Consequently, the changes and problems they experience with web accessibility vary. The organizational size, sector, culture, and web site are among the main indicators for the choice of web accessibility implementation strategy.

Still, it has been identified that web accessibility entails a variety of business benefits for organizations. The careful planning and design of its implementation process will countervail possible failure.

The findings of the organizational study in sections 4 and 5 reveal, amongst others, challenges of web accessibility implementation in terms of quality assurance and a lack of awareness. Section 6 of this contribution develops a business model for a web accessibility quality mark, an instrument that may overcome these problems. As already discussed before, the business impacts of web accessibility can only be fully exploited provided that adequate communication to the general public is ensured.

Besides visibility enhancement to foster awareness, the organizational study revealed that accessible web sites need a means for quality assurance. A quality mark can satisfy both needs as it represents the only impartial possibility to communicate an organization's efforts in terms of web accessibility to the general public and to guarantee the accessible web site quality. For these reasons, section 6 develops five alternatives for a web accessibility quality mark in Austria and evaluates them in terms of six criteria. Moreover, a business model for an Austrian quality mark is developed in order to facilitate and accelerate national implementation.

6 Business model for a web accessibility quality mark

Section 5 has revealed the impacts of web accessibility implementation for organizations in the private sector. However, the current lack of web accessibility realization procedures and mechanisms aggravates the implementation, even if the benefits, processes, and problems are identified. Moreover, organizations having implemented accessible web sites would want to disclose their effort to the public in order to profit from image enhancements. A quality mark for accessible web sites constitutes an impartial instrument for, on the one hand, certifying that an organization's web site meets web accessibility criteria and, on the other hand, publishing this effort. Without such a mechanism, an organization's commitment in terms of web accessibility may soon decline.

Currently, several web accessibility quality marks have been implemented in some member states of the European Union, each of them depending on slightly different criteria. In order to avoid further fragmentation, there have been harmonization efforts from the European Commission for a joint quality mark for the European Union. Austria has not yet developed a quality mark for accessible web sites.

The necessity for an Austrian quality mark can be seen as a direct consequence of section 5. The WAIP model developed in section 5.6 foresees a quality assurance and a dissemination stage for both of which a quality mark represents an important instrument. The identification of impacts of and experiences with web accessibility implementation may convince organizations if and only if the mechanisms for certification and marketing are given. This is the reason why in section 6, a business model for a web accessibility quality mark is developed and recommendations for a possible Austrian quality mark that fits into the European framework are made.

A quality mark for web accessibility seems to be an efficient possibility for addressing the deficits detected in sections 4 and 5 out of various reasons:

- **Awareness creation:** a web accessibility quality mark underlines the commitment of an organization to Corporate Social Responsibility. It may cause a snowball effect as it encourages other organizations to obtain the quality mark. This may result in a competitive advantage and a better corporate image of certified companies. Moreover, the access to international markets with a quality mark may be facilitated.

- **Process development:** a quality mark helps to turn complex and unstructured ideas into a process that complies with modern business processes and may therefore become part of the supply and demand portfolio of an organization.

- **Product development:** web accessibility may be incorporated into business and economic processes as a product by means of a quality mark which turns web accessibility into a calculable dimension.

- **Implementation assistance:** a quality mark provides implementation assistance for organizations internally and also for external purchase (e.g., by integration of the accessibility aspect in tendering or contracts).

- **Accessibility know-how demand:** a quality mark stimulates the demand and the awareness for web accessibility, also because they demonstrate its efficient implementation. Moreover, the demand for the web accessibility quality mark generates demand for expert know-how in this field. Web accessibility will therefore become an issue in the education and training of experts.

- **Quality assurance:** a quality mark provides evidence of the quality of a certain product and of the existence of a system designed to permanently improve the quality of the goods or services produced.

Section 6.1 gives an overview of the current state of web accessibility certification in Europe and is followed by a course of action in section 6.2 where the main research steps of this study are explained. Section 6.3 starts by giving a literature review of business models, and then presents the empirical findings of ten extant quality marks analyzed. In a next stage, four scenarios are developed and analyzed in terms of six evaluation criteria. Finally, a business model for an Austrian web accessibility quality mark is presented.

6.1 Conformity assessment in Europe

6.1.1 Terminology

The conformity assessment system in Europe is quite complex and requires a definition of the terminology and procedures used.

Accreditation is defined as the procedure by which an authoritative body gives formal recognition that a body or person is competent to carry out a specific conformity evaluation (ISO/IEC 17000 2004). The accreditation is issued by an *accreditation body* that verifies impartially and independently of the competency of conformance evaluators (certification, testing, and inspection bodies). The accreditation bodies' methodology is based on international criteria in order to ensure mutual acceptance of results. The European Co-operation for Accreditation (EA) acts as umbrella organization of the national accreditation bodies and ensures mutual recognition agreements between accreditation systems on international level. In Austria, the Federal Ministry of Economics and Labor (BMWA – Bundesministerium für Wirtschaft und Arbeit) represents the national accreditation body and is a member of the EA (Support-EAM 2005).

For *third party conformance evaluation* bodies (certification, testing and inspection bodies), an accreditation is mandatory. *Certification* is defined as the process by which an independent body evaluates an organization, product, process, service or person in terms of the compliance of what was evaluated with a standard or technical specification (ISO/IEC 17000 2004). *Inspection* means third-party evaluation by an organization performing inspection according to international standard ISO/IEC 17020.

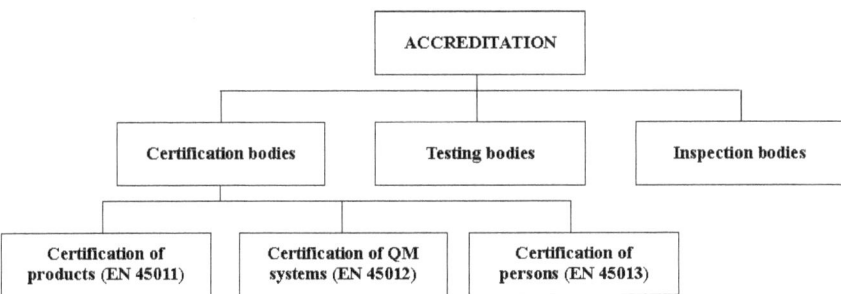

Figure 23: Conformity assessment overview

Figure 23 displays an overview of conformity assessment with a special focus on certification. Accreditation is necessary for certification, testing and inspection bodies. In the case of certification bodies, a certification of products, systems and persons is possible following the respective standards (EN 45011 for products, EN 45012 for QM Systems and EN 45013 for persons).

In contrast to this, *first party conformity assessment* does not involve any neutral accredited body for evaluation of the compliance with a normative document. In this case, the manufacturer commits to the compliance with certain criteria. The so called *supplier's declaration of conformity* constitutes a first party evaluation according to international standard ISO/IEC 17050 part 1 and 2.

Figure 24 depicts the principle of third party certification in contrast to the supplier's declaration of conformity. Third party certification involves an independent third party that certifies the compliance with underlying criteria. In case of supplier's declaration of conformity (self declaration), the manufacturer can only be evaluated by the customer, but no impartial third party is involved.

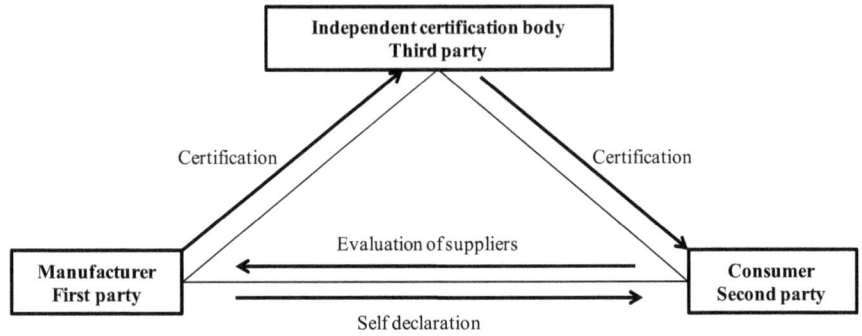

Figure 24: Principle of third party certification

A *standard* or *normative document* is a public technical document containing specifications of voluntary application, drawn up by consensus between stakeholders, based on experience and technological development, and approved by a standardization body recognized at national, regional, or international level (ISO/IEC 2004). The ISO (International Organization for Standardization), the CEI/IEC (International Electrotechnical Committee) for electrics, and the UIT/ITU (International Telecommunications Union) for telecommunications are the most important representatives for international standardization bodies. European standardization bodies, e.g., CEN, CENELEC and ETSI, develop regional standards and, in the case of Austria, the ON (Austrian Standardization Institute) creates national standards.

After both third and first party conformity assessment, a *quality mark* can be issued which is defined as a symbol that certifies that the products or services to which it is applied meet certain common requirements and comply with the corresponding quality specifications reference standards (Support-EAM 2005).

In sections 2 to 5, the relevance of web accessibility has been addressed. However, its implementation still seems to be a weak point. Reasons for this may be on the one hand the lack of awareness and understanding for the potential of web accessibility and, on the other hand, the lack of efficient procedures, processes and mechanisms for web accessibility implementation. The absence of reliable and normative concepts and products in the field of web accessibility may hamper organizations to take over the web accessibility concept.

6.1.2 Historical background

In some European countries, national web accessibility quality marks have been established, each of them predominantly based on the WCAG 1.0 but applying slightly different evaluation criteria.

Table 21 displays an overview of existing web accessibility quality marks in Europe.

Quality Mark	Country	Issuing Organization	Web site
Accessibility Mark	Italy	CNIPA	http://www.cnipa.gov.it
Accessiweb	France	Association BrailleNet	http://www.accessiweb.org
Anysurfer	Belgium	Réseau Anysurfer	http://www.anysurfer.be
DIN-Geprüft Barrierefreie Web site	Germany	DIN Certco	http://www.dincertco.de
Drempelvrij	Netherlands	Bartimeus Accessibility Foundation	http://www.drempelvrij.nl
Excellence through accessibility award	Ireland	National Disability Authority	http://www.nda.ie/
See it Right	UK	RNIB	http://www.rnib.org
Technosite	Spain	Grupo Fundosa	http://www.technosite.es

Table 21: Overview of existing quality marks in Europe

Table 21 lists eight quality marks that have already been implemented in European countries. Some of them are based on the W3C guidelines; some have made national adaptations and included them into reference documents. Consequently, (slightly) different criteria have to be met in different countries in order to be awarded the web accessibility quality mark. Given the fact that multinational organizations operate their web presences in different countries and different languages, this would imply that they would have to construct different web pages depending on the country and label they want to obtain. This situation entails a fragmentation process that is counterproductive to web accessibility efforts as organizations would rather refrain from implementing web accessibility in this case.

In order to overcome a resulting fragmentation process, the European Union has taken several measures for the creation and operation of a unified European web accessibility quality mark.

In 2004, the project "Supporting the Creation of an eAccessibility Mark" (Support-EAM) was launched in order to propose a strategy for the creation of a European web accessibility quality mark as part of the Action Plan eEurope 2005: An information society for all (Support EAM 2006). Support-EAM was conducted by seven partners from seven different countries: Association BrailleNet (France), Technosite (Spain), Bartimeus Accessibility Foundation (Netherlands), Dublin City University (Ireland), Universität Linz (Austria)[18], Katholieke Universiteit Leuven Research & Development (Belgium), AccessInMind Ltd (United Kingdom).

Within the Support-EAM project, a CEN (European Committee for Standardization) Workshop was launched in order to reach a consensus among different

---

[18] The author participated in the Support-EAM project on behalf of the University of Linz.

stakeholders in the European Union about specifications for a European web accessibility quality mark. The main objective of the CEN Workshop was to reach a "first level European agreement on how standard validation schemes commonly used in Europe can apply to web accessibility validation" (Support-EAM 2006). The CEN Workshop lasted for a year and consisted of five meetings in Brussels and Paris. Representatives of the industry, of several disability interest groups, members of the commission and of certification bodies throughout the world attended the CEN Workshop and discussed major issues in four editing groups:

1. Specifications for a European authority for web accessibility certification
2. Specifications for the organizations that can issue the web accessibility quality mark
3. Specifications for the process to be followed by each organization before issuing the web accessibility quality mark
4. Specifications for other good practices to be followed by organizations issuing the web accessibility quality mark[19]

The work of the editing groups was based on an analysis of existing European marking schemes and their possible applicability to the specific case of web accessibility. However, various different viewpoints, opinions, and interests of these stakeholders hampered the development of one distinct European model for a web accessibility quality mark.

6.1.3 Outcomes

The CEN Workshop Agreement (CEN 2006) resulted in specifications for a European Web Accessibility conformity assessment scheme consisting of one central European body, the European Authority for Web Accessibility Conformity Assessment (EAWAC), and three different national implementation options; each of them assuming the existence of one unique normative document (cf. Figure 25). The EAWAC is connected to the European Cooperation for Accreditation (EA), the European Committee for Standardization (CEN) and the European Union (EU). Moreover, the EAWAC is composed of a committee of experts, a complaints committee, stakeholders (users, web site owners) and participants. Figure 25 depicts a shortened version of the outcomes of the CEN Workshop.

---

19 The author took over the co-editor role of this editing group.

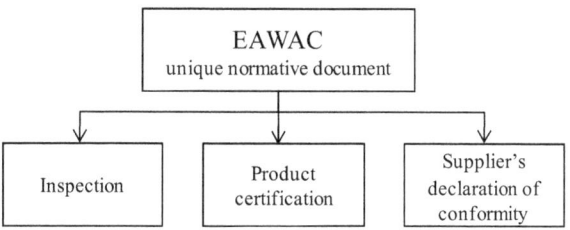

Figure 25: Conformity assessment scheme – shortened (CEN 2006)

1. **Inspection:** The ISO/IEC 17020 accredited inspection body issues the quality mark which is based on the normative document issued by the EAWAC (EN ISO/IEC 17020 2004). The inspection body performs regular surveillance of the certified web sites and withdraws the quality mark if the criteria have not been met. The membership at the EAWAC is mandatory.
2. **Product certification:** In this case, an EN 45011 (EN 45011 1998) accredited product certification body issues the quality mark which is based on the normative document issued by the EAWAC. The product certification body performs regular surveillance of the certified web sites and withdraws the quality mark in case of non-compliance with the criteria. The product certification body has to be a member of the EAWAC.
3. **Supplier's declaration of conformity:** The owner of a web site assures that his/her web site meets the criteria set in the normative document issued by the EAWAC. The owner accepts the specifications presented in the ISO/IEC standard 17050 part 1 (EN ISO/IEC 17050-1 2004) and 2 (EN ISO/IEC 17050-2 2004) about the Supplier's Declaration of Conformity. After registration with the EAWAC, the web site owner receives the quality mark. Regular surveillance is performed by the EAWAC. The web site user has the possibility to post complaints if the criteria have not been met. No third party controls or evaluates the compliance of the web site with the criteria set in the normative document or standard.

The type and number of options implemented is left open. The ownership as well as the creation and operation of a European conformity assessment scheme for web accessibility are among the main responsibilities of the EAWAC. These include the drafting of a normative document setting criteria to web accessibility as well as the establishment and administration of a quality mark. The EAWAC is intended to be implemented in the first place, coordinating the national follow-up establishments.

The current absence of a European authority and the difficulties involved with its creation forces to analyze alternate strategies that could be realized before or instead of the creation of a central European body. Furthermore, the existence of several national web accessibility quality marks in Europe, each of them based on different criteria, requires a harmonization process.

As a recent development of the Support EAM project and the CEN Workshop Agreement respectively, a European label, the "Euracert" has been established. Euracert represents a first attempt in the creation of a European label for web accessibility and has evolved as a partnership of three existing European quality marks in France, Belgium, and Spain. Based on the CEN Workshop Agreement, Euracert is awarded independently by the respective partners in combination with the local quality mark (Euracert 2007). Hence, awarded organizations have to display two quality marks on their web site (national and European). Further limitations of this model are that the Euracert mark is only available in the partner countries (currently France, Belgium and Spain). The Euracert mark represents a first step towards a European harmonization process that has to be enforced and boosted by national quality mark models that fit into this European framework.

6.2 Course of action

Given a European framework for web accessibility conformity assessment, our approach intends to develop a generic business model and the corresponding business processes in a way that they can be applied to any option proposed in section 6.1.3. Recalling the research question for this study from section 1.1, it can be formulated as follows:

How does a business model for an Austrian web accessibility quality mark have to be configured in order to be applied in a European context?

The research procedure for the development of a business model for a web accessibility quality mark is divided into five research steps:

Step 1: Analysis of existing web accessibility quality marks
In a first step, existing web accessibility quality marks in Europe, Australia, and the United States are analyzed in terms of their good practices (evaluation and testing processes, issuing procedures, etc.). Questionnaires are sent to 10 quality mark providers (results and analysis see section 6.3.2). Out of this qualitative data, suggestions for good practices of a harmonized quality mark were derived (cf. Table 23) that represent important input for the web site conformity assessment model (cf. Figure 30). Moreover, European quality marks in other areas (e.g., Keymark) were analyzed and subsequently served as input for the business model.

Step 2: Analysis of European and national directives
In a second step, European and national directives in terms of web accessibility are analyzed. This comprises a state of the art analysis of legal rules and regula-

tions in Europe and Austria (cf. section 2.4), certification and accreditation procedures and models (cf. section 6.1), and web accessibility criteria and evaluation processes (cf. section 2.3).

Step 3: Definition of actors, elements, roles and relationships
The results of step 1 and 2 serve as an input for step 3, in which the actors, elements, roles and relationships necessary for the development of a web accessibility quality mark are specified (cf. section 6.3.3).

Step 4: Scenario planning and analysis
Scenarios are a "description of a future situation and the course of events which allows one to move forward from the original situation to the future" (Godet and Roubelat 1996) and create "holistic, integrated images of how the future might evolve" (Ratcliffe 1999).

Scenario planning is a method to aid decision making in case of uncertainty by providing strategists with various possible futures (Mietzner and Reger 2005). Complex elements are combined to a coherent, systematic, comprehensive, and plausible story (Mietzner and Reger 2005). According to O'Brien (2004), scenario planning has several purposes: (i) a synthesis of important information for understanding future uncertainties, (ii) the development of a plausible set of descriptions of possible scenarios through the use of structured methodology, and (iii) the evaluation of implications of these scenarios for the organization today (O'Brien 2004). Specifically, scenario planning aids understanding of a situation while enhancing creativity (Wright et al. 2009).

In short, scenario planning is a method that supports decision making in case of uncertain future developments. This flexible method enables the development of realizable future alternatives and simultaneously challenges long term internal beliefs by introducing new ideas. However, scenario planning is a rather time consuming process that requires deep understanding and knowledge about the field of study (Mietzner and Reger 2005).

Thus, scenario planning represents a suitable method for tackling the research question in this quality mark study. The high degree of uncertainty of future development in web accessibility certification requires a specification of different scenarios in order to be able to compare and evaluate diverse alternatives.

Wilson (1999) recommends between two and four scenarios that should be plausible, structurally different, consistent, useful, and challenging (Wilson 1999). In sections 6.3.4 and 6.3.5, four possible implementation scenarios are specified and evaluated in terms of six evaluation criteria. In a subsequent scenario analysis, recommendations for implementation scenarios in Austria can be made.

Step 5: Implementation plan for an Austrian web accessibility quality mark

In step five, various different business model concepts have been analyzed and compared. Hedman and Kalling's (2003) model was chosen as a framework for description and analysis of the web accessibility quality mark.

6.3 Business model for web site certification

6.3.1 Business models – literature overview

Despite the term "business model" being relatively recent, various different perceptions and definitions of business models have been developed. Furthermore, business models have been examined by a variety of scientific disciplines. (Pateli and Giaglis 2004) discovered three main research areas covering business models: e-business, strategy, and information systems.

According to Pateli and Giaglis (2004), the initial and most often cited definition of business models was given by Timmers (1998). He defines a business model as "an architecture for the product, service and information flows", which identifies business actors and their roles, a description of their potential benefits, and their sources of revenue (Timmers 1998). A similar definition is given by Weill and Vitale (2001), who additionally focus on the flows of product, information, and money and the major benefits to participants. In short, a business model "describes, as a system, how the pieces of a business fit together" (Magretta 2002, p. 6).

Linder and Cantrell (2000) merge business models to the "organization's core logic for creating value" (Linder and Cantrell 2000, p. 1). Amit and Zott (2001), too, focus on value creation when defining business models. They denominate a business model as a unit of analysis which "depicts the content, structure and governance of transactions" in order to create value (Amit and Zott 2001, p. 511).

A more detailed definition of business models was developed by Osterwalder et al. (2005). This concept characterizes a business model as a "conceptual tool containing a set of objects, concepts and their relationships with the objective to express the business logic of a specific firm" (Osterwalder et al. 2005, p. 5). Furthermore, Osterwalder et al. (2005) include the concepts and relationships which describe the value provided to the customer.

Over the years, Osterwalder et al. 2005 discovered a progression in the definition of business models and in the evolution of research about business models. They developed five phases, ranging from a plain definition and classification of business models to the application of the whole business model concept (cf. Figure 26).

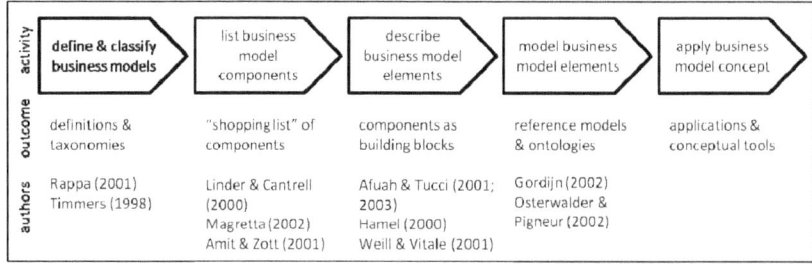

Figure 26: Evolution of the business model concept (Osterwalder et al. 2005)

The five phases outlined by Osterwalder et al. (2005) reflect the evolution of business model research and are based on an extensive literature review in business model concepts. Phase 1 comprises contributions who give first definitions and classifications of business models (Timmers 1998). Phase 2 indicates business model components that result in a kind of shopping list (Linder and Cantrell 2000; Amit and Zott 2001). In Phase 3, e.g., Weill and Vitale (2001) describe business model elements in further detail which resulted in phase 4, where reference models and ontologies are given (Gordijn 2002).

Hedman and Kalling's (2003) definition of a business model as a link between the strategy and the business processes of an organization reflects this section's main focus; the discussion of strategic planning alternatives and their depiction in terms of a business model.

This process oriented view is presented by Hedman and Kalling (2003) who split a business model into six different cross-sectional components: customers, competitors, offering, activities and organization, resources, and factor and production inputs (cf. Figure 27).

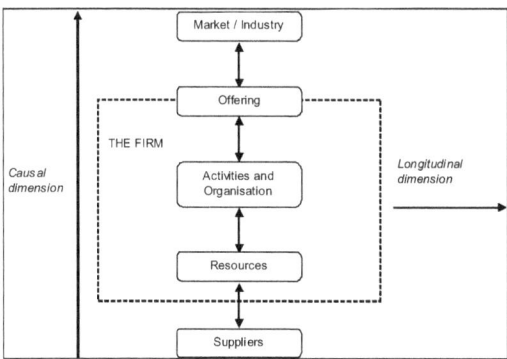

Figure 27: Business model components (Hedman and Kalling 2003)

157

The process from the supplier to the market traverses five different levels:
1. The market level analyzes customers and competitors.
2. In the offering level, the price strategy, quality, and service commitment is defined.
3. The activity and organizational level reflects value creation within the firm.
4. In the resource level tangible, intangible, and human resources are analyzed.
5. The market factor level deals with capital, labor, and production inputs.

The structure of Hedman and Kalling's (2003) process oriented view is used for describing business model alternatives in this work. In addition, Amit and Zott's value creation factors are consulted for evaluation purposes of these alternatives.

Amit and Zott (2001) define four main factors for value creation: efficiency, complementarities, lock-in and novelty (cf. Figure 28).

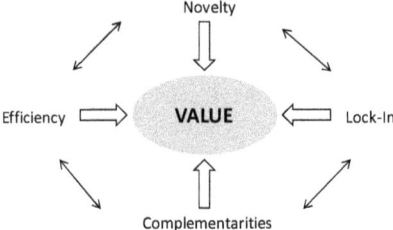

Figure 28: Value drivers of e-commerce business models (Amit and Zott 2001)

A business model's value increases with the extent of enhancements of the four factors depicted in Figure 28: Transaction *efficiencies* could be reached with a reduction of information asymmetries leading to benefits for both suppliers and consumers. A bundle of goods that is more valuable than each of the goods separately is referred to as *complementarities*. Furthermore, customer loyalty (*lock-in*) represents an important factor for value creation in a business model. Finally, the degree of innovation of business models and their processes leads to a higher value (Amit and Zott 2001).

6.3.2 Analysis of existing quality marks

As already discussed in section 6.2, an analysis of the best practices of existing web accessibility quality mark constitutes the first step in the business model development. For this purpose, questionnaires have been sent to 10 providers of web accessibility quality marks in Europe, Australia, and the USA.

Table 22 displays an aggregated overview of results where the most important instances have been extracted. All data giving information about the provider's identity have been dropped in order to preserve anonymity. The providers of web accessibility quality marks answered questions regarding their organizational form, the validity of the quality marks issued (in months), the withdrawal conditions (circumstances under which the label is removed from the web site), the frequency of controls by the provider, the transparency for the public (visibility of labeled sites to the public as well as the publication of reports), marketing efforts by the provider, the existence of a complaints channel for users, issuing levels of conformance, the criteria the quality mark is based on, and the national legislation the quality mark refers to.

Criteria	1	2	3	4	5	6	7	8	9	10
Organizational form	n/a	Non-Profit	Non-Profit	Non-Profit	Non-Profit	Non-Profit	Non-Profit	n/a	2 Non-Profits	n/a
Validity (months)	12	36	6	12	12	Not specified	24	12	Not specified	6
Withdrawal conditions	n/a	Non-conformance	Non-conformance	Non-conformance	n/a	None	Non-conformance, end of contract	Non-conformance, user complaints	Non-conformance after revalidation	None
Frequency of controls	"regular intervals"	n/a	Quarterly	Every 6 months	Once a year or on request from user	None	Once a year, controls may be made after 6 and 18 months	Once a year, or on request from users	Recheck only in case of user complaints	Every 6 months
Transparency for public	Gallery of awarded sites	Label on website	Label on website, Awards ceremony, custom client plans	Label on website, gallery of awarded sites	No	No	Label on website, gallery of awarded sites	Label on Website, gallery of awarded sites	Label on websites, gallery of awarded sites	Label on website, gallery of awarded sites
Marketing	n/a	n/a		None	None	None	Minimal; notoriety of provider sufficient	Commercial on TV	Contact to government, trainings, seminars	None
Complaints channel	User complaints channel	None	None	None	None	None	User complaints channel	Logo provides link to reaction page	User complaints per email	None
Levels	1	3 (committed/ quality/ excellence)	3	1	3 (1 up to 3 stars)	1	3 (bronze/ silver/ gold)	n/a	1	3 (A, AA, AAA)
Criteria	Own criteria	WCAG 1.0, AA	WCAG 1.0	Most of WCAG 1 A, some of AA, some of AAA	22 requirements (WCAG 1.0 and section 508	n/a	Based on WCAG 1.0	n/a	WCAG, slightly adapted	WCAG 1.0
Based on national legislation	No	No	No	No	Yes	No	Yes	n/a	No	No

Table 22: Analysis of 10 web accessibility quality marks

Table 22 shows that 7 out of 10 quality mark providers are nonprofit organizations. The validity of the quality mark ranges from 6 months up to 36 months. Mostly, the quality mark is withdrawn in case of non-conformance with the accessibility criteria. Only in one case, user complaints are taken into account for quality mark withdrawal. The frequency of controls ranges from once or twice a year up to unspecified time frames such as "regular intervals" or "in case of user complaints". Most of the quality marks dispose of a gallery where they list the awarded web sites in order to guarantee a certain transparency for the public. Marketing efforts for the quality mark are weakly developed. Only one quality mark issued commercials on television, another provider organized trainings and seminars. The majority of quality marks does not dispose of a complaints channel for the users; only 4 out of 10 have implemented such a possibility for the user to post complaints in case of inaccessibility. Regarding the levels of the mark, either one level is issued (accessible or inaccessible) or three levels are offered. In case of three levels, heterogeneity within these levels can be identified as they either refer to the A, AA and AAA criteria or are labeled individually (e.g., bronze-silver-gold, committed-quality-excellence). The majority of the quality marks questioned used the WCAG 1.0 as underlying criteria, but either different priorities (A, AA, AAA) or added additional criteria. Only two quality marks are based on national legislation.

The results in Table 22 show the heterogeneity of the existing web accessibility quality marks in almost every criterion analyzed. Different validities, withdrawal conditions and underlying criteria make direct comparisons of web sites in different countries impossible. Theoretically, a web presence in one country may be awarded the national quality mark, whereas it would not have been awarded the quality mark of the neighborhood country. Given this ongoing fragmentation process, the need for a unified web accessibility quality mark with identical evaluation processes and criteria becomes definite.

Based on the results presented in Table 22, a harmonized quality mark is defined after aggregation of the questionnaire data. Table 23 displays the items adopted for the harmonized quality mark. For this purpose, the most used items were adopted or – in case of heterogeneity – the best solution was taken over.

Criteria	Harmonized Label
Country	Europe
Org. Form	Non-Profit
Validity (months)	12, if conformance is met throughout the year
Withdrawal conditions	a) if web site fails a periodic evaluation (10-20 days delay for owner to repair, if not: withdrawal) b) in case of user-complaints (10-20 days delay for owner to repair, if not: withdrawal) c) at the end of contract
Frequency of controls	Mandatory 1 year after awarding, controls may be made after 6 and 18 months, after reported problems by visitors or after major modifications of the website "Regular intervals" throughout the year of certification.
Transparency for public	a) label visible on web site b) awarded web sites published on a gallery (scope and date of last evaluation) c) reports sent to owner who can decide if they are published d) logo image dynamically served by issuer (-> issuer can retract or change the logo if certification has been withdrawn)
Marketing	a) web site b) active contact to all levels of government to show the inaccessibility of their sites; c) organisation of trainings, participation in seminars and workshops d) collaboration with web design companies e) Separate list with organisations involved in the development of participation sites; ranked list --> organisations that have delivered more accessible sites are ranked higher
Complaints Channel	logo should provide link to reaction page visitors may use reaction form to post complaint reactions sent to inspection organisation if reactions are considered valid-> sent to owner -> 10-20 workdays to repair --> if not: withdrawal records are maintained of any appeals, valid complaints received by the website owner or certification body, and the subsequent remedial action.
Levels	More than 1, depending on different criteria
Criteria	WCAG 1.0
Based on national legislation	Yes

Table 23: Harmonized label

Table 23 suggests good practices for a harmonized web accessibility quality mark derived from the survey results depicted in Table 22. For a European quality mark, a non-profit organization should act as provider issuing the mark at a validity of 12 months. If a web site fails periodic evaluation (controls may be made after 6 and 18 months and after reported problems by visitors or major modifications of the web site) or in case of user complaints, the owner has a time window of 10-20 days to repair the problem. If the problem has not been solved within the proposed time window, the mark will be withdrawn. The same is true in case of expiry of contract. The quality mark has to be put on the web site which is listed on a gallery with indications of scope and date of last evaluation. Evaluation reports are sent to the web site owner who can decide on their publication. The logo is dynamically served by the issuer allowing him to retract or change the logo in case of withdrawal. Marketing efforts comprise the direct contact to all levels of government, the organization of trainings, participation in seminars, and workshops. Moreover, a tight collaboration with web design companies is aspired. As the logo disposes of a direct link to a reaction page, visitors and users obtain the possibility to post complaints that are sent to the issuing organization which checks their validity. If considered valid, the complaints are forwarded to the web site owner who has the possibility to fix these problems within a time frame of 10-20 days. In case of transgression of the time window, the mark is withdrawn. It is intended to issue a quality mark with more than one level, based on the WCAG 2.0 criteria and on national and European legislation.

The suggestions derived from this analysis serve as a direct input for the development of the quality mark structure, roles, and relationships.

6.3.3 Structure, roles, and relationships

In a first step, a generic business model defines the actors, their roles, and relationships without taking into account possible implementation strategies and their impacts on the business model. The generic business model is intended to outline the most important structures and can therefore be applied and adapted to any scenario.

Four main agents are involved in the business model for web accessibility conformity assessment:
(i) European authority as the owner of the quality mark,
(ii) Austrian organization issuing the quality mark,
(iii) partner organization performing web site evaluation, and
(iv) web site owner as the consumer.

As the resulting web accessibility quality mark is intended to be unified in Europe, the general business model structure is composed of a European and a national level. On European level, a central European body acting as the owner and licenser of the quality mark is responsible for provision and updates of the evaluation criteria and methodology, the surveillance of the national issuing organizations and the installation and operation of a complaints procedure. Any independent organization with know-how in the field of web accessibility and quality assurance may overtake the role of the European authority.

On national level, the organization issuing the quality mark acts as an intermediary between the European authority and the end customer; it licenses the quality mark from the European body and distributes and sells it to the end customer. The evaluation is performed by a partner organization disposing of specific technical web accessibility know-how. Figure 29 illustrates the relationships among the main agents and their roles.

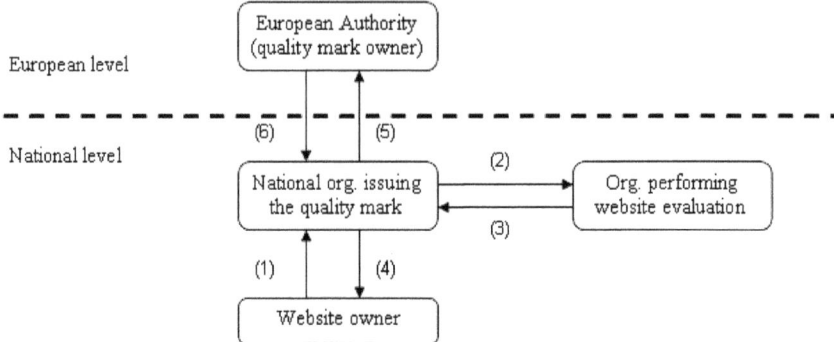

Figure 29: Business model structure

Figure 29 depicts the business model agents and their relationships. The web site owner submits an online application for conformity assessment (1). The organization issuing the quality mark verifies the identity of the customer and processes the request to a partner organization (2). The partner organization performs web site evaluation and sends the evaluation report back to the issuing organization (3). Based on the outcomes of the evaluation report, the quality mark is awarded to the web site owner (4) who is added to a list of awarded web sites published by the European authority (5). Regular surveillance is performed by the issuing organization (6). The issuing organization has to be immediately notified of notable changes of the awarded web site. Web site users have the possibility to post complaints in case of non-compliance of awarded web sites with the underlying criteria.

The flow chart in Figure 30 illustrates a conformity assessment process starting with the web site owner application. In case of negative evaluation results, the web site owner has the chance to amend his/her site and re-apply. In case of negative re-evaluation results, the quality mark is withdrawn.

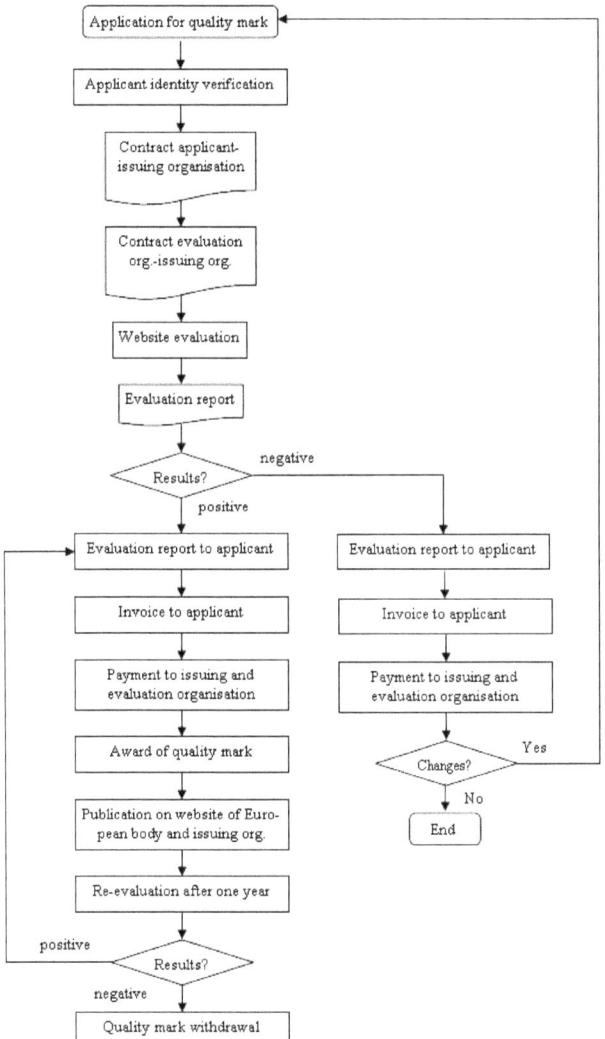

Figure 30: Web site conformity assessment flow chart

Two initially different implementation alternatives for a web accessibility quality mark are presented. On the one hand, the model may be based on standardization, accreditation, and certification procedures, thereby following the traditional way of implementation. Then again, the quality mark may be implemented as an independent framework without the application of standardization procedures. Figure 31 depicts the alternatives presented in our approach.

165

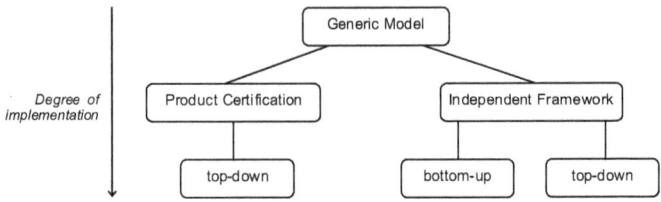

Figure 31: Overview of implementation alternatives

As already stated above, the generic model can be applied to any of the implementation alternatives. Alternative one, the product certification approach, is in line with the CEN Workshop Agreement framework. For reasons of simplicity and strong similarity with the product certification model, the inspection model is not explicitly covered. Alternative two, the independent framework, is out of scope of the CEN Workshop Agreement but, even so, represents an interesting implementation alternative as standardization is completely left out.

6.3.3.1 Quality mark based on product certification

This implementation alternative conforms to common standardization and certification processes and represents the initial attempt by the European Union for the creation of a web accessibility quality mark which was meant to be realized within the Support EAM project. However, different attitudes of the industry, stakeholders, and certification bodies led to serious discussion within an initiated CEN workshop. The parties involved could not agree on one distinct implementation model but proposed a conformity assessment framework consisting of a European Authority and three different national implementation options.

The European Authority consists of European organizations operating or supporting web accessibility quality marks. In a certification environment, this central European body has to be created in the first place (top-down approach) as two documents indispensable for certification have to be developed by the European authority.

(1) Normative document

A European quality mark should be based on a normative document that stipulates the specifications for certification. With regard to web accessibility, the requirements will include the World Wide Web Consortium's guidelines for accessible web presence. National stakeholders have pointed out that the development of these normative documents is a prerequisite for the implementation process. These documents can take the form of either a European norm or a CEN Workshop Agreement.

(2) Evaluation methodology

For the conformity assessment process an evaluation methodology is essential containing a procedure for testing the fulfillment of the requirements. At present, the EU Web Accessibility Benchmarking (WAB) Cluster (WAB Cluster 2008) is working on a Unified Web Evaluation Methodology (UWEM) (Nietzio et al. 2008) that could be used as a basis for that purpose. UWEM 1.0 has already been released and is based on WCAG 1.0. Requirements for an evaluation methodology include it to be scientifically repeatable, clearly interpretable, definite, and translatable. This methodology has to be issued as a standard or normative document.

Normative documents or standards represent official documents facilitating European and international cooperation. Standardization represents an elaborate process requiring mutual agreement of every party involved which is the reason why standards in the rapidly changing and dynamic field of web accessibility have not been elaborated.

Given a normative document and an evaluation methodology, the Austrian issuing organization can be established. The issuing organization has to be accredited by the Austrian accreditation body, the Federal Ministry of Economics and Labor (BMWA) following the norm EN 45011 (EN 45011 1998) for product certification bodies. The accreditation process is defined as a "third-party attestation related to a conformity assessment body conveying formal demonstration of its competence to carry out specific conformity assessment tasks" (ISO/IEC 17000 2004). This elaborate and time consuming process last for several years, however, the future product certification body is allowed to issue certifications and quality marks during that time. Once accredited, the issuing organization becomes a certification body being entitled to attest the conformity of a product with the requirements of a standard or a normative document and to subsequently award quality marks to the certified products.

The Austrian standards institute is one of various accredited Austrian organizations performing product certification and is currently issuing a European quality mark, the Keymark. The Keymark stands for the compliance of products with requirements of the relevant standards. It has developed as an umbrella label in the technical sector and currently consolidates 150 European standards (CEN/CENELEC 2001). These existing structures could be used and adapted for a potential web accessibility mark; nevertheless, the prerequisite of a normative document has to be fulfilled.

The European Authority for Web Accessibility Conformity Assessment, which should, according to the CEN Workshop Agreement, be the owner of the quality mark, has not yet been created. This top-down implementation requires the European Authority to be established in the first place, as the national realization is dependent on the normative documents issued by the European Authority.

6.3.3.2 Quality mark based on independent framework

This implementation alternative is not based on standardization, certification or accreditation procedures. This implies that the evaluation criteria and methodology do not have to be issued as a standard. Furthermore, the Austrian issuing organization does not need to be accredited and, as a consequence, does not act as a product certification body when issuing the quality mark.

As elaborate standardization and accreditation procedures drop out, this alternative gives room for two implementation strategies, a bottom-up and a top-down approach.

Analogously to alternative one, the top down approach starts with the establishment of a European body for reasons of creation of a guidelines document and an evaluation methodology. In a second step, an Austrian organization with expertise in the field of web accessibility and quality assurance is created. It issues the quality mark and outsources web site evaluation (based on the guidelines document) to a partner organization.

The European Computer Driving License (ECDL) was implemented following a top-down approach. The creation of evaluation criteria led to the establishment of a European body, the ECDL Foundation. Within a short time, national issuing organizations joined the ECDL Foundation, leading to the ECDL being currently available in 146 countries all over the world (ECDL 2008).

In a bottom-up approach, expert groups are trying to harmonize existing web accessibility quality marks in order to develop a unified guidelines document taking into account the different legal requirements for web accessibility in every European country. However, a bottom-up approach risks contributing to the ongoing fragmentation process within the European Union where several national quality marks already exist. The bottom-up approach must not result in another (e.g. Austrian) quality mark which is based on different criteria than the existing ones. The main objective is harmonization and therefore reflects the first big step in this approach. Once a guidelines document has been established, the creation of issuing organizations can be initiated. The European Authority may be established at a later stage. As the Internet represents a rapidly changing, dynamic environment where new technologies evolve, the experts group has to currently reconsider the accessibility guidelines and change them if necessary. Due to the non bureaucratic and slim structure of this alternative, eventual changes in the guidelines can be rapidly implemented. The up-to-dateness of the accessibility guidelines can be guaranteed this way.

On the other hand, as no certification or standardization processes are involved in this alternative, problems of trust because of lacks in impartiality may occur. Furthermore, legal commitment is not given which raises the question if this alternative overtakes the same significance to the customer than alternative one.

However, several success stories may illustrate the importance of a bottom-up approach without dependence on standards and certification procedures. In Austria, European quality schemes, e.g. the European Business Competence License (EBC*L) have been developed in a bottom-up approach. Starting with national organizations in Austria and Germany, a number of other countries joined, which led to the creation of a European body. Currently, the EBC*L is available in 16 countries in Europe (EBCL 2006).

6.3.4 Implementation scenarios

Discussions with national stakeholders in Austria about the CEN Workshop Agreement led to a serious debate that identified some weaknesses that the scheme had with regard to its implementation in the country.

Due to cost aspects, a simultaneous implementation of third party certification and supplier's declaration of conformity would make the third party certification obsolete. For this reason, national certification bodies might be less inclined to cooperate if the supplier's declaration of conformity were to be introduced in parallel.

European progress in establishing web accessibility certification suggests a variety of possible scenarios, whose individual applicability can be compared and analyzed by means of six evaluation criteria: complexity, costs, dependence, flexibility, impartiality, and time.

6.3.4.1 Evaluation criteria

1. *Complexity*
The complexity of implementation depends on the quality mark's background structures. This criterion represents a measure for the amount of prerequisites necessary for implementing the scenario. Thus, a scenario's complexity increases with the existence of ownership and license agreements at a national or at the European level.
2. *Costs*
A scenario's costs comprise the setup costs of the national issuing organization, the issuing costs of the quality mark or certificate (accreditation and testing costs) and the license costs for the quality mark imposed by the EAWAC. These costs, especially the setup and testing costs, cannot be specified, as they depend on a number of variables, such as the provider's organizational form (profit or non-profit), the sample size, or the evaluation procedure. All of these

variables must be specified in the normative document and the evaluation methodology; as a result, they are not known at present. This paper compares the scenarios in terms of the existence of various cost elements.

3. *Dependence*

Some scenarios can only be realized if certain prerequisites have been fulfilled. These may depend on national, European and international certification, accreditation, or legislation bodies. This criterion expresses the degree to which an implementation scenario is dependent on further authorities or institutions. The dependence on the normative document and the evaluation methodology holds true for every scenario and, subsequently, does not need to be taken into consideration.

4. *Flexibility*

The flexibility of implementation represents the issuing organization's degree of self-determination. For all of the scenarios presented in this paper, the quality mark must conform to a standard or a workshop agreement. However, the administrative background and, therefore, the degree of flexibility vary from scenario to scenario.

5. *Impartiality*

The quality mark system's impartiality is measured by this criterion, which compares third and first party conformity assessment in terms of their objectivity.

6. *Time*

The time period from the development of the normative document to the implementation of a particular scenario is covered by this criterion.

Section 6.3.4.2 to 6.3.4.5 outline four basic scenarios and analyze them by means of six evaluation criteria with the aim of supporting and accelerating the national implementation process, once a European normative document or a CEN Workshop Agreement has been released.

6.3.4.2 Scenario 1: Supplier's declaration of conformity

Scenario 1 includes a first party evaluation by a supplier according to the international standard ISO/IEC 17050. This approach is easy and cost-effective to implement, as no accredited third party is involved in this scenario. The owner of a web site can declare his/her commitment to a normative document or a CEN Workshop Agreement. He/she is authorized to place the quality mark on the web site (for a limited period, e.g., for one year), provided that the relevant criteria have been fulfilled and the supplier's intention to use the quality mark has been communicated to the EAWAC (CEN 2006). However, if the criteria have not been met, web site users may post complaints and the EAWAC can impose sanctions or withdraw the right to issue the quality mark in the event of violations.

Scenario 1 constitutes the least complex scenario, as it does not require third party involvement (as a consequence, no accreditation procedure accrues). For the same reasons, scenario 1 is an especially cost-effective and flexible solution. However, it is also highly dependent on existing structures, as it can only be established once the European Authority and a quality mark have been created. The impartiality of this scenario is a matter of great discussion. A study of e-commerce and financial web sites indicated that 30% of the web sites that had an accessibility quality mark claimed a higher level of accessibility than they actually provided (Petrie 2005). Because the quality marks concerned had been issued with a supplier's declaration of conformity, a certain lack of impartiality should be assumed for the first party system.

6.3.4.3 Scenario 2: Product certification without a quality mark

In the second scenario, an Austrian certification body would issue an explicit certificate stating conformity with the normative document or the CEN Workshop Agreement. Scenario 2 could provide a temporary alternative until the EAWAC, as the owner of the European quality mark, and the corresponding structures are established. This scenario requires neither the elaborate structure of a European quality mark nor ownership or license agreements.

Accordingly, scenario 2 is a third party solution with relatively low costs and high flexibility. The low complexity of this scenario is attributable to the fact that it is independent of administrative structures. The impartiality of third party certification makes scenario 2 a competitive solution that can be implemented immediately after the release of the normative document.

6.3.4.4 Scenario 3: Product certification with a quality mark

Scenario 3 assumes both the release and approval of a European quality mark and the establishment of an organizational structure for a specific web accessibility label. Thus, scenario three represents a follow-up or stage of expansion to scenario two. The quality mark in scenario 3 would be issued by national certification or inspection bodies.

This scenario involves the most elaborate structures. The EAWAC and the European quality mark system must be set up before scenario 3 can be realized, making the scenario highly dependent on European authorities and structures and therefore inflexible in its implementation. The costs for scenario 3 exceed the costs for scenario 2, due to the additional license costs incurred for the European quality mark. Because it results in the issuance of a harmonized European quality mark, scenario 3, like scenario 1, is in keeping with the final goal of the CEN Workshop Agreement.

6.3.4.5 Scenario 4: Product certification using existing structures

Scenario 4 relies on well-established organizational structures and quality marks, such as the Keymark. The Keymark is an existing quality mark that stands for the compliance of products with requirements of the relevant standards. It has developed as an umbrella label in the technical sector and currently consolidates 150 European standards (CEN/CENELEC 2001).

If the Keymark were to become the operating mark, the EAWAC would need to be embedded into CEN, the owner of the Keymark. Such a scenario goes beyond the scope of the CEN Workshop Agreement, which does not consider the use of existing structures for the creation of a quality mark. As the issuing organization has already been established, the costs, particularly the setup costs, may be lower than in scenario 3, provided that the owner of the existing mark refrains from any additional fees for the structure and label. This factor makes the implementation of scenario 4 highly dependent on the authority owning the existing mark. Adopting an existing structure assumes that the owner and issuer fully agree. In turn, such an agreement might require negotiations that could delay and hamper the implementation of scenario 4. Existing structures may decrease the complexity of implementation, but they also keep the flexibility to a minimum. A main advantage of this scenario lies in its not creating any additional administrative and bureaucratic structures. Its impartiality is given through third party certification.

6.3.5 Scenario analysis

The rough evaluation of the four scenarios by means of six criteria provides a basis of support for decision-making on the national implementation of the quality mark. Table 24 gives an overview of four alternative scenarios, taking into account the criteria complexity, costs, dependence, flexibility, impartiality, and time.

	Scenarios			
Criteria	Scenario 1	Scenario 2	Scenario 3	Scenario 4
Complexity	low	low	high	medium
Costs	low	medium	high	medium
setup	no	yes	yes	no
issuing	no	yes	yes	yes
licence	yes	no	yes	yes
Dependence	high	low	high	very high
Flexibility	high	medium	low	very low
Impartiality	low	high	high	high
Time	sooner	immediately	sooner	later

Table 24: Scenario evaluation (Leitner et al. 2006)

For reasons of better cross-comparison, an alternative illustration of the four scenarios by means of Kiviat diagrams is presented in Figure 32. The sizes of the resulting areas in the diagrams represent an indicator for the scenario quality: big areas indicate scenarios that dispose of good values in many criteria; small areas are a sign of complex and elaborate scenarios.

For this purpose, the evaluation criteria in section 6.3.4.1 had to be slightly amended as they had to fit to the scale ranging from 1 (very low) to 5 (very high). These values are not absolute but provide a means for operationalization of the qualitative evaluation in order to enable a comparison of the strategy alternatives.

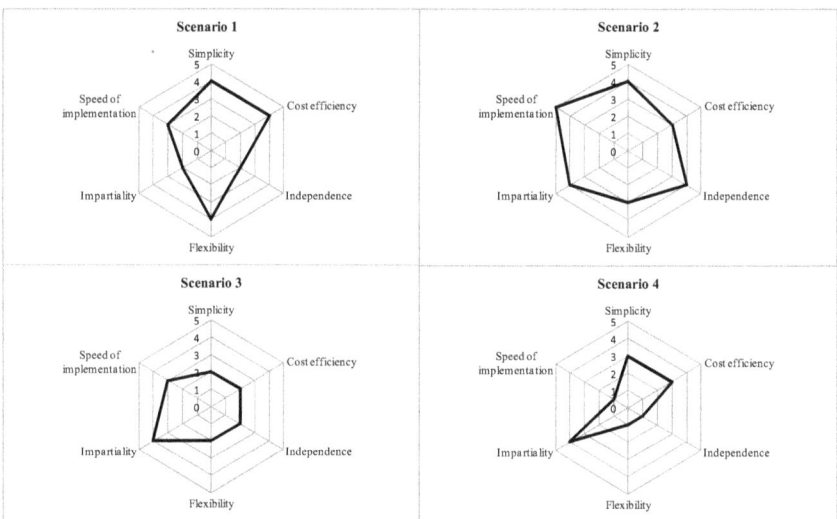

Figure 32: Scenario evaluation with Kiviat diagrams (Leitner et al. 2009b)

In an early stage of realization, scenario two is a reasonable strategy, as no explicit quality mark system is needed. Once the EAWAC and the quality mark are established, a follow-up choice can be made between scenario 1, as a cost effective solution with a lack of impartiality, or scenario 3, whose third party conformity assessment brings with it higher costs for the end user. Scenario 4 may require negotiations with existing quality mark owners, but could result in a cheaper and less complex alternative.

6.3.6 Business model and implementation plan

The specifications of the different levels of a business model are based on Hedman and Kalling's (2003) business model structure depicted in Figure 27. He defines five different levels: market, offering, activities and organization, resources and suppliers. Sections 6.3.6.1 to 6.3.6.5 describe and analyze these levels with regard to a web accessibility quality mark.

6.3.6.1 Market level

The market level defines the customer view of the web accessibility quality mark and the associated services, the relevant market, and the customer profile. This business model focuses on the penetration of the national Austrian market. Public facilities (e.g., government departments, facilities of care, educational institutions, geriatric centers, nursing homes, libraries, etc.), interest groups for disabled and elderly people, private organizations selling goods and services on their web sites and other organizations with (future) accessible web presences are among the main target group. For official web sites which provide information or electronic support for procedures there is the legally conditional need for meeting general standards about web accessibility since January 2008 (Austrian E-Government Act 2004). Therefore, visualizing their level of accessibility to the general public in terms of a quality mark will contribute significantly to image ameliorations and, on the other hand, help government officials control the abidance by the law. In Austria, no web accessibility quality mark has been established so far. Competition in this field is therefore not existent by now.

6.3.6.2 Offering level

The offered quality mark is positioned to be a high quality product and trusted solution with reliable service and experience offered by the issuing company. Social responsibility and social awareness are associated with the quality mark and will therefore be associated with the awarded web presences and organizations. The web accessibility quality mark will contribute significantly to the degree of corporate social responsibility (CSR) of an organization. The CSR approach reflects, among others, the promotion of social integration being an integral element for the economic success of a firm (Respact Austria 2005). In Austria, yearly rankings of organizations getting most involved with CSR foster their images (Center for Corporate Citizenship Austria 2008).

The quality mark is advertised on the web site of the issuing organization and the European authority and, in addition, placed on certified web sites, which again contributes to brand awareness among other organizations. Besides issuing the quality mark, the issuing organization offers helpdesk service and consultancy, periodic screening, and re-evaluation every year. The pricing strategy is composed of two models depending on the web site size and the degree of service. The models are all based on a one-year membership with the issuing organization.

6.3.6.3 Organizational level

The issuing organization, a non-profit association, has several sources of revenue. Membership fees constitute a major part of the issuing organization's income. As the award of a quality mark for web accessibility supports government interest, revenue streams in terms of government funding and sponsorship have to be provided.

The independent issuing organization outsources web site evaluation. Its major competencies rest with the conformity assessment and quality assurance processes. However, technical know-how in terms of web accessibility has to be available within the issuing organization, as it provides consultancy service together with the evaluation organization.

The issuing organization's accessible web presence represents its central marketing and distribution channel. Orders, deliveries, communication, and marketing are exclusively executed via a secure connection on the web site.

6.3.6.4 Resource level

The resources of an organization include the human, physical, and organizational capital creating the core competencies of a firm. In this business model, the core competencies are represented by web site evaluation, conformity assessment, web accessibility consultancy, and provision of a European network. In order to realize these competencies, specific physical, human, and organizational capital has to be available with every agent involved in this business model. The physical capital becomes manifest in web accessibility evaluation technology or conformity assessment technologies. These technologies cannot be used without the existence of human capital in terms of experience, skills, and intelligence in the relevant fields. Experts in web accessibility and conformity assessment have to be in key positions of the issuing company. Organizational capital (e.g., networking and cooperation, coordination systems) keeps the organization running and puts together the different fields of resources.

6.3.6.5 Market factor level

The supplier side of this business model is covered by the European authority, the owner of the quality mark acting as a licenser. The central European body regulates the quality mark design; it specifies and continuously updates the conformity assessment criteria and sets the evaluation methodology. This way, a unique European quality mark for web accessibility can be realized. Furthermore, the European authority has to set up a complaints channel for web site users.

This chapter outlined the structure and constitution of a business model for web accessibility conformity assessment based on Hedman and Kalling's (2003) business model definition.

6.3.7 Person certification

Additionally to the certification of products, persons can be certified. In case of web accessibility, experts in the field of accessible web design can be issued a certificate after giving proof of their knowledge. Given that accessible web sites become part of tenders or industry specifications, people disposing of knowledge about web accessibility are needed.

This person certification model represents an add-on feature to the classical web accessibility quality mark. A certificate is issued to persons who have given proof of their competency in accessible web design. The issue of the certificate may take over similar processes as the European Driving License issued by the Austrian Computer Society. The applicant has two possibilities: (i) attend courses about accessible web design or (ii) to learn about the required contents in an autodidactic way. The assessment is carried out by the issuing organizations or authorized test centers. The issuing approach can be divided into following subprocesses that are displayed in the flow chart in Figure 33.

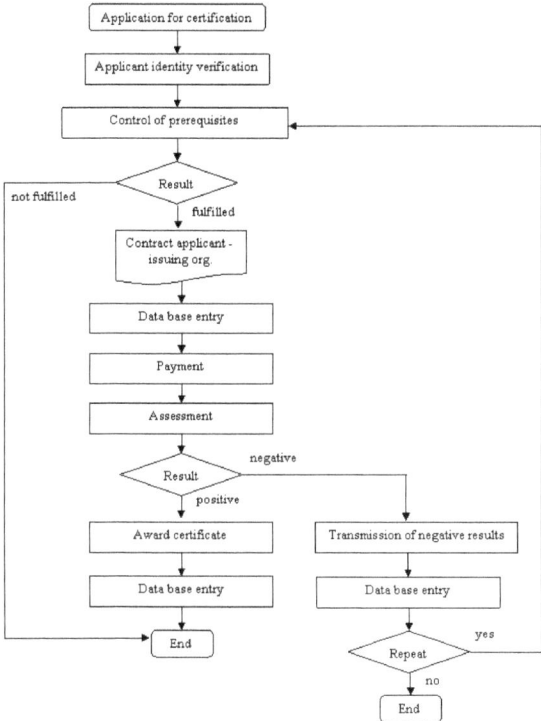

Figure 33: Person certification flow chart[20]

The steps of the person certification process depicted in Figure 33 are explained in further detail in the following paragraph.
1. Application for certification: The applicant hands in online an application for person certification.
2. Application identity verification: The identity of the applicant is verified.
3. Control of prerequisites: A certification assessment can only be repeated a predefined number of times in case of negative result. The control of these prerequisites takes place in this stage.
4. Contract applicant – issuing organization: After positive prerequisite control, a contract between the applicant and the issuing organization is signed.
5. Data base entry: The applicant is listed in a data base.
6. Payment: The payment of the applicant takes place before the assessment.
7. Assessment: The assessment is carried out at the issuing organization and at authorized test centers.

---

20 The issuing approach of a person certification has been developed in cooperation with the Institute Integriert Studieren at the University of Linz.

8. In case of positive results, two processes occur:
   a. Award of certificate: The certificate is awarded after a positive assessment.
   b. Data base entry: After a positive result and an awarded certificate, the candidate data is listed in the data base.
9. In case of negative results, three processes are followed:
   a. Transmission of negative results to applicant
   b. Data base entry: the negative result is listed in the data base
   c. Possibility to retake the assessment. (continue with 3)

A data base gives detailed indication about e.g., the applicant, the number of assessment repetitions, the results of the assessment, and the date of the award. This data base represents a means for quality assurance and visibility, repeatability, and traceability.

In order to realize this person certification model, a curriculum has to be provided from the issuing organization. Additionally, trainings for the assessments can be offered by other educational institutions. The assessment can only be conducted by the issuing organization or authorized testing institutions.

6.4 Summary and interpretation

Section 6 explores viable alternatives for implementing a European web accessibility quality mark in Austria. An intense literature review on current conformity assessment procedures identifies three possible structural models: (i) inspection, (ii) third party certification, (iii) and supplier's declaration of conformity. Research on the background of web accessibility conformity assessment in Europe revealed European and national attempts in this field. A number of national quality marks in European member states have been established that are dependent on different criteria and apply diverse evaluation methodologies. In order to stop this fragmentation process, a framework for a European quality mark for web accessibility has been proposed in the course of a European project (Support-EAM). Due to strong resistance from industry and a lack of a sustainable evaluation methodology and business model, its implementation has not been realized.

The current shortage of a quality mark for accessible web presences in Austria entails research considerations on its possible structure, business model and implementation strategy given a European framework. This contribution applies a look-ahead approach that assumes the release of a normative document and an evaluation methodology in the near future. Based on (i) the results of the Support-EAM project, and (ii) empirical data of current quality mark best practices, four alternatives of a possible Austrian quality mark for accessible web are developed by means of scenario technique. An evaluation of these scenarios in terms of the criteria complexity, costs, dependence, flexibility, impartiality, and time allows assumptions especially about the cost and time dimensions of their operability.

Additionally, a business model for an Austrian web accessibility quality mark is introduced which is based on established theoretical business model specifications. As an add-on feature, a process model for person certification is proposed. The conformity assessment of web sites together with a certification of experts in the field of web accessibility will contribute to quality assurance and awareness rising.

This section proposes an integrated look-ahead approach for an Austrian quality mark that fits into European conformity assessment structures. The development of viable implementation scenarios and a business model for this conformity assessment process shall facilitate and accelerate national implementation.

7 Conclusion

In European Union member states, the increasing importance of web accessibility becomes apparent by a growing number of initiatives in this area (cf. section 2.4.1). This development entails that not only public but also non-governmental web presences will have to account for this issue, which, in turn, causes business and management considerations to be made. However, besides few theoretical approaches for web accessibility benefit analysis (Puhl 2008) and cost-benefit scenarios (Heerdt and Strauss 2004), the issue of web accessibility has gained little attention from a business and managerial perspective so far.

This contribution draws on a holistic approach to fill this research gap and addresses business considerations of web accessibility out of two perspectives: (i) organization and (ii) authority. The organizational perspective identifies both business impacts of web accessibility implementation and develops a web accessibility implementation process (WAIP) model by means of exploratory case study research in three major industries. Research question one (RQ 1) relates to the organizational perspective.

RQ 1) *What business impact can be obtained from an implementation of accessible web presences in private sector organizations?*

The authority perspective explores viable alternatives for the development and implementation of a web accessibility quality mark by means of scenario technique and is addressed by research question two (RQ 2).

RQ 2) *How does a business model for an Austrian web accessibility quality mark have to be configured in order to be applied in a European context?*

Both perspectives are strongly interrelated. The identification of business impacts of web accessibility and the development of a web accessibility implementation process (WAIP) model represent an important knowledge base for organizations intending to consider accessible web presences. Due to the fact that the accessibility of a web site is not evident for the average user, a quality mark represents the only impartial means for organizations to both communicate their efforts to the general public and assure the quality of web site accessibility. In turn, the success of a web accessibility quality mark is reliant on organizations willing to consider accessibility for their web presences. Despite the fact that each of these two studies can be considered separately, even a greater added value is grounded in their joint conduction.

7.1 Key findings

The organizational perspective encompasses the analysis of business impacts of web accessibility implementation in three industry sectors (tourism, financial services, and information). This study reveals distinct findings for each sector analyzed, but also detects common patterns and phenomena that appear across each sector.

In the tourism sector (cf. section 4.1), 87% of 52 hotels analyzed failed web accessibility evaluation. A lack of awareness for the issue of web accessibility has been identified as a main reason for this inequality. Besides social aspects, quality enhancements of accessible web presences represent a major motivation for the implementation of web accessibility in the tourism sector. Due to, on the one hand, a high importance of a hotel web site (information, communication, and booking activities are conducted online at an increasing rate), and, on the other hand, low switching costs of the online consumer, the web site quality aspects (e.g., stability, security, simplicity, and usability) are fundamental for the success of the hotel. Accordingly, changes after web accessibility implementation encompass maintenance facilitations and an increase in usability, simplicity, and therefore, overall web site quality.

In the financial services sector (cf. section 4.2), 79% of 18 web presences analyzed failed web accessibility evaluation. However, financial institutions which succeeded in web accessibility implementation also conducted elaborate constructional accessibility adaptations (account statements in Braille language, cash machines with speech output). In the financial services sector, the awareness for this issue seems to be available to a differing extent. Four main motivations for web accessibility implementation could be identified as distinct for this sector: (i) the importance of trust and security due to sensitive information exchange in order to increase customer loyalty, (ii) strong social responsibility towards society acting as a medium to avoid financial exclusion, (iii) importance of differentiation and image enhancement due to a tendency of associating this sector with negative characteristics, and (iv) the growing customer group of elderly people that increasingly conduct their banking activities online. The main reasons for a failure of web accessibility implementation were misconceptions about the issue, incompatibilities with corporate design, and argumentation problems.

In the information sector (cf. section 4.3), 18 online media and service providing organizations have been analyzed 78% of which failed web accessibility evaluation. This study reveals a focus of the information sector on technical motivations for web accessibility implementation. Due to frequent data and content actualization, the web presences in this sector are subject to constant changes and face short time windows for this change process. Hence, online media organizations focus on high web site quality and ease of technical maintenance both of which occur with accessible web sites. Accordingly, predominantly technical impacts (web site quality, search engine ranking, and maintenance) after web accessibility implementation have been identified. In the information sector, accessibility is regarded as a side effect of high web site quality. However, data load and high frequency of changes provoke problems in terms of quality assurance especially in case of a high number of staff involved in content generation. In the information sector, the quality, stability, and device independency of the web presence has been identified as a crucial element for the organization's success.

Besides distinct findings for each sector analyzed, common patterns emerged across all three sectors (cf. section 5). The implementation of accessible web sites can be based on economic, social, and technical motivations (cf. section 5.2). Implementation considerations may be triggered by one or more of these motivation types, depending on the organizational sector and size, the corporate culture, and the purpose and complexity of the web presence. However, the focus on the type of motivation differs between the sectors analyzed.

The existence of key personalities as drivers for the web accessibility implementation process has been identified as crucial across all three sectors. These key personalities are sufficiently committed to the issue of web accessibility and may have learned about it either out of personal background (e.g., own disability, friends and family with disabilities) or business background (e.g., colleagues with disabilities, colleagues with technical expert knowledge, events and presentations about the issue). In every organization which has successfully implemented web accessibility, a key personality acted as a main driving force.

Overall, several characteristics of organizations which have successfully implemented web accessibility could be derived: (i) elaborate corporate culture with commitment to social values and corporate social responsibility strategies, (ii) high importance of extant web presence for core business, (iii) web site content subject to frequent changes, (iv) high relevance of elderly customers, and (v) existence of key personalities.

Changes after web accessibility implementation could be classified into economic, social, and technical changes (cf. section 5.3). Across all sectors, maintenance facilitations and an enhancement of search engine ranking could be identified. The perceived social and economic changes were highly dependent on the organization's motivations for web accessibility implementation and therefore differed according to the industry sector, organizational size, and purpose of the web presence.

The problems detected with web accessibility implementation (cf. section 5.3) were mainly associated with quality assurance aspects. A high number of web site editors raise the likelihood of accessibility errors that often remain undetected. Hence, for reasons of quality assurance the need for a quality mark for accessible web sites accrued.

The reasons why organizations fail web accessibility implementation (cf. section 5.4) include corporate design requirements, a lack of top management support, a lack of awareness (e.g., misconceptions about the issue), and a lack of argumentation. This work provides solutions in terms of development of two instruments to eliminate failure of web accessibility implementation: (i) a web accessibility implementation process model, and (ii) a business model for an Austrian web accessibility quality mark.

Initiators which failed web accessibility implementation proceeded on a "trial and error" basis which led to so called "ad hoc" implementation attempts that failed. For these reasons, one of the major research contributions of this work represents the development of a web accessibility implementation process (WAIP) model that is based on the implementation processes reported by organizations which successfully implemented web accessibility and has been developed for the first time in this contribution (cf. section 5.6). This model encompasses six phases: start, pre-analysis, business plan development, modification/implementation, quality assurance, and dissemination, in which detailed procedures are indicated. Organizations that stick to this implementation model may decrease or even eliminate the possibility of implementation failure.

Another reason for failure of web accessibility implementation identified in this contribution is a lack of awareness for the issue. A quality mark for accessible web presences issued by an independent third party may raise the awareness for web accessibility and simultaneously represents a means for quality assurance. Business impacts (e.g., customer loyalty, image enhancements, differentiation) are highly dependent on customer's perceptions of an organization and therefore can only be realized when the accessibility efforts of an organization are communicated accordingly to the general public. Hence, it can be stated that a quality mark is a prerequisite for full exploitation of the business impacts of accessible web presences.

The current lack of a web accessibility quality mark and the simultaneous existence of several quality marks in European member states led to the need for the development of a business model for an Austrian web accessibility quality mark that fits into a European framework and accelerates national implementation. In section 6, four alternatives of a possible web accessibility quality mark are developed by means of scenario technique: *supplier's declaration of conformity, prod-*

uct certification without a quality mark, product certification with a quality mark, and *product certification using existing structures.* An evaluation of these scenarios in terms of the criteria complexity, costs, dependence, flexibility, impartiality, and time allows assumptions about the cost and time dimension of their operability. In an early stage of realization, scenario two is a reasonable strategy, as no explicit quality mark system is needed. A follow-up choice can be made between the *supplier's declaration of conformity* scenario, as a cost effective solution with a lack of impartiality, or the *product certification with a quality mark* scenario, whose third party conformity assessment brings with it higher costs for the end user. The *product certification using existing structures* scenario may require negotiations with existing quality mark owners, but could result in a cheaper and less complex alternative. These scenario analyses provide an important decision support for organizations intending to implement a web accessibility quality mark.

Based on (i) established theoretical business model specifications and (ii) empirical data of ten extant quality marks, a business model for an Austrian web accessibility quality mark is introduced. This look-ahead approach for an Austrian quality mark fits European standardization efforts and may speed up national implementation.

Overall, this work represents a holistic approach that has four main contributions to research and managerial practice: (i) identification of business impacts of web accessibility implementation, (ii) development of a web accessibility implementation process (WAIP) model, (iii) development and evaluation of four scenarios for a possible web accessibility quality mark, and (iv) development of a business model for an Austrian web accessibility quality mark.

Considering accessibility as an innovation process, the fact that only 12% out of 89 web presences analyzed have passed web site evaluation leads to the suggestion that the innovation web accessibility has not taken off yet. Time and market factors at the time of its launch in 1999 have been identified as unfavorable. The change in market conditions (variety of technologies, web 2.0 aspects, variety of output devices, standardization attempts) provokes that the accessibility of web presences becomes increasingly relevant for organizations in the private sector. Despite other factors influencing innovation take-off, the findings of this contribution may further trigger the implementation of web accessibility and therefore speed up the integration process of this innovation.

7.2 Limitations

The studies presented here are also subject to several limitations. The study on the organizational perspective derives business impacts of web accessibility implementation from qualitative case studies. The main research instrument applied in this study is the semi-structured interview with representatives of various organizations. Despite other research instruments used (cf. Table 6), the semi-structured interviews represent a major database for derivation of the findings. Therefore, the study is dependent on the perceptions of organizational members which may be subject to bias. Several provisions have been undertaken in order to minimize interviewer induced bias (cf. section 3). However, the possibility of exaggerated claims by respondents cannot be eliminated. Future work may concentrate on observing a web accessibility process in an organization and determine the differences to this exploratory study. This may enrich these study's findings.

Moreover, the findings of this study are based on case study research in three distinct industry sectors. Qualitative research enables the identification of patterns in each of the sectors for the specific organizations analyzed. However, small sample size restricts generalizability of the findings.

7.3 Future Work

In this contribution, three industry sectors with high relevance in electronic business are analyzed, representing only a small fraction of the variety of extant sectors. Further research may therefore concentrate on a study extension that can both be conducted horizontally and vertically. The consideration of additional sectors represents a horizontal extension; a vertical extension can be carried out by an analysis of accessory organizations in each sector. Either way, the case study research framework developed in this work can be applied and enables sound cross-industry and cross-organizational comparisons. A constant enlargement may further reveal additional relationships and/or differences between industries, enrich the knowledge base for organizations, and thus increase relevance for research and organizational practice. This work constitutes a basis for a future knowledge management platform about web accessibility.

This case study is based on individual's perceptions and not on researcher observations. The analysis and observation of organizations before and after the implementation process may represent an area of future research which at the same time increases external validity and generalizability of this case study's findings.

In this contribution, two dimensions of the holistic research framework on web accessibility have been addressed. Areas of future research may involve online buying behavior of impaired customers and identify their needs in terms of online shopping.

The findings of both studies conducted are of high managerial relevance. Organizations intending to consider web accessibility for their web presences profit from the identification of other organizations' experiences. The sample consists of organizations of different sizes and therefore allows both SMEs and complex organizations to identify with the findings. Overall, this study represents a valuable knowledge base for organizations intending to implement web accessibility. The identification of benchmarks and good practices in terms of web accessibility implementation facilitates and accelerates other organization's implementation processes. The detection of obstacles and problems with web accessibility as well as strategies to overcome them may support and inspire other organizations. Moreover, the web accessibility implementation process model summarizes best practices and gives indications on how to trigger and develop a web accessibility implementation process in an organization.

8 References

Adams, J. S. (1965) Inequity in social exchange. In: Berkowitz, L. (Eds.) *Advances in Experimental Social Psychology*. Academic Press: New York.

Ahlers, D. (2006) News consumption and the new electronic media. *Press/Politics* 11 (1), 29-52.

Ahluwalia, R. (2002) Re-inquiries: How prevalent is the negativity effect in consumer environments? *Journal of Consumer Research* 29, 270-279.

Ambrose, I. (2007) Rights of tourists with disabilities in the European Union framework. *European Network for Accessible Tourism*.

Amit, R., Zott, C. (2001) Value creation in e-business. *Strategic Management Journal* 22, 493-520.

Anderson, R. E., Srinivasan, S. S. (2003) E-satisfaction and e-loyalty: A contingency framework. *Psychology & Marketing* 20 (2), 123-138.

Arch, A. (2008) *W3C, Web Accessibility for Older Users: A Literature Review*. online at http://www.w3.org/TR/wai-age-literature/#whatcog (last accessed 20/10/2009).

Austrian E-Government Act (2004) *Österreichisches E-Government Gesetz (Austrian e-government act)*.

Austrian Equalization Act (2005) *Österreichisches Bundesgesetz über die Gleichstellung von Menschen mit Behinderungen (Austrian equalization act for people with disabilities)*.

Austrian Federal Constitution (2008) *Oesterreichisches Bundes-Verfassungsgesetz (Austrian federal constitution law)*.

Baker, S. M., Holland, J., Kaufman-Scarborough, C. (2007) How consumers with disabilities perceive "welcome" in retail servicescapes: a critical incident study. *The Journal of Services Marketing* 21 (3), 160-173.

Baker, S. M., Stephens, D. L., Hill, R. P. (2002) How can retailers enhance accessibility: giving consumers with visual impairments a voice in the marketplace. *Journal of Retailing and Consumer Services* 9 (4), 227-239.

Bartunek, J. M. (1984) Changing interpretive schemes and organizational restructuring: the example of a religious order. *Administrative Science Quarterly* 29 (3), 355-372.

Brajnik, G. (2006) Web accessibility testing - when the method is the culprit. *International Conference on Computers Helping People with Special Needs*, Linz, Austria, Springer.

Brennan, R. L., Prediger, D. J. (1981) Coefficient kappa: some uses, misuses, and alternatives. *Educational and Psychological Measurement* 41, 687-699.

Brockhoff, K. (1999) *Forschung und Entwicklung: Planung und Kontrolle*. edition 5, Oldenburg: München.

Bryman, A. (2008) *Social research methods.* edition 3, Oxford University Press: New York.

Buhalis, D., Eichhorn, V. (2005) *Accessibility market and stakeholder analysis.* OSSATE.

Bullinger, H. (2001) *Knowledge meets motivation - Anreizsysteme im Wissensmanagement.* Fraunhofer Institut für Arbeitswirtschaft und Organisation: Stuttgart.

Burgelman, R. (1983) A process model of internal corporate venturing in a major diversified firm. *Administrative Science Quaterly* 28, 223-244.

Burnett, J. J., Baker, H. B. (2001) Assessing the travel-related behaviors of the mobility-disabled consumer. *Journal of Travel Research* 40 (1), 4-11.

Carrell, M. R., Dittrich, J. E. (1978) Equity theory: the recent literature, methodological considerations, and new directions. *The Academy of Management Review* 3 (2), 202-210.

Carroll, A. B. (1979) A three-dimensional conceptual model of corporate performance. *Academy of Management Review* 4.

CEN (2006) *Specifications for a web accessibility conformity assessment scheme and a web accessibility quality mark.*

CEN/CENELEC (2001) *Part 4: certification - 'the CEN/CENELEC European mark system'.*

Center for Corporate Citizenship Austria (2008) *CSR ranking 2008.* online at http://www.ccc-austria.at/index.php?option=com_content&task=view&id=22&Itemid=32 (last accessed 03/05/2009).

Chakrabarti, A. K. (1974) The role of champion in product innovation. *California Management Review* 17 (2), 58.

Chamber of Commerce for Individuals with Disabilities (2008) *Inspiration and history.* online at http://www.chamber4us.org/about/index.htm (last accessed 21/04/2009).

Chesbrough, H., Vanhaverbeke, W., West, J. (2006) *Open innovation: researching a new paradigm.* Oxford University Press: Oxford.

Clark, J. (2006) To hell with WCAG 2. *A List Apart* 217.

Clarkson, M. B. (1995) A stakeholder framework for analyzing and evaluating corporate social performance. *The Academy of Management Review* 20 (1), 92-117.

Commission of the European Communities (2007) *Communication from the commission to the European parliament, the council, the European economic and social committee and the committee of the regions, i2010 - annual information society report 2007.*

Council of the European Union (2008) *Council conclusions on accessible information society.* Brussels.

Cox, J., Dale, B. J. (2002) Key quality factors in website design and use: an examination. *International Journal of Quality and Reliability Management* 19 (7), 862-888.

Darzentas, J., Miesenberger, K. (2005) Design for all in information technology: a universal concern. *Database and Expert Systems Applications*, Springer.

Dean, D. H. (2004) Consumer reaction to negative publicity: effects of corporate reputation, response, and responsibility for a crisis event. *Journal of Business Communication* 41 (2), 192-211.

Decker, O. S. (2004) Corporate social responsibility and structural change in financial services. *Managerial Auditing Journal* 19 (6), 712-728.

Dewar, R. D., Dutton, J. E. (1986) The adoption of radical and incremental innovations: an empirical analysis. *Management Science* 32 (11), 1422-1433.

Doppler, K. (1994) *Change-Management. Den Unternehmenswandel gestalten.* edition 9, Campus: Frankfurt/Main.

Döring-Katerkamp, U., Trojan, J. (2002) Motivation und Wissensmanagement - Eine praktische Perspektive. In: Franken, R., Gadatsch, A. (Eds.) *Integriertes Knowledge-Management. Konzepte, Methoden, Instrumente und Fallbeispiele.* Braunschweig/Wiesbaden.

Dutton, J. E., Dukerich, J. M. (1991) Keeping an eye on the mirror: image and identity in organizational adaption. *Academy of Management Journal* 34, 517-554.

EBCL (2006) *European Business Competence Licence.* online at http://www.ebcl.at/ (last accessed 03/05/2009).

ECDL (2008) *Europäischer Computerführerschein.* online at http://www.ecdl.at/ (last accessed 03/05/2009).

Egan, R. W., Fjermestad, J. (2005) Change and resistance. Help for the practitioner of change. *International Conference on System Sciences*, Hawaii, IEEE.

Eisenhardt, K. M. (1989) Building theories from case study research. *The Academy of Management Review* 14 (4), 532-550.

EN 45011 (1998) *General requirements for bodies operating product certification systems (ISO/IEC Guide 65:1996).*

EN ISO/IEC 17020 (2004) *General criteria for the operation of various types of bodies performing inspection.*

EN ISO/IEC 17050-1 (2004) *Conformity assessment – supplier's declaration of conformity – Part 1: general requirements.*

EN ISO/IEC 17050-2 (2004) *Conformity assessment – supplier's declaration of conformity – Part 2: supporting documentation.*

ENAT (2007) *European network for accessible tourism: services and facilities for accessible tourism in Europe.*

Erdey-Gruz, M., Leitner, M.-L., Strauss, C. (2009) Web accessibility in the Austrian hotel sector. *International Conference on Business Informatics*, Vienna, Austria.

Euracert (2007) *Euracert label*. online at http://www.euracert.org/en/about/label/ (last accessed 28/04/2009).

Europe's Information Society (2008) *eInclusion: helping older people to access the information society*. online at http://ec.europa.eu/information_society/activities/einclusion/policy/ageing/index_en.htm (last accessed 12/02/2009).

European Commission (2005) *Standardisation mandate to CEN, CENELEC and ETSI in support of European accessibility requirements for public procurement of products and services in the ICT domain (M 376)*

European Commission (2006) *Ministerial declaration on e-inclusion*. Riga.

European Commission (2007) *The European e-business report*. E-Business Watch, Luxemburg.

European Commission (2008) *ICT and e-business impact in the banking industry. A sectoral e-business watch study by Rambøll Management.*

European Disability Forum (2001) *Facts and figures about disability*. online at http://www.edf-feph.org/Page_Generale.asp?DocID=12534 (last accessed 12/02/2009).

Eurostat (2007) *Measuring progress towards a more sustainable Europe*. European Communities: Luxemburg.

Federal Ministry of Economics and Labour (2007) *Tourismus in Österreich 2007*.

Fincham, R., Rhodes, P. (2005) *Principles of organizational behaviour*. Oxford University Press: Oxford.

Flavian, C., Torres, E., Guinaliu, M. (2004) Corporate image measurement. A further problem for the tangibilization of internet banking services. *The International Journal of Bank Marketing* 22 (5), 366-384.

Frank, J. (2008) Web accessibility for the blind: corporate social responsibility or litigation avoidance? *41st Hawaii International Conference on System Sciences*.

Friedman, M. (1970) *The social responsibility of business is to increase its profits*. 32-33.

Garriga, E., Melé, D. (2004) Corporate social responsibility theories: mapping the territory. *Journal of Business Ethics* 53, 51-71.

Gehrke, D., Turban, E. (1999) Determinants of successful website design: relative importance and recommendations for effectiveness. *International Conference on System Sciences*, Hawaii.

Gersick, C. (1988) Time and transition in work teams: toward a new model of group development. *Academy of Management Journal* 31, 9-41.

GfK Roper (2007) *Green gauge*. online at http://www.gfkamerica.com/practice_areas/roper_consulting/roper_greengauge/index.en.html (last accessed 20/09/2009).

Gioia, D. A., Chittipeddi, K. (1991) Sensemaking and sensegiving in strategic change initiation. *Strategic Management Journal* 12 (6), 433-448.

Gladwell, M. (2000) *The tipping point: how little things can make a big difference*. Little, Brown: Boston.

Glaser, B., Strauss, A. (1967) *The discovery of grounded theory*. de Gruyter: New York.

Godet, M., Roubelat, F. (1996) Creating the future: the use and misuse of scenarios. *Long Range Planning* 29 (2), 164-171.

Gordijn, J. (2002) *Value-based requirements engineering - exploring ennovative e-commerce ideas*. Dissertation, Vrije Universiteit Amsterdam: Amsterdam.

Goulding, C. (2005) Grounded theory, ethnography and phenomenology. A comparative analysis of three qualitative strategies for marketing research. *European Journal of Marketing* 39 (3/4), 294-308.

Granka, L., A., Joachims, T., Gay, G. (2004) *Eye-tracking analysis of user behavior in www search*. ACM: Sheffield, United Kingdom.

Gronroos, C. (1984) A service quality model and its marketing implications. *European Journal of Marketing* 18 (4), 36-44.

Hackett, S., Parmanto, B. (2005) A longitudinal evaluation of accessibility: higher education web sites. *Internet Research* 15 (3), 281-294.

Hallowell, R. (1996) The relationships of customer satisfaction, customer loyalty, and profitability: an empirical study *International Journal of Service Industry Management* 7 (4), 27-42.

Hannan, M. T., Freeman, J. (1984) Structural inertia and organizational change. *American Sociological Review* 49 (2), 149-164.

Hanson, V. (2001) Making the web accessible for seniors. *ICTA - International Conference on Aging*, Toronto, Canada.

Harris, L. C., Goode, M. M. H. (2004) The four levels of loyalty and the pivotal role of trust: a study of online service dynamics. *Journal of Retailing* 80, 139-158.

Harris, S., Sutton, R. (1986) Functions of parting ceremonies in dying organizations. *Academy of Management Journal* 29, 5-30.

Hartjes, R. (2009) *Web Accessibility: Techniken und exemplarische Erfolgsmessung*. Peter Lang Verlag: Wien.

Hayes, A. F., Krippendorff, K. (2007) Answering the call for a standard reliability measure for coding data. *Communication Methods and Measures* 1 (1), 77-89.

Hedman, J., Kalling, T. (2003) The business model concept: theoretical underpinnings and empirical illustrations. *European Journal of Information Systems* 12 (1), 49-59.

Heerdt, V., Strauss, C. (2004) A cost-benefit approach for accessible web presence. *International Conference on Computers Helping People with Special Needs*, Springer.

Herzberg, F., Mausner, B., Snyderman, B. B. (1959) *The motivation to work*. John Wiley & Sons: New York.

Holcomb, J. L., Upchurch, R. S., Okumus, F. (2007) Corporate social responsibility: what are top hotel companies reporting? *International Journal of Contemporary Hospitality Management* 19 (6), 461-475.

Howe, J. (2008) *Crowdsourcing: how the power of the crowd is driving the future of business*. Random House Business Books: London.

Hübner, H. (2002) *Integratives Innovationsmanagement: Nachhaltigkeit als Herausforderung für ganzheitliche Erneuerungsprozesse*. Schmidt: Berlin.

International Standards Organization (1994) *Ergonomic requirements for office work with visual display terminals. Part 11: Guidance on usability (ISO DIS 9241-11)*. London.

ISO/IEC 17000 (2004) *Conformity assessment - vocabulary and general principles*.

ISO/IEC (2004) *Standardization and related activities -- General vocabulary (Guide 2:2004)*.

Iyer, R., Eastman, J. K. (2006) The elderly and their attitudes toward the internet: the impact on internet use, purchase and comparison shopping. *Journal of Marketing Theory and Practice* 14 (1), 57-67.

JD Power and Associates (2007) *European hotel guest satisfaction index study*.

Jenkins, H. (2006) Small business champions for corporate social responsibility. *Journal of Business Ethics* 67 (3), 241-256.

Johnson, A., Ruppert, S. (2002) An evaluation of accessibility in online learning management systems. *Library Hi Tech* 20 (4), 441-451.

Jones, R. A., Jimmieson, N. L., Griffiths, A. (2005) The Impact of organizational culture and reshaping capabilities on change implementation success: the mediating role of readiness for change. *Journal of Management Studies* 42 (2), 361-386.

Kalisch, A. (2002) *Corporate futures: social responsibility in the tourism industry*. Tourism Concern: London.

Karmasin.Motivforschung (2006) *Mediennutzung ohne Barrieren? (Media Usage without Barriers?)*, study conducted on behalf of MAIN_Mediennutzung Integrativ.

Keaveney, S., Parthasarathy, M. (2001) Customer switching behavior in online services: an exploratory study of the role of selected attitudinal, behavioral, and demographic factors *Journal of the Academy of Marketing Science* 29 (4), 374-390.

Keen, P. (1981) Information systems and organizational change. *Communications of the ACM* 24 (1), 24-33.

Kelley, H. (1955) Salience of membership and resistance to change of group-anchored attitudes. *Human Relations* 8, 275-289.

Kelly, B., Nevile, L., Draffan, E. A., Fanou, S. (2008) *One world, one web ... but great diversity*. ACM: Beijing, China.

Kelly, B., Sloan, D., Phipps, L., Petrie, H., Hamilton, F. (2005) Forcing standardization or accomodating diversity? A framework for applying the WCAG in the real world. *International Cross Disciplinary Workshop on Web Accessibility*, Chiba, Japan.

Kempson, E., Whyley, C., Caskey, J., Collard, S. (2000) *In or out? Financial exclusion: a literature and research review*. Financial Services Authority: London.

Knauth, B. (2006) *Tourism and the internet in the European Union*. Statistics in Focus, Eurostat.

Krippendorff, K. (2009) Testing the reliability of content analysis data: what is involved and why. In: Krippendorff, K., Bock, M. A. (Eds.) *The Content Analysis Reader*. Sage Publications: Thousand Oaks.

Kroloff, G. (1988) At home and abroad: weighing In. *Public Relations Journal* 44, 8.

Krüger, M. (2008) Accessible flash is no oxymoron: a case study in e-learning for blind and sighted users. *International Conference on Computers Helping People with Special Needs*, Linz, Springer.

Lakhani, K. R., Jeppesen, L. B., Lohse, P. A., Panetta, J. A. (2007) *The value of openness in scientific problem solving*. Harvard Business School Working Paper.

Leitner, M.-L., Hartjes, R., Strauss, C. (2009a) Web accessibility issues for the distributed and interworked enterprise portals. *International Workshop on Design, Optimization and Management of Heterogenous Networked Systems (DOM-HetNetS'09)*, Vienna.

Leitner, M.-L., Miesenberger, K., Ortner, D., Strauss, C. (2006) Web accessibility conformity assessment – implementation alternatives for a quality mark in Austria. *International Conference on Computers Helping People with Special Needs*, Linz, Austria, Springer.

Leitner, M.-L., Miesenberger, K., Strauss, C. (2009b) Web accessibility - Implementierungsstrategien für ein Gütesiegel. *HMD - Praxis der Wirtschaftsinformatik* 265, 71-79.

Leitner, M.-L., Strauss, C. (2008) Exploratory case study research on web accessibility. *International Conference on Computers Helping People with Special Needs*, Linz, Austria, Springer.

Linder, J. C., Cantrell, S. (2000) *Changing business models: surveying the landscape*. Accenture Institute for Strategic Change.

Lofland, J. (1971) *Analyzing social settings: a guide to qualitative observation and analysis*. Wadsworth: Belmont, CA.

Loiacono, E., McCoy, S. (2004) Web site accessibility: an online sector analysis. *Information Technology & People* 17 (1), 87.

Loiacono, E., Watson, R. T., Goodhue, D. L. (2002) WebQual™: a measure of web site quality. *Marketing Theory and Applications* 13, 432-439.

Magretta, J. (2002) Why business models matter. *Harvard Business Review* 80 (5), 86-93.

Maidique, Z. A., Zirger, B. J. (1984) A study of success and failure in product innovation: the case of the US electronics industry. *IEEE Transactions on Engineering Management* 31 (4), 192-203.

Mankoff, J., Dey, A., Moore, M., Batra, U. (2002) Web accessibility for low bandwidth input. *ACM SIGCAPH Conference on Assistive Technologies (ASSETS 2002)*, Edinburgh, Scotland.

Marcussen, C. H. (2008) Trends in European internet distribution of travel and tourism services. online at http://www.crt.dk/uk/staff/chm/trends.htm (last accessed 27/11/2009).

Markham, S. K., Aiman-Smith, L. (2001) Product champions: truths, myths and management. *Research Technology Management* 44 (3), 44.

Matausch, K., Hengstberger, B., Miesenberger, K. (2006) "Assistec" – a university course on assistive technologies *International Conference on Computers Helping People with Special Needs*, Linz, Austria, Springer.

Mazlow, A. H. (1943) A theory of human motivation. *Psychological Review* July, 370-396.

McWilliams, A., Siegel, D. (2000) Corporate social responsibility and financial performance: correlation or misspecification? *Strategic Management Journal* 21 (5), 603-609.

Meredith, J. (1998) Building operations management theory through case and field research. *Journal of Operations Management* 16 (4), 441-454.

Mietzner, D., Reger, G. (2005) Advantages and disadvantages of scenario approaches for strategic foresight. *International Journal of Technology Intelligence and Planning* 1 (2), 220-239.

Miles, M. B., Huberman, A. M. (2005) *Qualitative data analysis: an expanded sourcebook*. edition 2, Sage Publications: Thousand Oaks, California.

Mitchell, T. R. (1982) Motivation: new directions for theory, research, and practice. *The Academy of Management Review* 7 (1), 80-88.

Mizerski, R. W. (1982) An attribution explanation of the disproportionate influence of unfavorable information. *Journal of Consumer Research* 9, 301-310.

Moir, L. (2001) What do we mean by corporate social responsibility? *Corporate Governance: International Journal of Business in Society* 1, 16-22.

Morello, G. (1986) The image of Dutch banks. *International Journal of Bank Marketing* 6 (2), 38-47.

Murillo, D., Lozano, J. M. (2006) SMEs and CSR: an approach to CSR in their own words. *Journal of Business Ethics* 67 (3), 227-240.

NatKo (2002) *Nationale Koordinationsstelle Tourismus für Alle: Tourismus für alle*. Mainz.

Neumann, P., Reuber, P. (2004) *Economic impulses of accessible tourism for all*. Federal Ministry of Economics and Labour (BMWA): Berlin, Germany.

Nguyen, N., LeBlanc, G. (1998) The mediating role of corporate image on customers' retention decisions: an investigation in financial services. *International Journal of Bank Marketing* 16 (2), 52-65.

Nietzio, A., Strobbe, C., Vellemann, E. (2008) The unified web evaluation methodology (UWEM) 1.2 for WCAG 1.0. *International Conference on Computers Helping People with Special Needs*, Linz, Springer.

Nonaka, I. (1994) A dynamic theory of organizational knowledge creation. *Organization Science* 5 (1), 14-37.

O'Brien, F. A. (2004) Scenario planning - lessons for practice from teaching and learning. *European Journal of Operational Research* 152, 709-722.

O'Connor, P., Frew, A. J. (2004) An evaluation methodology for hotel electronic channels of distribution. *International Journal of Hospitality Management* 23 (2), 179-199.

O'Grady, L., Harrison, L. (2003) Web accessibility validation and repair: which tool and why? *Library Hi Tech* 21 (4), 463.

O'Reilly, T. (2006) *Web 2.0 compact definition: trying again*. online at http://radar.oreilly.com/archives/2006/12/web-20-compact.html (last accessed 03/06/2009).

OECD (2003) *Transforming disability to ability*. Organisation for Co-Operation and Development (OECD): Paris.

OECD (2005) *Guide to measuring the information society*. Paris.

OECD (2008) *Globalisation, SMEs and tourism development - case study: successful alliances for SMEs in the Austrian tourism sector*.

Olsina, L., Lafuente, G., Rossi, G. (2001) Specifying quality characteristics and attributes for websites. *Web Engineering*, Springer.

Ortner, D., Miesenberger, K. (2005) Improving web accessibility by providing higher education facilities for web designers and web developers following the design for all approach. *DEXA - Database and Expert Systems Applications*, Copenhagen, Denmark, IEEE Computer Society.

Osterwalder, A., Pigneur, Y., Tucci, C. (2005) Clarifying business models: origins, present, and future of the concept. *Communications of the Associations for Information Systems* 15.

Oumlil, A. B., Williams, A. J. (2000) Consumer education programs for mature consumers. *The Journal of Consumer Marketing* 14 (3), 232-243.

ÖWA (2008) *ÖWA Plus 2008-IV Studie*. Österreichische Webanalyse: Vienna.

Pateli, A., Giaglis, G. (2004) A research framework for analysing e-business models. *European Journal of Information Systems* 13, 302-314.

Perrini, F., Russo, A., Tencati, A. (2007) CSR Strategies of SMEs and Large Firms. Evidence from Italy. *Journal of Business Ethics* 74 (3), 285-300.

Petrie, H., Badani, A., Bhalla, A. (2005) Sex, lies and web accessibility: the use of accessibility logos and statements on e-commerce and financial websites. *Accessible Design in the Digital World Conference*.

Petrie, H., Hamilton, F., King, N., Pavan, P. (2006) Remote usability evaluations with disabled people. *SIGCHI conference on Human Factors in computing systems*, Montreal, Canada, ACM.

Petrie, H., Kheir, O. (2007) The relationship between accessibility and usability of websites. *Proceedings of the SIGCHI conference on Human factors in computing systems*, San Jose, California, USA, ACM.

Pettigrew, A. M. (1990) Longitudinal field research on change: theory and practice. *Organization Science* 1 (3), 267-292.

Petz, A., Tronbacke, B. (2008) People with specific learning difficulties: dasy to read and HCI - introduction to the special thematic session. *International Conference on Computers Helping People with Special Needs*, Linz, Austria, Springer.

Pinto, J. K., Slevin, D. P. (1988) Critical success factors across the product life cycle. *Project Management Journal* 19 (3), 67-75.

Porter, M. E. (1998) *On competition*. Harvard Business Review: Boston.

Pühretmair, F. (2004) It's time to make e-tourism accessible. *International Conference on Computers Helping People with Special Needs*, Paris, France, Springer.

Puhl, S. (2008) *Betriebswirtschaftliche Nutzenbewertung der Barrierefreiheit von Web-Präsenzen*. Shaker Verlag: Aachen, Germany.

Quinn, R. E., Rohrbaugh, J. (1983) A spatial model of effectiveness criteria: toward a competing values approach to organizational analysis. *Management Science* 20, 363-377.

Ratcliffe, J. (1999) Scenario building: a suitable method for strategic property planning. *The Cutting Edge 1999 - The Property Research Conference of the RICS St. John's College*, Camebridge.

Ray, N. M., Ryder, M. E. (2003) 'Ebilities' tourism: an exploratory discussion of the travel needs and motivations of the mobility-disabled. *Tourism Management* 24 (1), 57-72.

Raymond, J. (2000) Senior living: beyond the nursing home. *American Demographics* 22 (11), 58-63.

Reichheld, F. F. (1995) Loyalty and the renaissance of marketing. *Marketing Management* 2 (4), 10-21.

Reichheld, F. F., Schefter, P. (2000) E-loyalty: your secret weapon on the web. *Harvard Business Review* 78 (4), 105-113.

Reifner, U. (1997) New financial products for inclusive banking. In: Rossiter, J. (Eds.) *Financial Exclusion: Can Mutuality Fill the Gap?* New Policy Institute: London.

Reisenwitz, T., Iyer, R., Kuhlmeier, D. B., Eastman, J. K. (2007) The elderly's internet usage: an updated look. *The Journal of Consumer Marketing* 24 (7), 406-418.

Respact Austria (2005) *The Austrian economic sector's guiding vision for corporate social responsibility.*

Ribbink, D., van Riel, A. C. R., Liljander, V., Streukens, S. (2004) Comfort your online customer: quality, trust and loyalty on the internet. *Managing Service Quality* 14 (6), 446-456.

Richer, S. (1976) Reference-group theory and ability grouping: a convergence of sociological theory and educational research. *Sociology of Education* 49 (1), 65-71.

Richins, M. L., Bloch, P. H. (1986) After the new wears off: the temporal context of product involvement. *The Journal of Consumer Research* 13 (2), 280-285.

Rickards, T. (1985) *Stimulating innovation: a systems approach.* Pinter: London.

Riordan, C. M., Gatewood, R. D., Barnes Bill, J. (1997) Corporate image: employee reactions and implications for managing corporate social performance. *Journal of Business Ethics* 16 (4), 401-412.

RNIB (2009) *Web access centre, business benefits.* online at http://www.rnib.org.uk/xpedio/groups/public/documents/PublicWebsite/pu blic_businesscase.hcsp (last accessed 21/04/2009).

Rogers, E. M. (1995) *Diffusion of innovations.* edition 4, Free Press: New York.

Rogers, E. M. (2003) *Diffusion of innovations.* edition 5, Free Press: New York.

Rogers, E. M., Singhal, A., Quinlan, M. M. (1996) Diffusion of innovations. In: Stacks, D., Salwen, M. (Eds.) *An integrated approach to communication theory and research.* Lawrence Erlbaum Associates: Mahwah, New Jersey.

Rothwell, R. (1994) Towards the fifth-generation innovation process. *International Marketing Review* 11, 7-31.

Roure, L. (2001) Product champion characteristics in France and Germany. *Human Relations* 54 (5), 663.

Ryan, R. M., Deci, E., L. (2000) Self-determination theory and the facilitation of intrinsic motivation, social development, and well-being. *American Psychologist* 55 (1), 68-78.

Sarv, D., Ming, F., Rajiv, K. (2003) E-loyalty: elusive ideal or competitive edge? 46 (9), 184-191.

Schein, E. H. (1990) Organizational culture. *American Psychologist* 45, 109-119.

Schmetzke, A. (2001) Web accessibility at university libraries and library schools. *Library Hi Tech* 19 (1), 35-49.

Schmid, K.-H. (1995) *Planung von Unternehmenskultur*. Dt.-Univ. Verlag: Wiesbaden.

Schmitt, R. (1972) *The reference other orientation*. Southern Illinois University Press: Carbondale and Edwardsville.

Schneider, B., Brief, A. P., Guzzo, R. A. (1996) Creating a climate and culture for sustainable organizational change. *Organizational Dynamics* 24 (4), 7-19.

Schon, D. A. (1963) Champions for radical new inventions. *Harvard Business Review* 41 (2), 77-86.

Schon, D. A. (1967) *Technology and change*. Dell Publishing: New York.

Scott, W. A. (1955) Reliability of content analysis: the case of nominal scale coding. *Public Opinion Quarterly* 10, 321-325.

Section508 (1998) *Section 508 of the Rehabilitation Act Section 508 of the Rehabilitation Act, 29 U.S.C. § 794d.*

Sethi, S. P. (1979) Institutional/image advertising and idea/issue advertising as marketing tools: some public policy issues. *The Journal of Marketing* 43 (1), 68-78.

Shneiderman, B. (2003) *Promoting universal usability with multi-layer interface design*. ACM Press: New York.

Sierkowski, B. (2002) *Achieving web accessibility*. ACM Press: Providence, Rhode Island, USA.

Sirdeshmukh, D., Singh, J., Sabol, B. (2002) Customer trust, value, and loyalty in relational exchanges. *Journal of Marketing* 66 (January), 15-37.

Snaprud, M., Sawicka, A. (2007) *Large scale web accessibility evaluation - a European perspective*.

Spector, A. J. (1961) Basic dimensions of corporate image. *Journal of Marketing* 25, 47-51.

Srinivasan, S. S., Anderson, R., Ponnavolu, K. (2002) Customer loyalty in e-commerce: an exploration of its antecedents and consequences. *Journal of Retailing* 78 (1), 41-50.

Srnka, K. J., Koeszegi, S. T. (2007) From words to numbers: how to transform qualitative data into meaningful quantitative results. *Schmalenbach Business Review : ZFBF* 59, 29.

Stake, R. (1995) *The art of case study research*. Sage Publications: Thousand Oaks, California.

Statistik Austria (2008) *Bevölkerungsprognosen*. online at http://www.statistik.at/web_de/statistiken/bevoelkerung/demographische_prognosen/bevoelkerungsprognosen/index.html (last accessed 26/04/2009).

Stummer, C., Günther, M., Köck, A. M. (2008) *Grundzüge des Innovations- und Technologiemanagements*. edition 2, Facultas AG: Vienna.

Suh, B., Han, I. (2002) Effect of trust on customer acceptance of internet banking. *Electronic Commerce Research and Applications* 1, 247-263.

Sullivan, T., Matson, R. (2000) *Barriers to use: usability and content accessibility on the Web's most popular sites*. ACM: Arlington, Virginia, United States.

Support-EAM (2005) *D 3.1: State-of-the-art of certification scheme in Europe.*

Support-EAM (2006) *Web accessibility evaluation curriculum*. online at http://www.support-eam.org/waec/en/index.html (last accessed 28/04/2009).

Support EAM (2006) *Fact sheet*. online at http://www.support-eam.org/supporteam/About_Supporteam/fact_sheet.asp (last accessed 26/04/2009).

Surowiecki, J. (2004) *The wisdom of crowds: why the many are smarter than the few and how collective wisdom shapes business, economies, societies and nations*. Anchor Books.

Thatcher, J., Waddell, C. D., Henry, S. L., Swierenga, S., Urban, M. D., Burks, M., Regan, B., Bohman, P. (2003) *Constructing accessible websites*. glasshaus: San Francisco.

Thompson, C. J. (1997) Interpreting consumers: a hermeneutical framework for deriving marketing insights from the texts of consumers' consumption stories. *Journal of Marketing Research* 34 (4), 438-455.

Thompson, C. J., Rindfleisch, A., Arsel, Z. (2006) Emotional branding and the strategic value of the doppelgänger brand image. *Journal of Marketing Research* 70, 50-64.

Timmers, P. (1998) Business models for electronic markets. *Electronic Markets* 8 (2), 3-8.

Trader-Leigh, K. E. (2002) Case study: identifying resistance in managing change. *Journal of Organizational Change Management* 15, 138-155.

Trocchia, P. J., Janda, S. (2000) A phenomenological investigation of internet usage among older individuals. *Journal of Consumer Marketing* 17 (7), 605-616.

U.S. Census Bureau (2001) *NAICS Sector: 51 Information* online at http://www.census.gov/epcd/ec97/def/51.HTM (last accessed 27/11/2009).

UNWTO (2007) *UN world tourism organization: tourism highlights 2007.*

Verband österreichischer Zeitungen (2008) *Abo und Einzelverkauf Tageszeitungen*. online at http://www.voez.at/b775 (last accessed 10/10/2009).

VID (2006) *Vienna institute of demography: data sheet 2006.*

Vigo, M., Aizpurua, A., Arrue, M., Abascal, J. (2008) *Evaluating web accessibility for specific mobile devices*. ACM: Beijing, China.

Vitaliano, D., Siegel, D. (2007) An empirical analysis of the strategic use of corporate social responsibility. *Journal of Economics & Management Strategy* 16 (3), 773-792.

Von Hippel, E. (1986) Lead users. A source of novel product concepts. *Management Science* 32, 791-805.

Von Hippel, E. (2005) *Democratizing innovation.* MIT Press: Boston, Mass./London.

Vos, S., Ambrose, I. (2007) *Services and facilities for accessible tourism in Europe.* European Network for Accessible Tourism.

W3C (1999) *Web content accessibility guidelines 1.0*. online at http://www.w3.org/TR/WCAG10/ (last accessed 12/02/2008).

W3C (2002) *Web accessibility implementation plan*. online at http://www.w3.org/WAI/impl/ (last accessed 20/10/2009).

W3C (2005a) *How people with disabilities use the web*. online at http://www.w3.org/WAI/EO/Drafts/PWD-Use-Web/#diff (last accessed 11/02/2009).

W3C (2005b) *Introduction to web accessibility*. online at http://www.w3.org/WAI/intro/accessibility.php (last accessed 12/02/2009).

W3C (2008a) *Preliminary review of web sites for accessibility*. online at http://www.w3.org/WAI/eval/preliminary.html (last accessed 10/02/2009).

W3C (2008b) *Web content accessibility and mobile web*. online at http://www.w3.org/WAI/mobile/ (last accessed 12/02/2009).

W3C (2008c) *Web content accessibility guidelines 2.0*. online at http://www.w3.org/TR/WCAG20/ (last accessed 20/02/2009).

W3C (2009a) *Developing a web accessibility business case for your organization*. World Wide Web Consortium (MIT, ERCIM, Keio), online at http://www.w3.org/WAI/bcase/ (last accessed 06/09/2009).

W3C (2009b) *Mobile web initiative.* online at http://www.w3.org/Mobile/About (last accessed 27/11/2009).

WAB Cluster (2008) *The EU web accessibility benchmarking cluster*. online at http://www.wabcluster.org/ (last accessed 01/05/2009).

Waddock, S. A., Graves, S. B. (1997) The Corporate Social Performance - Financial Performance Link. *Strategic Management Journal* 18 (4), 303-319.

Wargin, J., Dobiey, D. (2001) E-business and change – managing the change in the digital economy. *Journal of Change Management* 2 (1), 72-82.

Wartick, S., Cochran, P. (1985) The evolution of the corporate social performance model. *The Academy of Management Review* 4.

Webb, H., Webb, L. (2004) SiteQual: an integrated measure of web site quality. *The Journal of Enterprise Information Management* 17 (6), 430-440.

Webster, F. E., Jr. (1975) Determining the characteristics of the socially conscious consumer. *The Journal of Consumer Research* 2 (3), 188-196.

Weill, P., Vitale, M. (2001) *Place to space: migrating to e-business models.* Harvard Business School Press: Boston.

Werner, C. (2008) *Studie der Web Zugänglichkeit.* Vienna University of Technology: Vienna.

WHO (2001) *World health organisation, international classification of functioning, disability, and health.*

Williams, R., Rattray, R. (2003) An assessment of web accessibility of UK accountancy firms. *Managerial Auditing Journal* 18 (9), 710-716.

Williams, R., Rattray, R., Grimes, A. (2007) Online accessibility and information needs of disabled tourists: a three country hotel sector analysis *Journal of Electronic Commerce Research* 8 (2), 157-171.

Williams, R., Rattray, R., Stork, A. (2004) Web site accessibility of German and UK tourism information sites. *European Business Review* 16 (6), 577-589.

Wilson, I. (1999) Mental maps of the future. *The Cutting Edge 1999 - The Property Research Conference of the RICS*, Cambridge.

World Internet Usage Statistics (2008) *World internet usage and population statistics.* online at http://www.internetworldstats.com/stats.htm (last accessed 20/02/2009).

Wright, G., Cairns, G., Goodwin, P. (2009) Teaching scenario planning: lessons from practice in academe and business. *European Journal of Operational Research* 194, 323-335.

Yin, R. (2003) *Case study research - design and methods.* edition 3, Sage Publications: Thousand Oaks, California.

Yu, L. (2007) Measuring the culture of innovation. *MIT Sloan Management Review* 48 (4), 7.

Zaltman, G., Duncan, R., Holbek, J. (1973) *Innovations and organizations.* John Wiley & Sons Inc.: New York.

9 List of Tables

Table 1:	Research gaps and corresponding research contributions	15
Table 2:	Relationship between accessibility and usability	24
Table 3:	Core Techniques of WCAG 1.0	28
Table 4:	Overview of web accessibility in European Union countries	32
Table 5:	Process of building theory from case study research	43
Table 6:	Data matrix	48
Table 7:	Interview sample	52
Table 8:	Web site evaluation results in the tourism sector	61
Table 9:	Overview of results in the tourism sector	72
Table 10:	Web site evaluation results in the financial services sector	75
Table 11:	Overview of results in the financial services sector	96
Table 12:	Online media in Austria	98
Table 13:	Web site evaluation results in the information sector	100
Table 14:	Overview of results in the information sector	110
Table 15:	Reasons for web accessibility implementation	113
Table 16:	Key personality characteristics	117
Table 17:	Changes after implementation	119
Table 18:	Reasons for lack of implementation	124
Table 19:	Incentives for implementation	126
Table 20:	Web accessibility evaluation results	140
Table 21:	Overview of existing quality marks in Europe	151
Table 22:	Analysis of 10 web accessibility quality marks	160
Table 23:	Harmonized label	162
Table 24:	Scenario evaluation	172

10 List of Figures

Figure 1:	Web accessibility – the big picture	12
Figure 2:	Research design	16
Figure 3:	Research approach	18
Figure 4:	Roadmap	20
Figure 5:	Business aspects of web accessibility	37
Figure 6:	Population forecast for Austria	38
Figure 7:	Income differences	38
Figure 8:	Case study design	44
Figure 9:	Embedded, multiple case study design	46
Figure 10:	Conceptual framework for case study research	47
Figure 11:	Evaluation method	49
Figure 12:	Krippendorff alpha results	54
Figure 13:	Overview of the banking sector in Austria	74
Figure 14:	Economic changes after web accessibility implementation	120
Figure 15:	Social changes after web accessibility implementation	121
Figure 16:	Technical changes after web accessibility implementation	122
Figure 17:	Perceived changes of web accessibility implementation	123
Figure 18:	Web accessibility implementation process (WAIP) model	127
Figure 19:	Web accessibility implementation alternatives	130
Figure 20:	The innovation process in organizations	137
Figure 21:	Innovation process model vs. WAIP model	138
Figure 22:	Adopter categorization	141
Figure 23:	Conformity assessment overview	149
Figure 24:	Principle of third party certification	150
Figure 25:	Conformity assessment scheme	153
Figure 26:	Evolution of the business model concept	157
Figure 27:	Business model components	157
Figure 28:	Value drivers of e-commerce business models	158
Figure 29:	Business model structure	164
Figure 30:	Web site conformity assessment flow chart	165
Figure 31:	Overview of implementation alternatives	166
Figure 32:	Scenario evaluation with Kiviat diagrams	173
Figure 33:	Person certification flow chart	177

11 Appendix

A – Interview Guideline

Part 1: Company data
- Short description of own position in organization
- Description of organization (size, staff, turnover, industry, products, services)
- Role of CSR in organization

Part 2: Web site characteristics
- Description of web site (number of pages, technologies, maintenance, update, relaunch)
- Purpose of web site (sale, information retrieval)

Part 3: Reasons for (failure of) implementation of web accessibility
- Why did you implement accessible web? / Why did you fail in implementing accessible web?
- Experiences with web accessibility implementation (advantages, problems)
- Prerequisites for web accessibility implementation
- Cost factors
- Legal factors
- Social factors

Part 4: Experiences after implementation
- Changes after implementation (web site, customers, image, usability)
- Experiences with implementation process
- Business impacts of accessible web
- Measurement of accessibility
- Promotion measures
- Incentives for web accessibility implementation

Part 5: Future development
- Future development of web accessibility
- Expectations of organizations

B – Code lists

Sector	Code	Categorization	Quote
F	consumer consciousness	reason for implementation	The conscious consumer is a crucial factor for the disposal of products and services.
F	consumer consciousness	reason for implementation	Ethical criteria are being more and more included in the purchase decision process.
T	consumer consciousness	reason for implementation	Consumers become more and more conscious. This is an important aspect for the sale of products and services.
F	corporate image	reason for implementation	We want to be a decent bank; we roll up our sleeves and make an effort to do things properly.
F	corporate image	reason for implementation	For us, it was a mix of social commitment and PR considerations.
F	corporate image	reason for implementation	You can get indirect returns in terms of image.
T	design for all	reason for implementation	Elderly people appreciate if they do not have to climb steps - the same holds for websites.
F	design for all	reason for implementation	Interestingly, we learned that our new website catches on all our customers - not just the ones with disabilities.
F	design for all	reason for implementation	Our main reason was 'simple and for all'; the simpler the better and the more customers will understand and buy the product.
I	design for all	reason for implementation	The convertibility of font sizes represents a benefit for everybody, not just for people with sight disabilities.
F	differentiation	reason for implementation	We wanted to be different from other banks.
F	differentiation	reason for implementation	We tried to be the first to implement accessibility in order to be different from our competitors.
F	elderly customers	reason for implementation	Our website is being used by elderly people above-average; the fact that we have a lot of elderly customers has given a major reason for the initiation of the web accessibility project.
F	elderly customers	reason for implementation	If you look at the demographic shift in the next ten years, accessibility will be an issue.
F	elderly customers	reason for implementation	The wealthy customers are the elderly, they have the money.
F	elderly customers	reason for implementation	50% of our customers are older than 40. 71% of them receive newsletters.
F	elderly customers	reason for implementation	A majority of our customers are older than 40 years. These are people who have not grown up with a computer.
F	elderly customers	reason for implementation	We have argumented with the 50plus aspect. This customer group can use the accessible website more easily because they have the possibility to increase font size.
I	elderly customers	reason for implementation	We have realised a platform for a senior community where accessibility was a big issue.
F	fear of negative image	reason for implementation	We cannot afford negative headlines.
T	importance of website	reason for implementation	every new guest will see our web page first, judge it and then decide if he wants to come or not.
T	key personality	reason for implementation	My brother has a severe sight disability. He has to use magnification software when he uses the computer. He told me take care for the magnification aspect when designing a new site.
T	key personality	reason for implementation	My friend is an expert, he told me to make the site accessible.
T	key personality	reason for implementation	I have been at a lecture given by a sight disabled person. This has impressed me a lot.
F	key personality	reason for implementation	My grandmother uses a wheel chair. I know how inaccessible the town is. This all is a matter of awareness.

Sector	Code	Categorization	Quote
F	key personality	reason for implementation	A colleague from the technical department has a girlfriend with a hearing impairment. He had the first suggestions about this issue.
F	key personality	reason for implementation	We have worked in cooperation with the institute of the blind; a former colleague works now with them.
I	key personality	reason for implementation	According to my opinion, you can pique web developers' interest in accessibility. Sometimes they then implement it proactively without the management forcing it.
F	key personality	reason for implementation	"I initiated the project because the bank's website was not accessible with my screenreader".
I	key personality	reason for implementation	The project manager took over the initiative for web accessibility implementation.
I	key personality	reason for implementation	We have worked together with disability associations in the development process.
I	key personality	reason for implementation	The discussion about W3I standards, HTML standards and usability issues has led to our interest in accessibility and the involvement with the institute of the blind.
T	lack of awareness	reason for implementation	If you conduct a survey about web accessibility in Austrian hotels, I am sure you would not get any reasonable answers because they simply do not know what it means.
I	meaningfulness of own work	reason for implementation	For me, it has always been important to bring in social and user-centered aspects in my technical work. Technical work should comply with ethical standards.
T	social commitment	reason for implementation	Sustainability and climate protection are parts of our organizational philosophy.
F	social commitment	reason for implementation	This is a decent bank that takes care for societal matters.
F	social commitment	reason for implementation	The corporate culture has to be present; otherwise, such a project will fail.
F	social commitment	reason for implementation	We have a strong social awareness in the bank that is grounded in former environmental and ecological measures.
F	social commitment	reason for implementation	Our organization has always had a culture of awareness.
I	social commitment	reason for implementation	Small organizations like us do not think in CSR terms.
I	social commitment	reason for implementation	In my opinion, CSR is not an important driving force for web accessibility because, as a layperson, you would not notice the difference between an accessible and an inaccessible site. However, somebody complaining about an inaccessible web site of an organization may represent a huge problem from CSR point of view.
F	social commitment	reason for implementation	In our organization, the attitude is different. Web accessibility is regarded as something positive.
F	social commitment	reason for implementation	We have always had awareness for social issues. In this case, implementation of web accessibility is easier, when the awareness already exists.
F	social commitment	reason for implementation	When I joined this organization in 1989, social awareness already existed. I have grown in this culture and I experience it everyday.
F	social commitment	reason for implementation	CSR has a high significance in our company.
F	top management support	reason for implementation	You need somebody from top management in order to succeed with this issue.
F	top management support	reason for implementation	I can completely understand you. My wife uses a wheelchair.

Sector	Code	Categorization	Quote
F	top management support	reason for implementation	We had the advantage that one member of the management board was 150% web affine; this made it easier to convince him.
T	website quality	reason for implementation	We stumbled across it only because our old site was bad and poorly coded.
I	website quality	reason for implementation	Nobody was satisfied with the old website. It did not look good, did not work satisfyingly and did not have enough traffic.
I	website quality	reason for implementation	With our old website we finally reached our limits which is why we decided to start from scratch.
I	website quality	reason for implementation	We wanted a top-quality website that conforms to standards, is usable and accessible.
I	website quality	reason for implementation	User change the website if it is better usable than another one.
I	website quality	reason for implementation	We wanted a top-quality website that conforms to standards, is usable and accessible.
I	website quality	reason for implementation	Our customers want a neatly coded and high quality website that is usable and accessible and complies to actual standards.

Sector	Code	Category	Quote
I	competitive advantage	changes after implementation	With our accessible website we have definitely gained advantage in the market.
T	cost efficiency	changes after implementation	The website is much more cost efficient as we do not have to recode it so often. Therefore, the investment is a long term one.
T	cost efficiency	changes after implementation	No, it does not cost more. Costs have never been an issue.
I	cost efficiency	changes after implementation	If you want to change an existing site to an accessible one, this means high operating expense.
I	cost efficiency	changes after implementation	I cannot number the additional costs. I admit that some issues are more complicated to implement but maintenance facilitations cause a fast amortization of these costs.
I	cost efficiency	changes after implementation	If you code negligently you may perhaps save 3 % of the website costs.
I	cost efficiency	changes after implementation	Changing an existing site to an accessible one is like changing a motorbus to a Porsche.
I	cost efficiency	changes after implementation	We now have lower expenses concerning browser optimization.
I	cost efficiency	changes after implementation	The optimization for mobile portals is much less expensive with accessible sites.
I	cost efficiency	changes after implementation	Of course, some things are more complicated in the beginning. If you bear in mind that internet pages and content change constantly. Even if the user does not realize. Therefore, the expenses will be covered within a short timeframe because daily adaptations may drop out.
T	cost efficiency	changes after implementation	The ease in maintenance is a reason why we save costs.
F	customer feedback	changes after implementation	I receive many requests from people who have some kind of sight disability and are dependent on special software. Or from people who suffer from multiple sclerosis that may also cause sight disabilities. The whole problematic begins to move. People begin to talk about it. It has to be considered as something normal, something self-evident.
F	customer feedback	changes after implementation	After the relaunch we have received a lot of reactions, 90% positive ones.
F	customer feedback	changes after implementation	Customers can mail accessibility issues. Additionally, our sales force is trained and informed about accessibility. Also our call center staff. The whole bank is informed.

Sector	Code	Category	Quote
F	customer feedback	changes after implementation	I have not received direct feedback except from people with disabilities who have reported positive improvement.
I	customer feedback	changes after implementation	I have not received user feedback from blind or sight disabled people.
T	customer feedback	changes after implementation	We have had exclusively positive feedback.
F	customer feedback	changes after implementation	The frames are still a problem still critisised by our customers. We are aware of that. There is little direct feed back concerning the website.
F	customer loyalty	changes after implementation	Before the implementation of accessibility, 75% of the customers who wanted to open an account stayed with our bank, after the implementation this number increased to 95%.
F	design for all	changes after implementation	Everybody now profits from the new site, they have a faster site, can choose from where to read it.
F	image	changes after implementation	These days where banks are associated with negative things, it is very important to show that we are doing positive things.
F	image	changes after implementation	This is a decent bank. I will rather go there and not to one that treats people badly.
F	image	changes after implementation	The positive image, our banking institution has reached, is a major change after implementation. If you google us, you will find many positive media articles. This is very important, as banks are always presented in a negative light. It is important to show "we are doing positive things"
F	image	changes after implementation	In a long term view, decent organizations will be perceived in a better light than others. The product line of banking institutions is similar, so the differentiation takes place in the company attitudes and image.
I	increase in awareness	changes after implementation	For those who were not familiar with the issue, it has activated a thinking process.
F	increase in awareness	changes after implementation	We have organized the Disability Awareness day where we have worked with our 6000 employees.
F	increase in awareness	changes after implementation	We organize presentations and activities. We have planned to invite somebody from top management to take a wheelchair and try to do his work for one day.
F	increase in awareness	changes after implementation	We have communicated web accessibility in our internal newsletter as this word has not been part of our vocabulary before.
F	increase in awareness	changes after implementation	I realized for the first time when 1 organized presentations that most of the people did not know what web accessibility was.
F	increase in awareness	changes after implementation	It is important to raise awareness for web accessibility; to create awareness that it entails simplicity.
F	increase in awareness	changes after implementation	I receive many requests from people who have some kind of sight disability and are dependent on special software. Or from people who suffer from multiple sclerosis that may also cause sight disabilities. The whole problematic begins to move. People begin to talk about it. It has to be considered as something normal, something self-evident.
F	increase in awareness	changes after implementation	There was an event for pupils from the whole country in order to present current IT news. Our company was there as well in order to inform about accessibility. We have demonstrated how a sight disabled person performs online banking. We have also built up a cash mashine with speech output. This way we have tried to publish our efforts. I am sure that other organizations will also implement accessibility some time.
F	increase in awareness	changes after implementation	Our project has provoked great interest. We have also received an award. A big media echo was the consequence. We have included the disability interest groups from the beginning.
F	in-house knowledge exchange	changes after implementation	We have established the Disability Interest Forum where persons concerned and other interested people can meet and exchange information and experience.
F	in-house knowledge exchange	changes after implementation	There is the possibility to invite disability organizations in order to inform our employees.

213

Sector	Code	Category	Quote
F	in-house knowledge exchange	changes after implementation	I have made the experience that commited employees who work with the internet but come from different departments now talk about web accessibility. A knowledge exchange is happening.
F	integration	changes after implementation	With our accessibility initiative, we contribute to the integration of people with disabilities.
F	integration	changes after implementation	A sudden sensitization has occurred for employees with disabilities. [...] They have been given motivation and self-confidence.
F	integration	changes after implementation	People with disabilities have found an attentive ear, they could place their concerns.
I	learning process	changes after implementation	We are in a constant learning process as regards web accessibility.
F	long-term investment	changes after implementation	Accessibility is not something where I can say, I have invested the amount of x today and have saved the amount of y tomorrow.
F	long-term investment	changes after implementation	I think that the money invested (in accessibility) will draw long term profit.
F	maintenance	changes after implementation	Maintenance has become much easier. We can train new employees much faster because every webpage has the same structure now.
F	maintenance	changes after implementation	The website editors do not understand why some fields are now obligatory. [...] This is difficult to check because we have about 50 editors in our organization and we cannot check on every alt attribute inserted.
I	maintenance	changes after implementation	Changes and maintenance of our site have become considerably easier.
I	maintenance	changes after implementation	With accessible sites I can rename my navigation menu without having to phone a designer.
F	maintenance	changes after implementation	The release of a new browser used to provoke a crisis because we had to recode almost all the web sites. This is no longer the case.
F	maintenance	changes after implementation	If you are accessible you save a high amount of costs concerning the optimization for portable devices.
I	maintenance	changes after implementation	A first look on IE 8 shows that we will not have to do a lot to comply.
I	maintenance	changes after implementation	We did not have to adapt one single site for the new browser so far.
I	maintenance	changes after implementation	We now have lower expenses concerning browser optimization.
I	maintenance	changes after implementation	The optimization for mobile portals is much less expensive with accessible sites.
F	maintenance	changes after implementation	Maintenance has been outsourced. An external agency takes care for this now.
T	maintenance	changes after implementation	We have the site for the 3rd year now and it is unbelievably maintenance neutral. New content can be easily inserted and the site is still well received.
I	maintenance	changes after implementation	Maintenance has become considerably easier. We still notice the difference.
F	quality assurance	changes after implementation	Customers can mail accessibility issues. Additionally, our sales force is trained and informed about accessibility. Also our call center staff. The whole bank is informed.
F	quality assurance	changes after implementation	We have decided to measure customer satisfaction in half a year. From next week on, every 100th visitor will be questioned to our new website.
T	search engine ranking	changes after implementation	To us, a high search engine ranking is very important.

Sector	Code	Category	Quote
F	search engine ranking	changes after implementation	*I have read about better search engine ranking through accessibility, but in practice, it does not seem to work.*
F	search engine ranking	changes after implementation	*Google ranked us on top.*
F	search engine ranking	changes after implementation	*Our website is found more easily by search engines now because of the higher amount of keywords in the code.*
I	search engine ranking	changes after implementation	*You cannot be as clumsy as to not attain a better search engine ranking with accessible sites.*
I	search engine ranking	changes after implementation	*The most influential blind user is still Google.*
I	search engine ranking	changes after implementation	*It is difficult to measure if an increase in search engine ranking is caused by accessibility exclusively. The same holds for website traffic. But a semantically and structurally well defined website will contribute to a higher ranking.*
T	simplicity/usability	changes after implementation	*The website has become more intuitive.*
F	simplicity/usability	changes after implementation	*We used to have disputations within the organizations because some people wanted their text to be positioned above right, others below left and others again in bigger letters, etc. These conversations do not exist anymore as the structure is now predetermined. This also means an economy of time.*
F	simplicity/usability	changes after implementation	*It is not more difficult to create an accessible website when you know what to pay attention to.*
F	simplicity/usability	changes after implementation	*It would have been more complicated if I had staff to train.*
F	simplicity/usability	changes after implementation	*The description of an image represents one work step more than before. That has to be worth it.*
F	simplicity/usability	changes after implementation	*Accessibility has increased the usability of our site. The search engines find it more easily because of the increase in keywords. In this respect, we have had a double benefit.*
I	website quality	changes after implementation	*It is not comparable to the old version.*
I	website quality	changes after implementation	*The sequence in the code now complies with the journalistic weight of the article. The further up, the more important.*
I	website quality	changes after implementation	*It has shown that accessibility entails better structure of websites.*
F	website quality	changes after implementation	*Our site is still very fast in download.*
I	website traffic	changes after implementation	*Our accessible site has become a traffic driver. 94% of our website visits come from search engines.*
I	website traffic	changes after implementation	*We have experienced economic advantages since the website is technically better found.*
I	website traffic	changes after implementation	*Accessibility entails that the site is better found by search engines. This has been a trigger for increased website traffic and has entailed economic advantages.*
I	website traffic	changes after implementation	*Traffic has encreased enormously, the server react faster.*
F	website traffic	changes after implementation	*The website coding is not subject to trends anymore. It is long lasting.*

Sector	Code	Category	Quote
F	corporate design requirements	reasons for lack of implementation	*The headquarters issued requirements on how a web presence had to look like that were contrary to our accessible website proposal. It was completely impossible for us to succeed.*
F	corporate design requirements	reasons for lack of implementation	*We had to compromise with the corporate design department as regards several design elements.*
I	corporate design requirements	reasons for lack of implementation	*It would be necessary that organizations adapt their corporate design guidelines to accessibility standards. But unfortunately, they do not do that.*
F	corporate design requirements	reasons for lack of implementation	*We had a tough discussion and then we lost. The project failed because of the page width that needs to be fixed and not dynamic.*
F	corporate design requirements	reasons for lack of implementation	*Perhaps it was our mistake. We have chosen a design that did not catch on.*
F	differences in accessible layout	reasons for lack of implementation	*In my opinion, accessible websites do not look 'up-to-date'". It is a matter of taste.*
F	differences in accessible layout	reasons for lack of implementation	*If we had implemented accessibility, our website would be worse compared to our competitors' sites.*
F	differences in accessible layout	reasons for lack of implementation	*From a design perspective, you do not have as many possibilities as with non-accessible sites.*
F	lack of arguments	reasons for lack of implementation	*If I had had a plan on how to present the subject to decision makers, I would not have been turned down so easily.*
F	lack of arguments	reasons for lack of implementation	*I have only pointed out the social argument which was the reason why it has not been considered further.*
F	lack of arguments	reasons for lack of implementation	*I did not succeed in presenting the subject in a way the others could follow.*
F	lack of arguments	reasons for lack of implementation	*If I had more arguments at hand, I would have succeeded. Normally, that is what convinces the marketing department.*
I	lack of awareness	reasons for lack of implementation	*The basic understanding of accessibility is not available.*
F	lack of top management support	reasons for lack of implementation	*We had numbers, statistics, arguments but it was of no use. It was completely illegitimate.*
F	lack of top management support	reasons for lack of implementation	*The marketing department turned my effort down with the words: "We do not have many sight-disabled customers. As long as this is not stated in the law, we do not implement it.*
F	misconceptions	reasons for lack of implementation	*Blind People don't buy cars.*
F	misconceptions	reasons for lack of implementation	*We do not have blind customers. This would not be profitable.*
F	misconceptions	reasons for lack of implementation	*We do not have that many sight disabled customers.*
F	misconceptions	reasons for lack of implementation	*Accessible websites are ugly.*
F	misconceptions	reasons for lack of implementation	*We do not need such things.*
F	misconceptions	reasons for lack of implementation	*Blind people cannot afford cars.*

Sector	Code	Category	Quote
F	competition	incentives for implementation	If 90% of organizations in our sector had implemented web accessibility and we had not, it would be an absolute must for us.
T	government aid	incentives for implementation	Money – in which form ever – is a big incentive but it is not the solution. The basic attitude cannot be changed by financial incentives.
F	government aid	incentives for implementation	I think government incentives are an issue.
I	internal drivers	incentives for implementation	The ORF has such a dominating position in radio, TV, and internet but I still do not think the market will regulate web accessibility implementation on its own. The initiation has to come from internal driving forces.
F	law	incentives for implementation	Law is the top incentive.
F	law	incentives for implementation	law as an incentive is always bad. Something that is regulated by law will always result in compromises.
I	law	incentives for implementation	Legal incentives and public sponsorship shall provoke a more charitable thinking of organizations.
I	law	incentives for implementation	I think a law in this area makes more sense than market related measures.

Sector	Code	Category	Quote
T	accessibility project initiation _physical accessibility marking	procedure	In our organization, we have implemented accessibility features, even though not many employees know that. We need to demonstrate the accessibility efforts on our website. We took pictures, we borrowed a wheelchair. We took pictures of the seminar rooms and I assured myself that we do have accessible facilities since we cannot claim our accessible status otherwise. Eleven seminar rooms are accessible by elevators except for one room, that is accessible by stairways. Raked floors and elevators are provided throughout the building. Thus, we decided to make it public. Since it is of no advantage to anybody if nobody knows. That's how we got the idea.
F	accessibility implementation	procedure	We've got a wiki-page where the editors may download all the necessary files, such as the published guidelines.
F	accessibility implementation	procedure	This was the company's multiple stage process. At first, we had an analysis made by a firm, which belongs to XY association, to find out what is not in line with the accessibility guidelines. We received a competence system from XY and support by the company's subsidiary, which also implemented the system. That means, that following questions have been worked out: "What are we doing?", "What are we capable of doing?". "What stages are necessary?. We charged the subsidiary with the adjustment, which took six months. Our employees developed titles, keywords and abstracts. Afterwards, we had the audit report made by the training project-team and everything was completed after a last adjustment. All in all, the whole process took half a year for its completion. We had to finance it from resources of our budgets, since the IT-department couldn't give us any financial support. However, it wasn't too expensive, so that we could finance it without big troubles.
F	accessibility implementation	procedure	Yes, this may even be due to the fact, that we had to provide a precise business plan. When we relaunched a product during the Easy One Project last year, we discovered an increase in sales due to the clear and simple definitions of our business plan. Our plan worked out even and we can proof it now.

Sector	Code	Category	Quote
F	accessibility implementation _screenreader tests	procedure	At that time we acquired the former homepage-reader, which helped me to read it by showing the access topology.
F	accessibility implementation	procedure	We developed guidelines for accessible websites, which became the company standard in particular for open-access content. There are a thousand of pdf files, which have to be adjusted to web accessibility but this is a very difficult task since the pdf files have been produced differently. Either on a server or within a word document or with the help of many other programmes. Therefore, we made a selection of most important documents, which are not older than three years, to be adjusted. In future, all documents, will be generated according to the web accessibility.
F	accessibility implementation	procedure	That's not the problem but the learning process. You need to repeat it ten times in order not to forget it.
F	accessibility implementation	procedure	The other thing is that one organizes trainings - especially in the IT Accessibility Training sector - this we did at the academy in Winterthur and organized a course "Accessible Webdesign". Accessibility then is - as already mentioned, we wrote guidelines and the people should stick to it - mandatory. In this way we can guarantee that accessibility doesn't get lost from today to tomorrow. I am in some sense an accessibility motor, in order to assure this. But I think that through certification we had a good mechanism in order to control it. Like Branding Guidelines we also just have Accessibility Guidelines and to we can guarantee that it remains like that.
F	accessibility implementation	procedure	Another measure is that as soon as the website is certificated, the process starts all over again in order to be certificated next year. In case of failures, measures of troubleshooting and correction have to be taken.
F	accessibility implementation	procedure	We have already received the Biene award for online banking once. We have been given a reviewer report for the sales process. Thus, before everything else, we first checked our status in accordance with the web accessibility guidelines. Time told us that we can even improve our sales process.
F	accessibility implementation	procedure	We had the problem of already existing Content Management System. Therefore we had to adjust our websites to the accessibility requirements. In order to do so, we cooperated with an organization that even evaluated our websites and the assessment results.
F	accessibility implementation	procedure	What happened after this, was sort of my initiative, so that I went to the disability interest group and that we then made all of it this way. And he has been so kind and reviewed it. I think, 2 or 3 times, mailed me back some remarks, what has been criticized by the experts, this I then corrected and then sent it back to him again.
F	accessibility implementation	procedure	We reconvert CMS according to visible definitions versus non-definitions including help-comments. For example, if the alt-text is not defined with the WYSIWYG-tool, the non-definition is visible to the authors. Furthermore, introducing help-comments clarifies the meaning of the alt-text and its usability to the users.
F	accessibility implementation	procedure	We adapted our websites to the accessibility requirements at the expense of four total working days.
T	accessibility implementation: external agency	procedure	We switched to different agencies several times. After all, this is the third agency which is already providing the second version. In fact, the last version is one which counts.
F	accessibility implementation: external agency	procedure	We charged an external company with the adjustment, which took six months.
F	accessibility implementation _business plan	procedure	Yes, this may even be due to the fact, that we had to provide a precise business plan.

Sector	Code	Category	Quote
I	accessibility implementation_cms adaption	procedure	No, the CMS itself is still not accessible. This has some handling related reasons. Because it is a fact that if you make a website accessible its usability usually increases. But if I need so-called special functions/applications with CMS, it can absolutely happen that this depends on Javascript, for example. And an editor for example cannot be accessible at all because of Javascript. And such editors, that work without Javascript, are not existing yet.
E	accessibility implementation_cms adaption	procedure	that we rebuild the CMS in a way, that if for example WYSIWYG Tool is used and the alt-Text is not defined, this is reported
E	accessibility implementation_cms adaption	procedure	We had the problem of already existing Content Management System. Therefore we had to adjust our websites to the accessibility requirements.
I	accessibility implementation_cms adaption	procedure	The Content-System is an in-house development. Yes, we developed it internally.
E	accessibility implementation_decision on acc level	procedure	That means, that following questions have been worked out: "What are we doing?", "What are we capable of doing?", "What stages are necessary?"
I	accessibility implementation_effort	procedure	If I say that I create this site accessible compared to a standardconform website, then the effort is comparative, the extra effort will be relatively low. If I say that I create it compared to a 0815 Templates and any design or so, then the effort can surely
I	accessibility implementation_expert consultation	procedure	It appeared from the inside, moreover there also has been, at least for a certain time, a tight contact with an association, I don't know much, as I wasn't involved
E	accessibility implementation_expert consultation	procedure	We cooperated with an organization that evaluated our websites and even the assessment results. A blind woman was very helpful in this matter.
T	accessibility implementation_expert consultation	procedure	Mr K. gave me advise to do so, and I got together with the software engineer.
E	accessibility implementation_expert consultation	procedure	And then there has been another check with him and our site was at that time reviewed by Mr. L. and Mr. L. could even win Ms. P. over for the issue, also Ms. P. was concerned with our site.
E	accessibility implementation_expert consultation	procedure	looked for Mr. L, who fortunately installed the contact to Ms. P., who met with Mr. L. 2 or 3 times, I think. What happened after this, was sort of my initiative, so that I went to Mr. L and that we then made all of it this way. And he has been so kind and reviewed it, i think, 2 or 3 times, mailed me back some remarks, what has been criticized by the experts, this I then corrected and then sent it back to him again
T	accessibility implementation_expert consultation	procedure	I met a young man, who has been in the business for a long time and who owns a large agency with 60 employees by himself.
I	accessibility implementation_expert consultation	procedure	We have been working there with disabled persons, with visually handicapped and took at it together with them, tested the websites together and took a close look on what they were actually doing. And one of our discoveries was, and that was sort of a exciting core for the "EASY2SEE".
E	accessibility implementation_guidelines	procedure	We developed guidelines for accessible websites, which became the company standard.

Sector	Code	Category	Quote
I	accessibility implementation_high costs changing existing sites	procedure	If you want to make an existing site accessible, this is a great effort. Because in principle you sit there, so with a bigger site, and I reviewed the sites of a few companies and compiled these advices with the request, what to do alltogether. And just the reviewing took three, 4, 5 days. If you start working through these sites, looking: how are the forms designed, it is also about syntactical issues. So it is for example absurd, what you have to take a look at on some sites. There is for example a form, where there is stated: first name, asterisk, there is name, asterisk, there is mail adress, asterisk, adress, asterisk, there is word, there is country, asterisk, subject, asterisk and then there is stated text. Then there is stated send, and below send there is stated: arrays with asterisks are compulsory arrays. So how should someone who for example clicks through this form as a blind user and then appears the send-button. He will never get to this information. So there are very often so many errors in reasoning inside, that I am actually wondering how someone doesn't has the idea to write this at the very beginning. Which is actually absurd even for the normal user. So that means, if you rebuild a site to an accessible state, in principle you have to look at all sample sites. So I say that If there are 20 article sites I probably don't have to do this, but if I have a newsletter registration
I	accessibility implementation_high costs changing existing sites	procedure	Yes. Unfortunately, that's often the only way, somehow comparable with converting the bus into Porsche.
I	accessibility implementation_learning process	procedure	we are of course in time very strongly engaged in the topic visual impairment, which was quite easy and very fast to learn, was how to create a site for blind persons. This is relatively simple, because I can work with the theme: throw away the stylesheets and then I know sort of how this thing has to look.
F	accessibility implementation_learning process	procedure	The learning process means, that you need to repeat it ten times in order not to forget it.
I	accessibility implementation_learning process	procedure	Basic improvements have been accomplished for the last two years. This is even a constant process within our company.
I	accessibility implementation_low costs relaunch	procedure	The development process will not become more expensive, if we focus on the accessibility from the beginning of a website development.
F	accessibility implementation_pre-analysis	procedure	We had an analysis made by a firm, which belongs to XY association, to find out what is not in line with the accessibility guidelines.
I	accessibility implementation_quality assurance	procedure	We generate articles via the system, then this is kind of sent to the translation. The translation office receive in principle a message, that a new article is there. They log in, enter the content, send this kind of back to us, we review it. Take care of the fact that the links are nevertheless marked accessible. There are also errors within the system, but we try to handle this. We cater for the fact that the languages are tagged correctly. And the audio readout is reading it correctly. Because this is sort fo the main point for these language awards.
F	accessibility implementation_screenreader tests	procedure	Yes, indeed. At that time we acquired the former homepage-reader, which helped me to read it by showing the access topology.
I	accessibility implementation_simple language	procedure	simple language, that you just create short sentences, without using to many foreign words, and stay comprehensible for everyone, maybe also for people, who are not that capable of the german language, we have by now versions in 5 different languages
T	accessibility implementation_trainings	procedure	yes, we train other companies, in doing so, we put a focus more on the training of institutions and execute this inhouse. Not other agencies.
F	accessibility implementation_trainings	procedure	a web editorial team, that carries this out and these members of staff are of course trained and informed, for example "How do I have to fill this, if I create something new?" and so on, in order to keep it accessible also in the future.

Sector	Code	Category	Quote
F	accessibility_implementation_trainings	procedure	You can also take courses, HTML Web Publisher or Guidelines, where you can see, that you should create more headings in html, that you need to specify alt attributes reasonably and so on. They don't have great elbowroom.
F	accessibility_implementation_trainings	procedure	this reorganization was made by an external company, as the website was also created by this company. We had to convey them the Know-How on how to create accessible websites.
F	accessibility_implementation_trainings	procedure	The other thing is that one organizes trainings - especially in the IT Accessibility Training sector - this we did at the academy in Winterthur and organized a course "Accessible Webdesign". Accessibility then is - as already mentioned, we wrote guidelines and the people should stick to them - mandatory. In this way we can guarantee that accessibility won't get lost from today to
F	accessibility_implementation_trainings	procedure	I just had to train myself, I just had to immerse myself into the criteria. I then programmed it myself, yes.
F	accessibility_implementation_trainings	procedure	It is easier. You can train the editors much faster
F	accessibility_implementation_trainings	procedure	Sure, I did two trainings in Hagenberg, but this is just half the way
F	accessibility_implementation_trainings	procedure	First there was an editor training, because it was another CMS than before - just from the handling point of view - for all editors. During this training we also haven't hardly ever mentioned the term accessibility
F	accessibility_implementation_trainings	procedure	The other thing is that one organizes trainings - especially in the IT Accessibility Training sector - this we did at the academy in Winterthur and organized a course "Accessible Webdesign".
F	accessibility_implementation_trainings	procedure	If you do something, always look at it from the accessible perspective, if it is okay there, from the display point of view, " and then you also have to create compulsory arrays, more than one would maybe usually create, for alternative texts, because otherwise it won't be filled.
F	accessibility_implementation_trainings	procedure	We did text trainings, but less concerning accessibility, just: how do I write comprehensible. I then sat down with Ms. P. and said, now we just go through the website with the voice output of her computer and also with Braille and then I sat one afternoon totally fascinated beside her and watched her using it - and my colleague from the banking sector also.
F	accessibility_implementation_wiki	procedure	When the guidelines them were put into action, there was a Wiki at our company, there the editors can get all the material
I	accessibility_marketing	procedure	developed together with the visually impaired association our label "EASY2SEE". Technically and with regards to content it is actually about trying to, so accessibility is sort of something, that refers in principle to all possible impairments, restrictions, special needs.
F	accessibility_marketing	procedure	At our site pure information about the fact that we are oriented towards this direction, can be found under "help" and "instructions for use"
F	accessibility_marketing	procedure	Okay, if you open an account with us with eBanking, you even have the benefit, that you can adapt everything personally, you can see it excellently!", that is something to probably take along. With the SMS-Banking, I don't know, how much that cost, there was also not argued with the statement "That returns so and so much.". That way just, if I say: "I am the new bank, the new BAW4G!", then I need a few things and there this actually fits just as well, if I say, I am new, make something different than the others, at our company there is the accessible eBanking.
F	accessibility_marketing	procedure	And there we informed our giro customers, that now there is the new XY.de, that we positioned everything easier and faster and more structured
F	accessibility_marketing	procedure	Easy for all - that is how we marketed the relaunch. Not accessibility - we just called it "Easy for all".

221

Sector	Code	Category	Quote
F	accessibility marketing	procedure	there has actually just been a press release. It was just announced more popular on the homepage for a certain period of time, that this ist possible now. I think, there has also been an attachement to the account statement, where it referenced to this fact
I	accessibility marketing	procedure	Label or something similar? J: We are not that far. We are not 100% conform, in this respect we can not state this, yes? That is the problem.
I	accessibility marketing	procedure	with the users that sit in front of it and have no idea what accessibility is and moreover for the internal PR and for the communication of the company outwards it is actually not necessary to drape oneself somehow with flowers and crowns to tell this. That means, I don't have to mention this on the homepage.
I	accessibility marketing	procedure	more or less marketing measure into the direction accessible websites. This is embedded within Regiotours
I	accessibility marketing	procedure	There has been a press release related to the last relaunch, at which one has to say, press releases from certain media can hardly be found in other media, so in this respect, yes
F	accessibility marketing	procedure	It was just communicated within the barriers of accessibility, that we stick to those guidelines
F	accessibility marketing	procedure	if you click on the menu item "accessible" on the website, this press release can be found. But it actually had, I have to say, at least in the economy sites not that echo, that we expected, from which we were thinking, that...But obviously journalists aren't less interested in this or it is simply not such a topic
F	accessibility marketing	procedure	Since the relaunch we just communicate the pole positions. We came in first at the Ibi Website Creating, then at Tech Channel with the topic security and now at Chip with the topic online banking and at the moment it is the best installment credit online, that places first. We created a site 2 weeks ago that refers to those awards. Biene is also very important for us, but I tell you quite clearly, as sales department I am fully honest, such a thing like "best installment credit" compared to 20 other banks would support us more than the Biene award. We had at that time, when we got the Biene for Online Banking, it is by the way in this cupboard over there. At that point in time nobody knew what this was. We now applied for the Biene. If we core, we will use this also, that we are placed somewhere - without a doubt. But just to let you know the emphasis of XY.de. We consider this maybe some kind of running along than self-evident.
I	accessibility marketing	procedure	but I am actually content with the fact, that I introduced a function, attracted people in a manner, this is what we now from observations of users and also of normally-sighted people, to make people curious to find out what this is good for. What that should be doing.
F	accessibility investment	procedure	Yes. We had a budget-related press conference in January, where we announced that we invested about 4 million CHF in the sector of accessibility.
F	accessibility investment	procedure	At that time, in retrospective we said "Thank God!", that we had plenty of rope in this matter and that it was up to us to take decisions and therefore we didn't had to justify this in advance.

Sector	Code	Category	Quote
F	awareness raising	procedure	The best way is to pick a concernate person, who works with this tool. One should without any doubt pick someone, who is concerned. And then explain, how he or she works, what the difficulties are respectively what the barriers are. And this wakes a light bulb moment - this I also experienced over and over again. People are very impressed. I often do this for IT project managers, for the management. This is something, I have heard often, that people are impressed. I think, one has to approach this in a practical way. Go there yourself and absolutely show with a demo so that people experience it live. One always takes about accessibility - but many don't know what that is. One can also argue with the demographical development. Accessibility means for all people - one doesn't have to be handicapped. There are achromates, there are elderly people, who hear, see, feel poorly. This is also a huge market. Also of course the positive effect, the CSR, there you can provide examples. One time you can design statistics, how many articles have been edited about XY in Switzerland because of the change to accessibility. There are a lot of organisations, that have written about this. So one can also deliver examples, they will be considered by the management, because it also wants to have these positive information. Especially for a bank this is very important. Web Accessibility has to became actually a matter of course for a company. That all people want this as a service. And there isn't existing the danger, that one's costs are too high. Through accessibility one also has the advantage, that usability is increased. This is also an important argument.
F	complaints mechanism	procedure	We provide an email-address (accessibility@XY.de) for customers in case of difficulties with downloading files or comprehension difficulties.
F	compromises	procedure	Actually this relaunch was already ordered at the agency as accessible. As we had to go online at the 4.10., the criteria for accessibility have been given low priority. It was cut down. One said: "We can not check this right now, we will do that afterwards!". But that then was such a point, where one said: "We don't have to do that today, that can also happen tomorrow!". And I shouldn't have accepted this compromise at that point in time, because ex-post it was something, I had to do myself. But it should have been integrated from the beginning. We thought about organising this relaunch in a way, that accessibility is introduced as a must-criteria. The technique was there, that was the big advantage. Apart from that it wasn't really such an effort.
F	cost/benefit	procedure	I think, we cannot make every inch count in this matter.
F	cost/benefit	procedure	The company XY used strictly cost-benefits analysis.
F	cost/benefit	procedure	When we designed the businessplan and said, how many more deals can you generate, if it is easier. There was this business plan. Now those amendments we had to do especially for the accessibility, the ones we did, were that marginal, that we said, that is an also-ran. We don't have to execute a cost-benefit analysis - we just do it.
F	decision maker marketing department	procedure	but this is, if it doesn't exist within the marketing, this though, then you can forget about this now. If marketing insists on this and says "We need that, that's what we have do to, otherwise there will be negative headlines or we market this in a positive way,". it will be done and then also the investors and most of the time the investor is the marketing, will also say yes.
F	decision maker marketing department	procedure	If a company's marketing strategy declines web accessibility due to the fact, that blind people don't drive a vehicle, the web accessibility won't be an issue, not even if the project manager is in favour of the accessibility implementation. Thus, the integration of web accessibility depends on the company's marketing strategy.
F	goals	procedure	We will be assessed by our sales output. We have to achieve our aims and we do our best to reach the pre-specified aims.
F	idea selling	procedure	This is something we did internally. We didn't inform the board of director or someone else, because we had regular presentations in front of the board about the actual state of affairs, this is a project and a project has to face some comittees.

Sector	Code	Category	Quote
F	idea selling	procedure	The idea I mentioned was that one introduces accessibility sort of reversely. Because with accessibility itself, that is at least my experience, one doesn't get through or at least we didn't get through with it. If I now go the other way and say "We keep on working normally and gradually implement accessibility." But I don't start right away with accessibility, with some probably technical expressions and explanations. [...] Then I have more likely a foot in the door.
F	importance of layout	procedure	The basic principle is an attractive layout, with which everyone can identify him or her in any way and I would then move away from this, so no one has to move away and take a look if I can trim this in a way, that also these WAI-criteria are fulfilled and if it fulfills additionally these criteria, other people don't care at all and then one has both.
T	no awareness	procedure	This was very exciting for me. No one has had awareness for this issue before. Nobody has thought about it.
F	project initiation	procedure	I financed it actually out of my own budget.
F	project initiation	procedure	It was not designed specifically for accessibility, as far as I know.
F	project initiation	procedure	The basic starting position was, actually the story with 50-plus and so on, that has been in vogue back then. And as we are a bank with a lot of elderly customers, we also have strong relationships to the retiree association. This was actually the reason to redesign our web site.
I	project initiation	procedure	So, we started in 2002. There I first dealt with the topic WAI, intensively, at that time the company XY was there, not als a company, but as department within our Media company. Actually we started at the end of 1999.
F	project initiation	procedure	There has been a project at our company over the last year, which was called "EasyOne". EasyOne had 3 part projects, first the revision of the presence, die revision of the concluding processes, so the sales processes and the introduction of a new finance center, so the OnlineBanking. Everything was found under the big label "easy". So it shouldn't be accessible for the accessible target group, but we said, it should be easy of everyone. The customer takes a look at it, he has to understand it und there should be no questions remaining. And under this aspect we renewed in principle the online section of XY.
F	project initiation	procedure	The stimulation was set by the agency. The agency stated that there are these rules and that it would be nice, if we fulfil them anyway to a great extent, if we would then again refinish there and we say that we fulfil them completely. The stimulation was set by the agency. By XY.
F	project initiation	procedure	First there were considerations to differentiate us from other banks. That hasn't resulted into an adequate PR echo.
F	project initiation_agency	procedure	The agency provided us with the incitement.
I	project initiation_bad quality of old website	procedure	We also changed the background of the architecture completely. A second not unimportant reason was also that we wanted to get away from the former table layout.
I	project initiation_bad quality of old website	procedure	at two places relatively at the limit with the old version. So on one hand technologically
T	project initiation_bad quality of old website	procedure	I only hit on this, because the old websites have been unsatisfactory and very poorly developed.
F	project initiation_design for all	procedure	The slogan was simply "easy". It is not the accessibility that is most important but the easy-handling for every user, not only for target groups which depend on the accessibility but for everyone.
F	project initiation_elderly customers	procedure	And as we are a bank, that has a lot of elderly people within the customer base, we also have strong relationships to the retiree association. This was actually the reason to rebuild this to an accessible state.

Sector	Code	Category	Quote
T	project initiation_famous website archetypes	procedure	that big, well-known websites are very very banal or just simply designed, very clearly laid-out.
T	project initiation_keyperson	procedure	that was initiated by the former project leader
T	project initiation_keyperson	procedure	together with the webmaster, but the initiation came from us
T	project initiation_keyperson	procedure	an expert for a friend who said, one has to make all of it accessible
F	project initiation_management level	procedure	That was an initiative from my boss at that time, who said "Let us make it accessible!"
I	project initiation_standard conformance	procedure	Exactly, yes, neat working and, yes, I don't know exactly. So concerning myself it is clear that I always try: so, I am also a technician from the educational point of view, but
I	project initiation_standard conformance	procedure	so standard conform design of websites
I	project initiation_standard conformance	procedure	that encourages a lot of people, especially in the technical sector. So you can really excite people. Webdeveloper, with the topic accessibility, that is interesting. This I often experienced already: They pick this up an often they do it on their own initiative also without their management and bosses forcing it
I	project initiation_standard conformance	procedure	Well, I was convinced by the W3C Standards and the topics on Usability and we got into contact with the Blindenverband in Vienna.
T	project initiation_usability problems	procedure	That was just a feedback from many guests, some couldn't open the site at all, some had a very very bad Internet connection, for example especially in upper Italy, Southern Tyrol nearly no one of our guests could view the site because the waiting times were too long and the system was overstrained, then it wasn't that optimally programmed, but we just thought, one has to make a modern website, one has to have flash animations, with a lot of moving pictures, with a lot of music and entertainment and action. That was the former version.
F	relaunch	procedure	At that time it was the case that we made a relaunch of the site or sort of wanted to in advance and in the course of this relaunch, one can say, these WAI criteria appeared. At that time, I think, this EU law was published, that all public sites need to be capable in the future. And the basic thoughts then were actually, if we start working with it and do a relaunch, then we just make the work in this way, this is just a minimal thing in addition and pick this up as well. And then it sort of started and we made this as well right away.
F	relaunch	procedure	We had a major relaunch with the merger of Bank Austria and Creditanstalt.
F	relaunch outcomes	procedure	Moreover we make smooth relaunches, which means that we more or less took the way, that we countinously developed our website. So it is not that we say, we do the big Big Bank, but there are really continous improvements, every year something new. May it be that we for example labelled the pictures - that was not the case at the beginning - may it be that we (at the main navigation) swapped the gifs, may it be that we changed the whole navigation, to make it more understandable. If you look at this point, there was stated for example "accrual", but no one accrues, everyone saves. These are things, where we say, we work on it continously, of course also the needs of people change all the time, people get more web-affine, they are more used to the Internet, there is more broadband access, less modems. We have exact data about it, how many people use which browser, if they visit our homepage, exactly these data we modify routinely.
F	relaunch outcomes	procedure	I also think that this smooth adaption is more reasonable. Of course, a site will generally be relaunched after a few years. But, to say: so here I am now and I change it every 5 years, this is not our way. Our way is a continous adaption - a smooth adaption. At this moment, where we see or get feedback, either through studies, either through customer feedback, that we need a development - at this moment we also try to do it. However with the restriction - the budgetary situation. We try of course, to handle it as cost-effective as possible, which means we try to do those things primarily that cost the company least. Just out of the simple reaction, taht we want to use our money carefully. At the moment when I know, there is a big relaunch occuring, I will not make massive technical changes in advance but try to implement them during the relaunch. Everything that is easy, simple or cost-effective, is changed constantly.
F	year of acc launch	procedure	We hold our position since 2007.

225

Electronic Business

Herausgegeben von Christine Strauss

Band 1 Rudolf Hartjes: Web Accessibility. Techniken und exemplarische Erfolgsmessung. 2009.
Band 2 Natalia Kryvinska: Converged Network Service Architecture. A Platform for Integrated Services Delivery and Interworking. 2010.
Band 3 Marie-Luise Leitner: Business Impacts of Web Accessibility. A Holistic Approach. 2010.

www.peterlang.de

www.ingramcontent.com/pod-product-compliance
Ingram Content Group UK Ltd.
Pitfield, Milton Keynes, MK11 3LW, UK
UKHW021829210426
5322IPUK00004B/97